SHEE͟ METAL LAYOUT

Second Edition

Leo A. Meyer

Coordinating Author
Sheet Metal Industry Training Fund

Gregg Division/McGraw-Hill Book Company

New York
St. Louis
Dallas
San Francisco
Auckland
Bogotá
Düsseldorf
Johannesburg
London
Madrid

Mexico
Montreal
New Delhi
Panama
Paris
São Paulo
Singapore
Sydney
Tokyo
Toronto

Library of Congress Cataloging in Publication Data

Meyer, Leo A
  Sheet metal layout.

  Includes index.
  1. Sheet-metal work—Pattern-making. I. Title.
TS250.M542   1979   671.8'21   78–11343
ISBN 0–07–041731–8

Sheet Metal Layout, Second Edition

1 2 3 4 5 6 7 8 9 0   KP KP   7 8 6 5 4 3 2 1 0 9

Printed and bound by Kingsport Press, Inc.

Contents

Preface

This book is for the student who already has gained a knowledge of the basic principles of pattern drafting. It presents the practical shop layout methods used by the sheet metal journeyman to lay out shop problems. The text covers the standard seams and edges used in the sheet metal shop and the short-cut methods of layout that are standard shop practice.

Sheet metal work, like other skilled trades, places a high value upon speed and efficiency. Consequently, the "right" methods of laying out a pattern have been replaced in the shop by short-cut, or "jump," methods. The journeyman has developed these short-cut methods to get the job done faster with the necessary accuracy. To understand any jump method one must have a thorough understanding of the principles of pattern drafting on which the method is based.

To further assist the student toward practical shop layout, three new chapters have been added to this new edition: Sheet Metal and Metal Gauges; Notching Patterns; and Cutting Patterns. These chapters have been added because modern sheet metal shop practice usually requires that the sheet metal drafter not only develop the pattern on metal, but also be able to cut and notch the pattern, to make it ready for fabrication.

Practice problems are included at the end of each chapter in order to provide the student with an opportunity to apply the methods discussed. If shop facilities are available, the patterns may be fabricated and joined into a line of fittings. It is recommended that the patterns be fabricated whenever possible. This not only gives the most complete test of pattern accuracy but also provides the experience needed by a competent layout man.

Leo A. Meyer

Laying Out Patterns

Trade terms

In every trade, experienced workers use specialized terms. The sheet metal trade has its share of these terms; ability to use them labels a person as experienced or as a beginner. Some of the common terms are listed below. Learning their definitions is as much a part of pattern drafting as is learning to make the pattern for an elbow.

Layout. Although the proper term for the development of patterns is *pattern drafting,* the term commonly used in the sheet metal trade is *layout work.* Drafting books refer to *developing a pattern,* but the sheet metal layout worker always speaks of *laying out a pattern.*

Stretchout. *Stretchout,* though very commonly used, is a rather vague term. Generally it means the distance across the pattern if the object were stretched out flat. The stretchout of a round pipe is its circumference; the stretchout of a square pipe is its perimeter.

Pattern. The *pattern* of an object is the surface of that object stretched out flat, including all the allowances for seams and edges and all the notches. The difference between a pattern and a stretchout is that the stretchout refers only to the distance around or across an object, whereas the pattern refers to the complete flattened-out surface of the object.

Fitting. Another general term used in the trade is *fitting.* A fitting is an object for which a pattern will have to be developed. In general, a fitting is an irregular object; a straight piece of pipe is not called a fitting. Duct elbows, round-pipe offsets, and transitional pieces are all classed as fittings.

Jump methods. Any shortcut used in laying out a pattern is called a *jump method.* It usually means that the method is faster but not so accurate as the conventional method.

Choosing the right method of layout

To learn layout work, a student should first learn to develop patterns by the technically correct method, since this gives an opportunity to learn all the fundamental principles involved. However, in a shop, where time is important, it is necessary to use the fastest layout method that will produce the desired results.

The choice of layout method is governed by many things. If the material is stainless steel, its high cost indicates that more time should be spent making an accurate pattern. If the finished product is to be placed where hundreds of people will see it every day, more time should be spent making an exact pattern. On the other hand, if the job is to be done with galvanized iron and installed in an attic where it will not be seen, a fast, approximate layout method may be used.

Another condition governing layout method is the number of pieces that will be produced from the same pattern. If only one piece is to be made, a short method may be used. If a hundred pieces are to be made, the pattern must be as accurate as possible.

A third important consideration in the choice of layout method is the type of shop in which the work is done. In a shop that requires high-quality work, layout workers take more pains laying out patterns. A shop that wants work turned out speedily, without too much regard for quality, will use jump methods of layout.

The ability to choose the best layout method is just as important as knowing how to lay out the pattern. A good layout worker usually knows several methods of laying out common fittings and is able to choose the most suitable method. The beginner who learns to consider the various methods of laying out a fitting before beginning, will eventually develop the ability to select the proper method almost automatically.

Principles of shortcut methods

Learning shortcut methods is mainly a matter of experience and practice. However, there are certain principles involved that the beginner should know. If these principles are kept in mind, many shortcut methods suggest themselves to the alert layout worker.

All shortcuts are essentially the elimination of all unnecessary processes. The worker should always look for lines on a layout that do not contribute anything to the accuracy of the pattern. If only essential lines are drawn on developments, work will speed up immensely.

Learn the shapes of patterns. In order to use shortcuts, it is important to learn the typical shapes of patterns. All fittings of a general class have patterns of similar shape. The gore pattern of a round elbow, for example, is always of the same general outline. The same is true for the pattern of a square to round and for many other types of fittings. The general shape that a pattern follows can only be learned by experience and by alert observation. An expert layout worker knows the shape of a pattern and often can lay it out by determining the location of a few essential points and then drawing in the rest of the pattern freehand. Knowing the general shape of a pattern also enables the layout worker to tell quickly if a mistake has been made in the layout.

Know the principles of pattern drafting. As stated previously, shortcuts usually consist of the long methods with all unessential lines eliminated. It follows, therefore, that no one can learn shortcut methods without a thorough grounding in the basic principles of pattern drafting. The fastest way to learn shortcuts is to master the fundamentals of pattern drafting and then develop shortcuts by the logical elimination of nonessential steps from the long methods of layout. Unless the layout worker understands pattern drafting, shortcuts will always be nothing more than a series of memorized steps that are followed blindly and unintelligently.

Know the accuracy of the method being used. Some shortcuts are more accurate than others. Generally, the shorter the method, the less accurate it is. The layout worker should know not only several shortcuts for common problems, but also the approximate degree of accuracy of each method. It is useless to use a shortcut if it does not give a fitting accurate enough for the job requirements.

Know the limitations of the method being used. Typically, shortcut methods have some limitations. Some shortcuts work only on fittings that are equally tapered; other methods work only if the taper is sharp enough; still other methods work only if one side is flat. If the limitations of the method are not known, the shortcut is useless.

"Trimulation" and "guessulation." No discussion of shortcut methods would be complete without a mention of *trimulation* and *guessulation*. Though these terms are used jokingly within the trade, they are useful as shortcut methods; however, they are used only in emergencies or for very rough work. Trimulation means simply forming up the sheet metal into the approximate shape desired and then trimming it down to the right size by a cut-and-fit technique. Guessulation means roughly the same thing, although it usually involves sketching a pattern out by guess and then forming and trimming to closer fit.

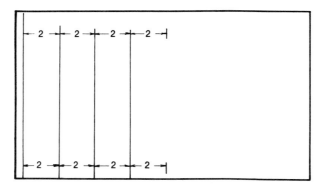

Fig. 1-1   Layout Out Lines on Sheet Metal.

Basic layout procedure

Sheet metal layout is basically the same as pattern drafting; but although it employs the same principles, it does not employ the same methods. In drafting, the T square and triangles make it easy to square and project lines. In layout work, it is slow and awkward to square and project lines on a sheet of metal; therefore, these operations are eliminated as far as possible. Each layout worker develops an individual, particular procedure, but, in general, the following rules are observed.

Check the bottom edge for straightness. The bottom edge of a sheet is usually straight enough for normal accuracy. However, if a very accurate pattern is to be laid out, a 10-ft straightedge should be used to determine whether the sheet edge is bowed. Sheet edges are often bowed inward or outward from stress in the mill rolling operations.

Square the left-hand end of the sheet. When starting a layout, check the left-hand end of the sheet for squareness. Usually the end of the sheet is square to the bottom edge; if it is not, draw a line about ¼ in from the left end and square to the bottom. The most common tool used for squaring a sheet is a 2-ft framing square.

Work from the bottom and left edge. After the left edge of the sheet has been squared, no more lines are squared up in a normal layout. All other lines are measured from the squared left-hand edge and from the bottom. For instance, if parallel lines are to be drawn across the sheet 2 in apart, 2 in is measured at the bottom and 2 in at the top of the sheet and parallel lines drawn at these two points. The process is repeated for as many lines as needed. Figure 1-1 illustrates this method. The same method is used for drawing lines the length of the sheet.

This technique is preferred to squaring and projecting lines because it is faster and more accurate. It is difficult to line up a square with the edge of a sheet and be consistently accurate.

Draw horizontal lines and then vertical lines. Lines drawn across the width of a sheet are called vertical lines, and lines drawn the length of the sheet are called horizontal lines.

To lay out a pattern, the easiest method is usually to start with either the vertical lines or the horizontal lines and draw in all the required lines. First all the lines in one direction are drawn and then all the lines in the other direction. When both sets of lines are completed, the outline of the pattern is usually evident and only a few extra lines are needed to complete it.

Draw only necessary lines. This seems obvious, but unless the layout worker constantly watches for unnecessary lines, it is easy to get into the habit of drawing them in on every pattern. As the layout worker develops more skill, it becomes easier to eliminate lines that at first seemed necessary.

Always use the first layout for the pattern. Many times, after a pattern is laid out, duplicates are copied from it to make several fittings. When making more than one pattern, always use the original pattern to mark the duplicates. Whenever a duplicate is marked there is a slight change from the original. If the original is not used for all duplicates, this variation increases with each change of pattern until there is considerable difference between the original pattern and the last reproduction.

Shop pattern methods

Shop pattern methods are techniques for processing sheet metal patterns. The suggestions that follow are good basics for the beginner, who can then alter them as experience is acquired.

Prick marking patterns. After a pattern is laid out, it is good practice to prick mark *every* bend line. It is common for beginners to prick mark only the bend lines that will have to be bent from the opposite side of the metal. This is poor practice for two reasons: first, if any duplicates have to be made, every bend line must be prick marked; second, if only the lines for the opposite side are marked, it is often found, when a fitting is half-formed, that a line has been overlooked. This means an extra trip back to the bench in order to prick mark the lines. In the long run, it is not only faster but also safer to prick mark all the lines, as there is then less chance of bending a line that should not be bent.

Notches. After a pattern is laid out, it must be notched before it can be formed. The purpose of notching is to remove extra metal that would otherwise interfere with forming the fitting. Proper notching is an important part of doing a good job, and the skill can only be acquired by experience.

When work does not have to be accurate, bends are sometimes made from the notches. This is especially true in fabricating ducts in shops that have ductnotching machines that can notch the whole end of a pipe in one operation.

Marking patterns. Often a layout worker will stand at the bench laying out patterns for several days before starting to form up. Often someone else forms and assembles the patterns. Therefore, it is essential that each pattern be marked with clear instructions for forming. Each layout worker carries some type of grease pencil or brush pen to make notations on the metal for the future use of whoever is to form up the material. Some shops have a definite system of marking patterns, but most shops leave this up to the layout worker.

Layout workers should develop a systematic method of marking that will be clear to everyone who is to use the patterns. The amount of marking to be put on a pattern depends upon the job. A duct elbow or a piece of straight duct needs little or no marking because it is a common pattern that is easy to recognize. However, an odd-shaped gravel stop, for example, might need a complete notation of the direction and degree of the bends.

In marking patterns, care must be taken that all directions are clear and can be interpreted in only one way. "Make 2" can be interpreted as "make two more" or as "make two, including the pattern." "Bend up" or "bend down" can be interpreted in two ways, depending upon which side is regarded as up.

To make directions exact, the layout worker should make all marks on the side of the pattern that is to be the inside of the fitting. If a pattern can be formed in such a way that it would be inside-out, the layout worker should always mark "in" or "inside" on the pattern to indicate the inside. If "in" is not marked on the pattern, experienced people always form the pattern so that the marking is on the inside. If there is no marking, it will be assumed that it makes no difference which side is formed to the inside.

Beside marking "in" on the pattern, the layout worker should indicate whether more of the same pattern are to be made. "Make 2 more" means that a total of three of the particular piece is needed. If there are unusual bends, the bends should be marked "90° in" or "bend out to fit template," or give whatever directions make the finished shape clear. If the fitting is one that changes size from one end to the other, the sizes of both ends should be marked. In marking patterns, it is standard practice that the first dimension is the size of the pattern on which the marking is made. For example, if the pattern for one side of a piece of rectangular duct is marked "8 × 6," it means that the pattern marked is 8 in across and the matching side is to be 6 in. Conversely, if the piece were marked "6 × 8," it would mean that the pattern marked was 6 in across and the matching side is to be 8 in.

Numbering the fittings, if a large number of them are being made, is an important time-saver. To make a long run of duct from a blueprint, the worker first plans how to make it, deciding on the lengths to use, and what type of fitting will work best at each spot. With a red pencil, the layout worker marks the connecting points of each duct fitting; then, starting from one end of the line of duct, numbers each piece in consecutive order. When laying out the patterns for the pieces, the patterns are also numbered with the designated number. If a fitting is made in four different pieces, each piece is given the same number. Numbering is helpful in two ways: the formed pieces are easily identified for assembly into a fitting, and the installer can readily determine the sequence of fittings when assembling the duct.

Effective marking is a matter of experience. Too little marking leads to confusion and wasted time; too much will do the same.

Drawing in curves on patterns. Many patterns have irregular curves that the layout worker must learn to draw in quickly and accurately. The most common method of doing this is to bend a flexible steel rule through the points and have a helper draw in the curve. This is shown in Fig. 1-2.

An even more satisfactory method is to learn to draw these curves freehand. This is not so difficult as it seems; with a little practice, anyone can draw a smooth, even curve through the guide points. When drawing a curve freehand, watch the point through which the curve will be drawn—do not watch the pencil. This helps to form a smooth curve that runs through the desired point. Try to avoid moving the pencil with the fingers, as this limits the sweep of the pencil; instead, use wrist action and movement of the forearm. By using the

Fig. 1-2 Drawing in a Curve with a Flexible Steel Rule.

forearm as a pivot, a smooth curve can be drawn in much the same way that a compass is used.

Using a scribe. To mark a line that is to be an inch or less from the edge of the metal, a scribe can be used. A sheet metal *scribe* is a piece of scrap metal that is notched as shown in Fig. 1-3. The distance x is made the distance desired from the edge of the sheet; then the scribe is held so that point A is against the edge of the sheet and point B is scratching a line on the sheet, as shown in Fig. 1-4.

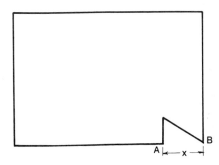

Fig. 1-3 A Sheet Metal Scribe.

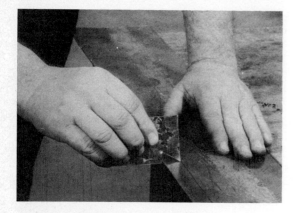

Fig. 1-4 Using a Scribe.

Conserving metal. Speed is important in layout, and so is the location of the pattern on the sheet. Whenever a pattern is to be laid out, it should first be examined to see if any changes in design or size can be made in order to cut the sheet more economically. Lay the pattern out in the lower left-hand corner of the sheet so that it will be cut out with the least amount of waste.

Practical mathematics

Mathematics is an important part of layout work. In fact, layout work is, essentially, applied geometry. Listed below are some of the practical mathematical shortcuts used in layout work.

Changing decimals to nearest sixteenth. The layout worker must often figure the circumference of a circle using arithmetic instead of a circumference rule. Other problems may require arithmetic instead of reference to a table. Decimals are used for easy figuring and then converted to fractions. The ordinary method of changing decimals to fractions is inadequate, because the only fractions that can have any meaning to a sheet metal worker are the multiples of $1/16$ in; these are the divisions on the rule. If the decimal is changed into a fraction such as $28/58$, it must be figured again to determine the nearest sixteenth.

To change the decimal to the nearest sixteenth, multiply the decimal by sixteen and change the answer to the nearest whole number. This whole number is the nearest sixteenth. For example, to convert the number 18.345 into a fractional number to the nearest sixteenth, first multiply 0.345 by 16. The answer is 5.520. Rounding 5.520 off to the nearest whole number gives 6, which means that there are six-sixteenths or three-eighths. Therefore, the measurement to the nearest sixteenth of 18.345 is 18⅜.

Example. Convert 3.692 to the nearest sixteenth.

Solution. $0.692 \times 16 = 11.072$.

The nearest whole number to 11.072 is 11. Therefore, the nearest sixteenth is eleven-sixteenths; the nearest sixteenth to 3.692 is $3^{11}/_{16}$.

This method of changing decimals to the nearest desired multiple may be used for any desired fraction. If the nearest desired fraction is one-eighth, the decimal is multiplied by 8.

Dividing a circle into equal parts. Dividing a half circle into equal parts is a necessary step in many kinds of layout problems. Because it is done so often, a short method has been developed. In almost all cases, the half circle is divided into six equal parts, since this is easiest.

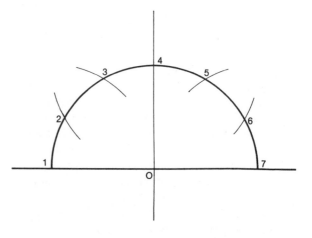

Fig. 1-5 How to Divide a Circle into Six Equal Parts.

Figure 1-5 shows how a half circle is easily divided into six equal parts. After the half circle is drawn, a line is squared up from the center point *O* in order to divide it into two quarter circles. Then, with the dividers still set to the radius of the circle, an arc is swung, with point 4 as a center, to intersect the circle at points 2 and 6. After these arcs are swung, point 7 is used as center and an arc is swung to intersect at point 5. Similarly, using point 1 as center, an arc is swung to intersect at point 3. This makes three equal spaces to the quarter circle and six to the half circle.

This division of spaces can be made quickly and accurately and can be used for almost all layout problems. Only for a very large diameter circle would it be necessary to use more divisions.

Dividing a line into equal spaces. The layout worker is required to step off a line into equal parts as well as to divide a circle into equal spaces. The division of a circle is a mechanical operation that can be easily accomplished as long as the proper procedure is used. The quick division of a line calls for skill and practice as well as knowledge. The layout worker should be able to divide a line into twelve equal spaces in three tries or less.

To divide a line into twelve equal spaces, first divide the line in half. This can usually be done easily by mental arithmetic. The halfway mark acts as a guidepost in determining the rest of the divisions.

After the halfway mark is established, the dividers are set at an estimated one-sixth of one of the half spaces. In most layouts, a half circle has already been drawn and divided into six equal spaces. If so, set the dividers to slightly more than one of the circle spaces. With this setting start at one end of the line and step the spaces off to the halfway mark. Usually the first setting is not right, and the six steps with the dividers will be too short or too long. Whatever the amount of error, estimate one-sixth of this amount and readjust the dividers; then step off the distance again to see if the setting is right. If the spacing is still wrong, readjust the dividers and try again. With practice one can learn to attain the exact spacing on the

second or third trial. After the dividers have been adjusted properly by this trial and error method, step off the full length of the line into even spaces.

Some layout workers use measurements to divide the line into quarters as well as into halves. If this can be done conveniently, it simplifies finding the twelve spaces because the first quarter space can be stepped off by trial and error into three spaces.

Dividing dimensions mentally. In many cases, such as stepping off a line into equal spaces, it is necessary to divide a measurement in half quickly. This can usually be done mentally. To simplify the procedure, first separate the whole number from the fraction; then mentally divide the whole number in half; next divide the fraction in half and add it to the first number. In the measurement 18⅞, for instance, first separate the 18 from the ⅞. One-half of 18 is 9. One-half of ⅞ is $7/_{16}$. (Any fraction can be divided in half by just doubling the bottom number.) Therefore, one-half of 18⅞ is $9^7/_{16}$.

Example. (1) Take one-half of 9¾.

Solution. One-half of 9 is 4½; one-half of ¾ is ⅜. Therefore, one-half of 9¾ is 4½ plus ⅜, which is 4⅞.

Example. (2) Divide 18¼ into fourths.

Solution. One-half of 18 is 9; one-half of ¼ is ⅛. Therefore, one-half of 18¼ is 9⅛. To obtain one-fourth of 18¼, divide 9⅛ in half. One-half of 9 is 4½; one-half of ⅛ is $1/_{16}$. Therefore, one-fourth of 18¼ is 4½ plus $1/_{16}$, which is $4^9/_{16}$.

Adding with two rules. A layout worker is constantly adding and subtracting fractions. The accuracy of the work depends upon these calculations, so it is very important that they be correct. Most layout workers have found that hasty calculations in the shop are often wrong; therefore, they have devised a positive method of speedily adding and subtracting fractions.

This is done by means of two rules. By sliding them alongside each other, fractions can be figured quickly. Figure 1-6 shows how $9^7/_{16}$ is added to

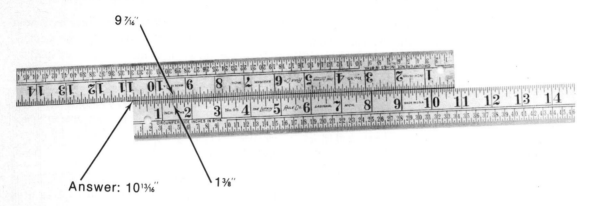

9 ⁷⁄₁₆″

Answer: 10¹³⁄₁₆″   1⅜″

Fig. 1-6 Adding Fractions with Two Rules.

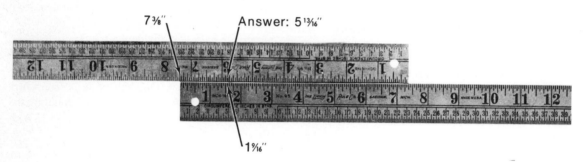

7⅜″   Answer: 5¹³⁄₁₆″

1⁹⁄₁₆″

Fig. 1-7 Subtracting Fractions with Two Rules.

1⅜. The 1⅜ mark of the first rule is set even with the $9^7/_{16}$ mark of the second rule. The sum of the two numbers is read on the second rule at the point even with the end of the first rule.

This method is actually a simplified method of drawing out the two distances and measuring them. Subtraction can be accomplished by reversing this method. Figure 1-7 shows the two rules used to subtract $1^9/_{16}$ from 7⅜.

This is so simple a device as to seem almost ridiculous, but it is the use of just such simple devices that makes the difference between an expert layout worker and an average one.

Electronic calculators. The cost of pocket electronic calculators is now so low that anyone who does layout work should have one. Many formulas that were previously too time-consuming can now be used because of the speed and accuracy of calculators. Even for simple addition and subtraction, calculators are desirable because they are fast and reduce human error. The calculator to be used should have a square root key, since this will make many shop calculations easier and faster. If the worker understands trigonometry, a calculator that can perform trigonometric functions will make it possible to use many time-saving formulas that would otherwise be impractical.

Checking a square and a straightedge for accuracy. Although layout is not done to precise measurements, the layout worker must have a square and a straightedge that are reasonably accurate. Because of the rough usage that shop tools receive, there is sometimes a question whether the square or the straightedge is accurate.

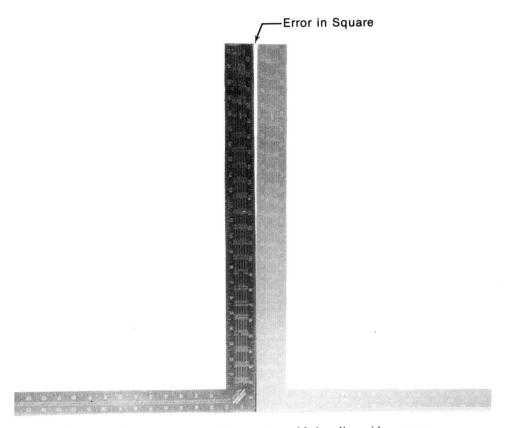

—Error in Square

Fig. 1-8 Checking a Square for Accuracy. Mark a line with a square in left-hand position. Then place square in right-hand position.

The square can be checked by squaring up a line and then reversing the square to the other side of the line. If the square is correct, it will show the line to be square from the reverse side also. The error in an inaccurate square is shown in Fig. 1-8.

The straightedge can be checked in the same manner. First draw a line with the straightedge, then set the straightedge on the other side of the line. If the straightedge is exact, the line will match it from this other side also.

This same principle of checking from opposite positions may be used to check many other tools. A level, for example, can be checked by setting it on a flat surface and noting the position of the bubble, then turning the level end for end and setting it in the same spot. If the level is exact, the bubble will appear in the same relative position as in the first setting.

Circumference rule. A standard tool for any layout bench is a 3-ft or 4-ft circumference rule, such as that shown in Fig. 1-9. In addition to its use as a measuring rule and as a straightedge in layout work, it is also used to determine the circumference of a circle.

To find the circumference of a circle, look on the circumference scale that is directly below the standard scale. To find the circumference of a 3-in diameter circle, look directly under the 3-in mark of the standard scale. The reading on the circumference scale is $9^7/_{16}$ in, which is the circumference of a 3-in-diameter circle. Using the same

Circumference Scale

Fig. 1-9   Steel Circumference Rule.

method, the circumference of a 6-in-diameter circle is found to be 18⅞ in.

The circumference scale can also be read backward when the circumference is known but the diameter is not. To find the diameter of a circle with a circumference of 18⅞ in, locate 18⅞ on the circumference scale and read upward to the regular scale. In this case, of course, the diameter is 6 in.

The area of a circle can also be found on a circumference rule. To do this, square the radius of the circle and look up this number as if finding the circumference for this number. For a 6-in-diameter circle, the radius is 3 in; 3 times 3 equals 9, which is the square of the radius. Nine on the circumference scale indicates 28¼ in, which means that the area of a 6-in-diameter circle is 28¼ sq in. By working backward, the radius of a circle can be found if the area is known.

Beginners will often overlook the tables and formulas listed on the reverse side of the circumference rule. It is a good idea to look over the material listed there so that it may be used when needed.

Shortcut for figuring the area of a circle. Layout workers should be able to figure the approximate area of a circle quickly. This must often be done mentally. A rule that is accurate to within 4 percent is "three-fourths of the diameter squared"; multiply the diameter of the circle by itself and take three-fourths of the result. For instance, in figuring the area of a 10-in-diameter circle, multiply 10 times 10, which is 100. Three-fourths of 100 is 75, which means that the area of a 10-in-diameter circle is about 75 sq in. This is not strictly accurate—the area of a 10-in circle is actually 78.54 sq in—but it is close enough for the layout worker who needs to know the approximate

area in order to design a job. If greater accuracy is needed, it can be calculated more closely later.

Example. Find the area of an 8-in-diameter circle.

Solution. 8 × 8 = 64; three-fourths of 64 is 48. Therefore, there are approximately 48 sq in within an 8-in-diameter circle.

Finding the equivalent total diameter for two circles. A common problem for the layout worker is to figure what diameter circle has the same area as the combined area of two other circles. An example of this type of problem is shown in Fig. 12-1, page 134. This is a Y-branch fitting, where two smaller pipes are joined together to form one large pipe. The large pipe must have an area as great as the combined area of the two small pipes in order to carry enough air.

This problem can be solved by mathematics—by figuring the area of both small pipes, adding them together, and then working from this to find a diameter appropriate to the combined area. This, however, involves considerable arithmetic, which is not only time-consuming but also liable to error. The layout worker uses a simpler method—measuring across a framing square.

In a Y branch, if the two small diameters are 6 in and 8 in respectively, the diameter of the large pipe is found as follows. With a rule, measure from the 6-in mark on the tongue of the framing square to the 8-in mark on the blade of the square. The measurement on the rule from the 6-in to the 8-in mark gives the diameter of the large pipe, 10 in. Fig. 1-10 shows the solution of this problem.

Example. Find the equivalent diameter of a 4-in-diameter circle and a 9-in-diameter circle.

Solution. Measure from the 4-in mark to the 9-in mark of the square. This measurement is 9⅞ in.

Therefore, the equivalent diameter of the 4-in and the 9-in circles is 9⅞ in.

Metric measurement

Metric measurements are gradually being adopted in American industry. When they become a part of the sheet metal trade, their use will simplify layout work because it will eliminate the use of clumsy fractions. Conversion from one unit to another will also be simplified. For example, changing from meters to centimeters is done by simply moving the decimal point in the number.

The layout worker should become familiar with the metric system in anticipation of the time when it will be adopted by the building industry. This may still be a few years away because industry-wide standards must first be developed and adopted. This includes such things as new sheet metal gauges, widths of sheets, and standard distances between the wooden parts of a building.

PRACTICE PROBLEMS

Problem 1-1

Purpose. To learn some of the trade terms used in the sheet metal trade.

Study. *Trade terms.*

Assignment. Write *in your own words* definitions of the following terms:

1. Layout
2. Stretchout
3. Pattern
4. Fitting
5. Jump methods

Problem 1-2

Purpose. To learn some of the considerations in choosing the proper method of layout.

Study. *Choosing the right method of layout.*

Assignment. List at least three conditions that govern the choice of layout method.

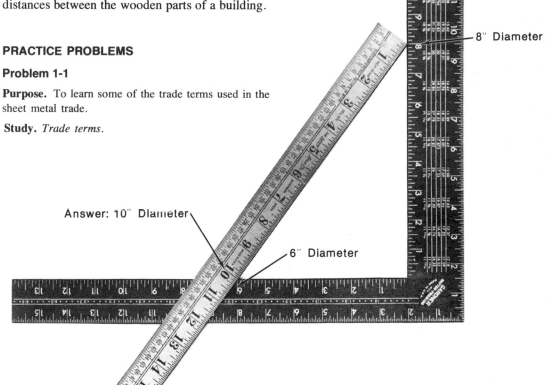

Fig. 1-10 How to Find the Diameter of the Large Pipe in a Y-branch Fitting.

Problem 1-3

Purpose. To learn the basic principles that govern the use of shortcuts.

Study. *Principles of shortcut methods.*

Assignment. Answer all the questions that follow.

1. In what way are shortcuts related to the long, technically correct method?

2. What advantages will layout workers have if they know the general shape that the pattern should take?

3. In *your opinion,* can a layout worker *thoroughly* understand shortcut methods without having a solid understanding of the principles of pattern drafting? You need not agree with the book, as long as you are able to give logical reasons for your answer.

4. In your opinion, why are the shorter layout methods less accurate than the longer ones?

5. Would a good layout worker use "trimulation" or "guessulation"? Give reasons for your answer.

Problem 1-4

Purpose. To study some basic layout methods.

Study. *Basic layout procedure.*

Assignment. Lay out the pattern for the square duct shown in Fig. 1-11. Use a piece of drawing paper 12-by-18-in for the layout. Lay out to full size. In doing the layout, use the first five rules listed in the assigned reading. Be prepared to answer any questions about how you used these principles.

Problem 1-5

Purpose. To study the methods of prick marking a pattern.

Study. *Prick marking patterns* and the introductory paragraph of *Shop pattern methods.*

Assignment. On the pattern made in Problem 1-4, indicate by small penciled circles the points at which the pattern should be prick marked.

Problem 1-6

Purpose. To gain practice in notching patterns.

Study. *Notches.* Examine the patterns in the other chapters in this book and those in any other pattern books available to discover the manner and purpose of the notches.

Assignment. With a red pencil, mark in the notches for the pattern drawn in Problem 1-4.

Problem 1-7

Purpose. To study methods of marking a pattern.

Study. *Marking patterns.*

Assignment. Answer the following questions:

1. Look at the pattern from Problem 1-4. Is it necessary to mark the inside? Why?

2. If a total of ten pieces exactly like this one were needed, how should the pattern be marked?

3. In an average shop, would any more directions need to be marked on this particular pattern? Why?

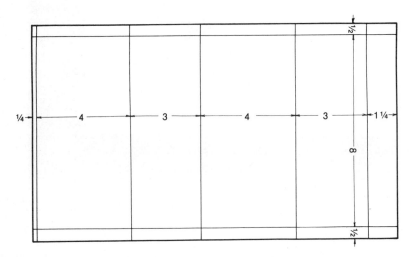

Fig. 1-11   Pattern for Square Duct.

4. If the inside is not marked on this pattern, but there are other marks, which side is assumed to be the inside?

5. If one of these patterns is marked with a 1, and another similar piece is marked with a 2, what do these numbers indicate?

6. Is it possible to put too much marking on a pattern? Why?

Problem 1-8

Purpose. To gain practice in drawing curves.

Study. *Drawing in curves on patterns.*

Assignment. Divide a sheet of 12-by-18-in drawing paper into quarters. In each quarter make a series of six dots to form an irregular curve. On the upper left-hand quarter, use a flexible rule to draw in a smooth curve through these dots. On the other three, practice drawing a curve through the dots freehand, using the technique outlined in the text. If these curves are not satisfactory, turn the sheet over and try four more curves.

Problem 1-9

Purpose. To study the use of a scribe.

Study. *Using a scribe.*

Assignment. Cut out a piece of sheet metal—or cardboard, if sheet metal is not available—about 3-by-4-in. Using each of the four corners, make a scribe for a ¼-in, a ½-in, an $^{11}/_{16}$-in, and a ⅞-in marker. If it is made from sheet metal, use it to mark each of the distances on another piece of metal.

Problem 1-10

Purpose. To learn how to convert decimals to the fractions desired.

Study. *Changing decimals to the nearest sixteenth.*

Assignment. Do the following problems:

1. Change the following measurements to the nearest sixteenth, in fractions that could be measured on the circumference rule.
   a. 18.742
   b. 3.593
   c. 7.029

2. Change to the nearest thirty-second.
   a. 1.091
   b. 5.693
   c. 24.798

Problem 1-11

Purpose. To practice dividing a circle into six equal parts.

Study. *Dividing a circle into equal parts.*

Assignment. Draw a half circle with a 4-in radius. Divide it into six equal parts according to the instructions given in the assigned reading.

Problem 1-12

Purpose. To practice dividing a line into equal spaces.

Study. *Dividing a line into equal spaces and circumference rule.*

Assignment. On a sheet of 12-by-18-in drawing paper, draw lines of the following lengths. Divide each according to the instructions given, and write next to each line the number of tries that were necessary before the division came out evenly.

1. A line equal to the circumference of a 6-in-diameter circle.

2. A line equal to the stretchout of a 3½-in-diameter circle.

3. A line equal to the circumference of a 4-in-diameter circle.

4. A line with a 3¾-in stretchout.

Problem 1-13

Purpose. To practice dividing mixed fractions mentally.

Study. *Dividing dimensions mentally.*

Assignment. Without using a pencil and paper, divide the following into halves. Give the answers to the nearest sixteenth.

1. One-half of 18⅞
2. One-half of 9$^{7}/_{16}$
3. One-fourth of 25¾
4. One-fourth of 13$^{7}/_{16}$
5. One-half of 12½

Problem 1-14

Purpose. To practice adding and subtracting by the use of two rules.

Study. *Adding with two rules.*

Assignment. Solve the following problems by the use of two rules:

1. $1^3/_{16} + 4^5/_8$
2. $7^{13}/_{16} + 4^{11}/_{16}$
3. $8^5/_8 + 17^{15}/_{16}$
4. $19^3/_{16} - 7^{13}/_{16}$
5. $12^7/_{16} - 11^{15}/_{16}$

Problem 1-15

Purpose. To learn how to check a square and straightedge for accuracy.

Study. *Checking a square and a straightedge for accuracy.*

Assignment. Obtain a square and a straightedge. On a piece of drawing paper 12-by-18-in, check both for accuracy. Write the results of the check next to the lines. If there is an error, indicate how much. If a level is available, check it for accuracy also.

Problem 1-16

Purpose. To learn all the uses of a circumference rule.

Study. *Circumference rule.*

Assignment. Solve the following problems by use of the circumference rule:

1. Find the circumference of a circle with a *radius* of $5^5/_{16}$ in.
2. If a circle has a circumference of 44 in, what is its *diameter*?

3. Find the area of a circle with a diameter of 4½ in.
4. Find the area of a circle with a circumference of 25⅛ in.

Problem 1-17

Purpose. To learn to figure the approximate area of a circle.

Study. *Shortcut for figuring the area of a circle.*

Assignment. Figure the approximate area of the following circles. Try to make all calculations mentally.

1. Figure the area of a 9-in-diameter circle.
2. Figure the area of a 6-in-diameter circle.
3. Figure the square feet in a 7-ft-diameter circle.

Problem 1-18

Purpose. To learn how to figure the proper diameter for Y-branch fittings and similar fittings.

Study. *Finding the equivalent total diameter for two circles.*

Assignment. Solve the following problems:

1. Find the equivalent diameter for a 6-in and an 8-in circle.
2. Find the equivalent diameter for a 5-in and a 7-in circle.
3. The large diameter of a Y-branch is 13 in; one of the small diameters is 6 in. What must the other small diameter be in order to balance the total area?

A skill as important as pattern layout is the ability to choose proper seams and edges, and to make suitable allowances for them. This chapter will discuss the most common edges, their uses, and their allowances, using the names by which they are most generally known.

The hem

One of the most common sheet metal edges is the hem. A hem is simply the edge of the metal, bent over and flattened down. Figure 2-1 shows a sectional view of a ¼-in hem, and a smaller drawing showing the allowance.

The purposes of the hem are to eliminate the raw edge of metal and to stiffen the edge. The hem is used around the tops of boxes and pans to make a stiff and smooth edge. It can be used for the edge of any fitting that would otherwise have an exposed raw edge. Because it is so simple to form, it is the most commonly used edge.

Double hem

A double hem is just what the name implies; a hem that has been doubled. It is a hem in which two folds are made instead of one. Figure 2-2 shows a sectional view of a ¼-in double hem and the allowance for it. Note that for a ¼-in double hem, the allowance is ¼ in and $^3/_{16}$ in. The outside allowance for a double hem is always $^1/_{16}$ in less than the size of the hem. Thus, for a ⅜-in double hem, the outside allowance would be $^5/_{16}$ in.

A double hem has the same purposes as a single hem; to eliminate a raw edge and to stiffen the edge. The advantage of the double hem is that it is much stiffer than the single hem and almost as easy to make.

Wired edge

Another edge that is used for stiffening and making a smooth edge is the wired edge. This edge

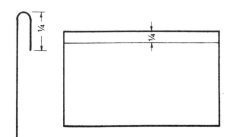

Fig. 2-1 Single Hem.

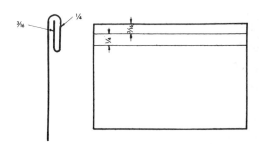

Fig. 2-2 A ¼-in Double Hem.

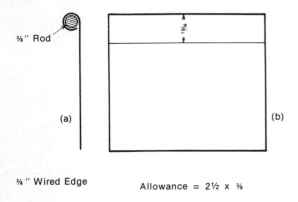

¾″ Rod

(a)

⅜″ Wired Edge   Allowance = 2½ x ⅜

Fig. 2-3   A ⅜-in Wired Edge.

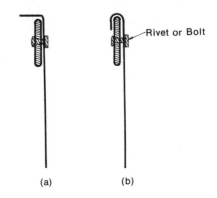

Rivet or Bolt

(a)   (b)

Fig. 2-4   Band-iron Edge.

consists of metal wrapped around a rod or wire. A sectional view of a ⅜-in wire edge and its allowance is shown in Fig. 2-3.

The allowance for a wired edge varies. Much depends upon the experience and judgment of the worker. The rule for the allowance is "2½ times the diameter of the wire" when the sheet metal used is lighter than 22 gauge. If 22 gauge or heavier is used, the allowance should be increased to three times the diameter of the wire. This allowance, however, depends upon the skill of the user. Usually a beginner either draws too much metal around the wire or not enough.

Band-iron edge

An edge that gives even more stiffness than any yet mentioned is the band-iron edge (Fig. 2-4). This is quite similar to the wired edge, in that it is a piece of band iron with the sheet metal wrapped around it. Figure 2-4 also shows how this edge is formed. It is usually used on round objects, such as trash cans, to give a stiff edge that will withstand a lot of pounding. The band-iron edge and the wired edge can be used interchangeably. The band-iron edge is often used because it requires less skill and time to make than the wired edge.

The allowance for the band-iron edge is usually ½ in. If ⅛-in thick band iron is used, there will be about ⅜ in of metal to fold down over the band, since ⅛ in of metal will be required to span the thickness of the band.

If possible, a square bend is made at the ½-in mark by the brake, as shown in Fig. 2-4*a*. The band is then riveted on, and after it is in place, the metal is pounded around into the finished position with a hammer and dolly. If the fitting is a round object, and it is not practical to make a bend before it is formed, then the edge is left straight. After the object is formed, the band is riveted on so that the top of the band is even with the ½-in mark, and then it is pounded over with hammer and dolly.

Angle-iron edge

The angle-iron edge (Fig. 2-5) is similar to the band-iron edge. It is made in the same manner except that angle iron is used. The advantage of the angle-iron edge is added stiffness; it is one of the stiffest sheet metal edges, and is used exclusively

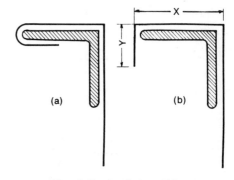

(a)   (b)

Fig. 2-5   Angle-iron Edge.

on rectangular objects. It is not practical on round objects because of the difficulty in rolling angle iron. The angle-iron edge is shown in Fig. 2-5a.

Fig. 2-5b illustrates how the metal is bent to form the edge. The distance indicated by x should be made $1/16$ in larger than the width of the angle iron. The distance shown by y varies with the thickness of the angle and should be ⅜ in plus the thickness.

After the bends are made, the angle is set in place and held by a few rivets. Then the metal is pounded around the angle with a hammer and dolly.

Split-pipe edge

A simple edge that is very rigid is the split-pipe edge (Fig. 2-6). This is probably one of the simplest edges to make, and is also one of the stiffest. It is used principally for the edges of sinks and drainboards in restaurant kitchens. No allowance is used. The sheet metal is formed as if the object is to be made with a raw edge. The split pipe, which is already formed, either in galvanized iron or in stainless steel, is purchased, cut to length, and slipped over the raw edge. The miters are welded or soldered, and the pipe is fastened to the metal by either tack welding or soldering.

The flange

On many jobs the drawing will have a notation for a "⅞-in flange." This means simply that ⅞ in is to

be bent out square. A flange can be any size, but ¾- and ⅞-in are the most common. The flange is most commonly used to stiffen a long span.

The flange and hem

A variation of the flange is the flange and hem (Fig. 2-7). This is a combination of two edges. The hem gives added stiffness to the flange and provides a smooth, safe edge.

The allowance for this edge is simply the allowance for the flange plus the allowance for the hem. When it is formed, the hem is bent first and then the flange.

Fig. 2-7 Flange and Hem.

PRACTICE PROBLEMS

Problem 2-1

Purpose. To study the uses of various sheet metal edges.

Study. All of Chapter 2, with special emphasis on the stiffness of each edge.

Assignment. List the eight edges described in Chapter 2, in order of their stiffness, the most flexible first. This list may vary according to your own opinion.

Problem 2-2

Purpose. To study the difficulty of forming edges.

Study. All of Chapter 2, with emphasis on how edges are formed.

Assignment. List the eight edges in order, from easiest to most difficult to form.

Problem 2-3

Purpose. To study the shape and allowance of each edge.

Study. All of Chapter 2, with emphasis on the sectional views of each seam and the allowance for each seam.

Assignment. On a sheet of 12-by-18-in drawing paper, make a sectional view to the scale indicated, and a full

Fig. 2-6 Split-pipe Edge.

scale pattern 2-in long, with dimensions of the allowances of the following edges.

1. ¼-in hem (double scale)
2. ¼-in double hem (double scale)
3. ⁵/₁₆-in wired edge (double scale)
4. Edge with 1-by-⅛-in band iron (double scale)
5. Angle-iron edge for 1-by-⅛-in angle (full scale)
6. Split-pipe edge with ¾-in split pipe (full scale)
7. ⅞-in flange with ¼-in hem (full scale)

Problem 2-4

Purpose. To study the forming of edges.

Study. Chapter 2, with reference to the forming of edges.

Assignment. Make the following edges out of sheet metal, according to the directions given:

1. Cut a piece of 26-gauge galvanized iron, 8 in by 4 in. On the long side form a ¼-in double hem. On the opposite edge form a ¼-in wired edge.

2. Cut a piece of 26-gauge galvanized iron, 6 in by 8 in. On one long side form a ½-in flange with a ⅜-in hem. On the opposite edge form an angle-iron edge or a flat-bar edge with whatever angle or flat bar is available.

3. On a piece of 26-gauge galvanized iron, swing an arc with a 12-in radius. Cut out a portion of this arc about 10 in long. Around this arc form a ⅛-in wired edge.

3

Clips and Connectors

Standard methods have been developed for connecting joints of sheet metal duct and pipe. In exceptional cases certain unusual connections may be used, but normally the clips in this chapter are used. These have been found to meet all the requirements for speed and strength. The beginning sheet metal worker should know thoroughly the uses, the allowances, and the forming of all the clips shown.

Fig. 3-1 Government Clip.

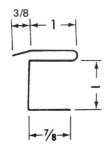

Fig. 3-2 Allowance for Government Clip.

Government clip

The government clip, shown in Figs. 3-1 and 3-2, is sometimes called the ''cup'' or ''pocket clip.'' A most widely used clip, its principal use is in joining sections of large, rectangular duct. It is comparatively easy to make, and most shops are set up to produce it on a semiproduction basis. Almost every shop has a clip machine that properly notches the end of the clip blank and punches the rivet hole in one operation. In addition, most shops have a lock-forming machine that automatically forms the clips.

The corners of the clip are either riveted or stapled together. When the clips are completed, they are fastened onto the duct. The allowance on the duct for the clip is 1 in, as shown in Fig. 3-4. This allowance is not bent but is left straight for the clip to fit on. After the clip is set on the duct, it is fastened with a clip punch or by riveting. To complete fastening the clip onto the duct, the corners of the clip are tapped in as far as possible, so that they will not hit on the corners of the duct that is to fit into the clip.

On the joint of pipe that is to fit into the clip, a ⅞-in flange is allowed for, as shown in Figs. 3-3 and 3-4. This flange is then bent and fitted into the clip, as shown in Fig. 3-5a. After the flange is set into place, the edge is knocked over to connect the two sections together, as shown in Fig. 3-5b. The edge of the clip is pounded over with the side of the hammer while the clip is supported underneath with a dolly bar. The edge is usually pounded over

1" Allowance for
Government Clip

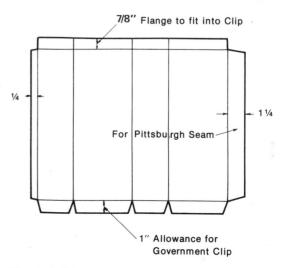

7/8" Flange to fit into Clip

¼

1 ¼

For Pittsburgh Seam

1" Allowance for
Government Clip

Fig. 3-4   Flange and Allowance for Government Clip.

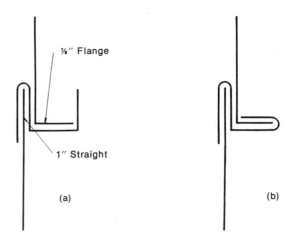

⅞" Flange

1" Straight

(a)

(b)

Fig. 3-5   Sectional View of Government Clip.

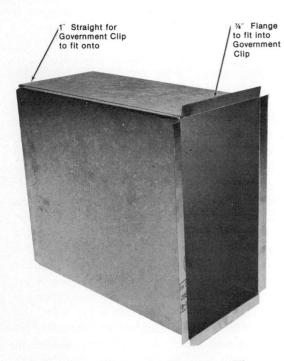

1" Straight for
Government Clip
to fit onto

⅞" Flange
to fit into
Government
Clip

Fig. 3-3   Allowance for Government Clip.

about halfway and finished with a pair of tongs. Finishing the edge with tongs results in a smoother edge and is used especially when appearance is important. If appearance is of no consequence, the edge is often pounded over completely with hammer and dolly.

Figure 3-6 shows the finished government clip on a section of duct. Note that the finished clip leaves a 1-in standing edge all around the duct.

Fig. 3-6 Government Clip in Use.

This is both an advantage and a disadvantage. It is an advantage because the standing edge acts as a stiffener for the duct. However, a 1-in edge projecting from the sides of the duct is sometimes a disadvantage because of limited space. S-and-drive clips have an advantage over government clips when space is a factor because they lay flat against the duct.

When connecting ducts that have government clips, first try to hook one side in and get it temporarily fastened; then swing the duct around into the rest of the clip. This method of hooking one side and swinging the other sides in applies to other clips as well. It is always easier to swing in a connection than to try to make all four sides fit at once.

Drive clips

Drive clips are sometimes called *cap strips,* and are usually used in conjunction with S clips. When

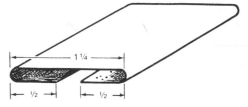

Fig. 3-7 Drive Clip.

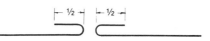

Fig. 3-8 Edges for Connecting Drive Clip.

they are, the connection is called an *S-and-drive clip.* The drive clip is bent as shown in Fig. 3-7. Normally the dimensions for the clip are to fit a ½-in bend, as shown, but they can be varied to fit special conditions. For the standard clip, the width of the pattern is usually 2¼ in. For a special clip

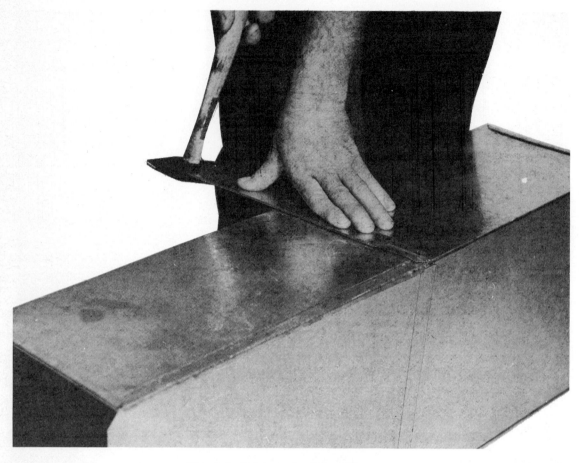

Fig. 3-9   Driving on a Drive Clip.

the allowance is four times the width of the bend it is to fit plus ¼ in. For the standard clip, the pieces to be connected usually have a ½-in edge bent on them, as shown in Fig. 3-8. Note that these edges are not smashed down completely flat, as with a hem. They are squeezed down until they lie parallel to the main piece but still have a gap between them. After the edges are formed, the clip is slipped into place and driven on with the side of a hammer, as shown in Fig. 3-9. A sectional view of the fitted clip and pieces is shown in Fig. 3-10.

On most connections, it is usual practice to bend about ½ in of each end of the clip around the corner of the duct to lock the clip in place. This is shown by the arrows in Fig. 3-11.

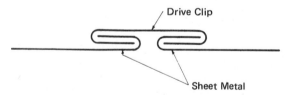

Fig. 3-10   Sectional View of Assembled Drive Clip.

Sometimes drive clips do not slide on easily, but heavy blows might bend the clip. To avoid bending the clip, hold it with a pair of clamping pliers, as shown in Fig. 3-12, and pound on the pliers instead of on the metal. This will burr the end of the clip slightly but will keep the main part

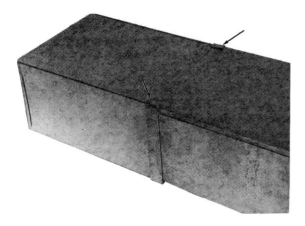

Fig. 3-11 Finished Drive Clips. Arrows Indicate How the Ends of the Clips Are Bent Around the Corner to Lock Them in Position.

of the clip intact. The bent part may be trimmed off after the clip is in place. A clip may be removed by the same process; hold the end with a pair of clamping pliers and pound on the pliers.

Drive clips are usually formed on a bar folder. If the strips are cut 2¼ in wide, the gauge is set at about ½ in. After one clip is bent, adjustments are made on the gauge to make the gap of the clip the size desired. Depending on individual preference, the gap will vary from ⅛ to ¼ in. Clips are also formed on lockforming machines.

S clips

S clips or *slips* are used either alone or with drive clips. When they are used with drive clips, the connection is known as an *S-and-drive clip*. The

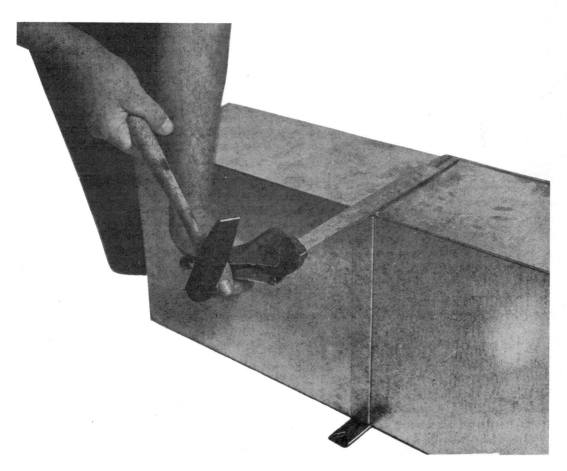

Fig. 3-12 Driving on a Tight Drive Clip.

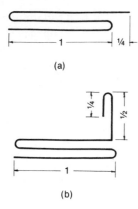

(a)

(b)

Fig. 3-13 Sectional View of S Clips.

name derives from the shape of the clip, as can be seen in Fig. 3-13*a*. S clips are usually formed on the bar folder with the gauge set at 1 in.

The standard dimensions for the S clip are shown in Fig. 3-13*a*, but this size can be varied for special jobs. Note that a ¼-in tail extends from one side of the clip. This makes it easier to slide the second piece of metal into the clip.

An extra ½-in allowance is added to both pieces of duct that fit into the S, so there is a total overlap of the two pieces of 1 in, as shown in Fig. 3-14.

When an S clip longer than about 18 in is used, it is usually made with a strongback. A sectional view of an S clip with a strongback is shown in Fig. 3-13*b*. The height of the strongback varies with the length of the clip but is usually about ½ in. The strongback is used on this clip because a long S has little rigidity and will sag without reinforcement. An S clip with a strongback is often called a *bar slip*.

Unlike the drive clip, the S clip will not hold two pieces of metal together; it merely makes a tight, smooth connection between the two pieces and keeps the two pieces of metal from lapping over more than 1 in. (See Fig. 3-14.)

The S clip is easy to install, because it slides over the first piece and the second piece is slid into it. If the clips are formed up too tightly, it is good practice to run a screwdriver through them; this opens them slightly and permits the metal to slide in more easily. When using a screwdriver to open a clip, take care not to run the hand across the edge of the clip, since a serious cut can result.

S-and-drive clips

The drive clip and the S clip are frequently combined as the S-and-drive clip to connect air-conditioning ducts together. It is standard practice to use the S clip on the two longest sides of the duct because it is the easiest clip to install. The drive clips are driven on the two short sides.

To start making the duct connection, slide the S clips onto the end of one duct. They are generally lapped as shown in Fig. 3-15. Note that the tail of one S is inside the pipe and the tail of the other S is outside. This means that, when the other duct is slid into the S, one side of it will lap inside the first duct and the other will lap outside. It is easier to make the connection if they are lapped this way rather than with both tails in or both out.

S-and-drive clips are easy to form and easy to use; they also make a flat seam that does not stick

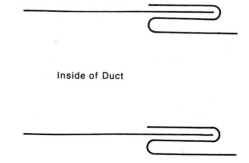

Inside of Duct

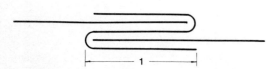

Fig. 3-14 Sectional View Showing the Total Lap of Metal When a 1-in S Clip is Used.

Fig. 3-15 Sectional View Showing How S Clips Are Lapped Inside and Outside of Duct.

out from the duct when it is finished. They are especially handy to use when a duct has to be run up against a wall where it would be impossible to reach behind to make up a government clip.

S-and-drive clips are not as stiff a connection as government clips and are usually used on ducts with the widest side 18 in or less. Generally, if they are used on ducts wider than 18 in, the S clip is made with a strongback in order to make the connection stiffer.

Double S clip

A double S is a wide strip of metal with an S formed on each edge, as shown in Fig. 3-16. This is used in spots that require a connection between two sheets but in which the sheets have a little gap between them. By making a double S instead of an S, a gap of several inches may be filled in.

The double S clip is also used to fasten sheets to a wall without the nails or screws showing. Figure 3-17 shows how this is done. The clip is fastened securely to the wall, and when the sheets are slipped into the clip, the nails are hidden but the sheet is held firmly.

Nailing clips

Nailing clip is not the name of any definite clip but of a number of different clips that accomplish the same purpose; to hold a sheet nailed down to a

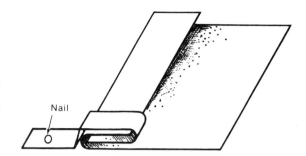

Fig. 3-18 Nailing Clips.

wood surface while hiding the nails from sight. In addition, some are designed to hold the sheets down but to allow for expansion and contraction of the metal.

A common type of nailing clip that was originally designed for use on lock-seam roofing is shown in Fig. 3-18. This clip is usually about 1 in wide. It hooks over the edge of the lock seam and is nailed into the wood surface. When the next sheet is hooked over the lock-seam edge, the nailing clip is completely covered. Nailing clips are used whenever there is a possibility that expansion and contraction of the sheets will pull up the nails. Nailing in this manner allows movement of the metal so that there is little strain on the nails.

Another common nailing clip is shown in Fig. 3-19. This clip is usually used when the sheet can be nailed down but the nail should not show. In this clip, a strip as long as the sheet itself is bent as shown in Fig. 3-19a. The clip is then inserted and nailed as shown in Fig. 3-19b. Care must be taken to keep the nails as close to the edge of the sheet as possible. After all the nails are in, the edge is

Fig. 3-16 Sectional View of Double S Clip.

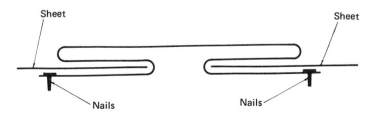

Fig. 3-17 Sectional View Showing How a Double S Clip Is Used to Fasten Sheets to a Wall with No Visible Nails.

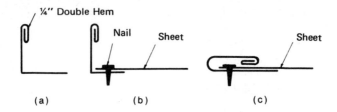

Fig. 3-19   Nailing Clip Used on Blind Seam.

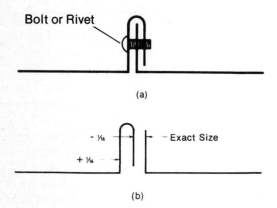

Fig. 3-20   Sectional Views of Standing Seam.

tapped over as shown in Fig. 3-19c. This edge hides the nails and looks like a double seam or a lock seam. In fact, this clip is often called a *blind seam*. The edge is tapped over with either a wooden mallet or a piece of wood held against the edge and hit with a hammer. This eliminates dents in the metal and looks better. The width of the finished clip is usually about ⅜ in.

Standing seam

The standing seam is used to connect large sheets together. Its principal advantages are that it acts as a stiffener as well as a connector, and that it can be bent as part of the sheet, with no extra pieces needed. The standing seam is shown in Fig. 3-20a. The seam is usually made at least ¾ in high and is secured by either rivets or bolts at intervals of about 12 in.

The size of this seam will vary with the job. Common sizes are ¾, ⅞, and 1 in. Whatever the

size of the seam, proper allowances for the edges have to be made. Figure 3-20b illustrates the proper allowances for the edges. The single edge is made to the exact size of the seam; the inside of the double edge is made $1/16$ in larger than this; and the outside edge of the double edge is made $1/16$ in smaller than the exact size. For a 1-in standing seam, the single edge will be exactly 1 in. The outside edge of the double edge will be $15/16$ in and the inside allowance $1^{1}/16$ in.

PRACTICE PROBLEMS

Problem 3-1

Purpose. To study the shape and dimensions of each type of connector.

Study. All of Chapter 4 with emphasis on the sectional views and dimensions of each connector.

Assignment. On a sheet of 12-by-18-in drawing paper, make a sectional view to full scale of the following connectors, and make a pattern to the size and scale indicated. Show full-scale dimensions.

1. Government clip: make a pattern for one side of a clip to fit a 4-in wide duct. Make it full size. (Remember that the government clip has a mitered corner and a rivet hole.)

2. S-and-drive clip: make patterns full size to fit a 3-by-5-in duct. (S clips are made ¼ in less than width of the duct.)

3. Standing seam: make patterns of two pieces of 3-by-4-in metal, with a ¾-in standing seam on the 4-in side. Make it full size.

4. Double S: make it 6 in long, to join two sheets that are 2 in apart. Make it full size.

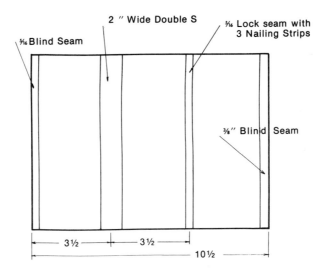

Fig. 3-21 Problem 3-4, Using Nailing Clips.

Problem 3-2

Purpose. To study the use of the government clip.

Study. *Government clip.*

Assignment. Make the patterns and form up a government clip to fit the duct shown in Fig. 4-24.

Problem 3-3

Purpose. To study the use of S-and-drive clips.

Study. *Drive clips, S clips, S-and-drive clips.*

Assignment. Make a set of S-and-drive clips to fit the tap-in shown in Fig. 4-27.

Problem 3-4

Purpose. To study the uses of nailing clips.

Study. *Double S clip, Nailing clips.*

Assignment. On a piece of 1-in pine board 6 by 12 in, nail down three strips of metal by use of the seams shown in Fig. 3-21. Make the seams 5½ in long at exactly the position indicated.

Problem 3-5

Purpose. To study the use of a standing seam.

Study. *Standing seam.*

Assignment. Join two pieces metal, 4 by 6 in, with a ⅞-in standing seam along the 6-in side.

4

Seams and Locks

Knowing how to design a job is just as important as knowing how to lay out the patterns. No matter how accurately the patterns are laid out, if the job is poorly designed, it will be unsatisfactory.

One of the most important features in job design is the proper choice of seams and edges. In Chapter 2, the common edges were described. In this chapter the most common seams are illustrated. These two chapters, plus the preceding chapter on clips and connectors, provide the background necessary to the layout worker.

Groove seam

The groove seam is also called the *Acme lock* in some areas. The shape of this lock is shown in Fig. 4-1. This is a flat seam; that is, it is not used on corners. The groove seam is frequently used to join two large pieces of metal together, but its most frequent use is in seaming round pipe and fittings.

A lockforming machine that can form an Acme lock is available, but many seams are still formed on a bar folder and by a hand groover. For some production work a grooving machine is used to set down the seam, but in the ordinary shop it is usually done by hand. Since both the lockformer and the grooving machine do not require any training or special knowledge for their use, the student should concentrate on learning to make a

neat groove seam by hand. If he or she learns to do this, then the operation of the special machines is simple.

Allowances for the groove seam are always a problem for the beginner, who usually assumes that the groove seam will take twice the amount of the bend because there are two bends. This is not the case. *The correct allowance for a groove seam is three times the amount of the bend.* Close examination of the sectional view in Fig. 4-1 will show that three laps of metal must be added in order to make the seam.

The allowance rule for a groove seam is "three times the bend equals the full allowance." One-half the full allowance is added to each end of the pattern. For a ¼-in groove seam, the full allowance will be 3 × ¼ in, which is ¾ in. Half of this, or ⅜ in, must be added to each end of the pattern.

The ¼-in seam is the most common size for a groove seam because it is the easiest to form. Smaller seams are difficult to keep hooked together, and larger seams are too wide to make a neat job. Smaller seams are sometimes used on special jobs, but larger seams are seldom used.

Double seam

The double seam is a corner seam. In its finished form, it is shaped somewhat like a groove seam, as shown in Fig. 4-2. This is a very strong seam and is neat in appearance when done skillfully. However, it is a difficult seam to form, and those done by a beginner are usually very unsightly.

Fig. 4-1 Sectional View of Groove Seam.

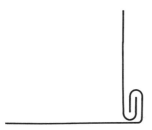

Fig. 4-2 Sectional View of Double Seam.

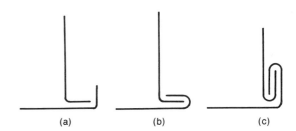

(a)   (b)   (c)

Fig. 4-4 Steps in Forming a Double Seam.

Formerly, the double seam was used frequently on any fitting requiring a corner seam. However, other seams, principally the Pittsburgh seam, have gradually replaced it. The double seam is still sometimes used to seam bottoms on round cans and tanks, but even here the Pittsburgh seam has replaced it to some extent. Nevertheless, the double seam is still a very necessary seam for the sheet metal and layout worker to know.

Although the double seam is difficult, requiring great accuracy in layout and skill in forming, it has the advantages of strength and of the ease with which it can be soldered and made watertight. The beginner can attain competence after forming a dozen or so practice seams, and will then know how to make the neatest looking of all the common seams.

The usual size of the double seam is ¼ in, but other sizes may be made. On any size seam, the same differences in measurements are allowed. Figure 4-3 shows the allowances for a ¼-in double seam. On the two pieces of metal, the patterns end at point *A* and at point *B*. On the single edge, a full

¼ in is allowed. On the double edge, the inside allowance is $9/32$ in, which allows an extra $1/32$ in of metal to clear the ¼-in edge. The outside allowance is made $7/32$ in to ensure that it can be clinched over without being too large. Some layout workers use slightly different measurements for a ¼-in double seam, but the system of allowing $1/32$ in over and $1/32$ in under on the double edge is always observed.

To form this seam, three definite steps are followed, as shown in Fig. 4-4. First, the single edge is set into the double edge, as shown in Fig. 4-4*a*. Then the double edge is clinched down over the single edge, as shown in Fig. 4-4*b*. Next the double edge is formed around the corner to finish the seam as shown in Fig. 4-4*c*.

Coffin lock

The coffin lock, shown in Fig. 4-5, is also called the *pocket lock*. This lock requires solder to hold it together, but once it is soldered, it is a very strong seam. Its purpose is to provide a corner seam that is smooth on the outside, and it is used on corners

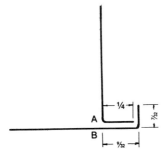

Fig. 4-3 Allowances for a ¼-inch Double Seam.

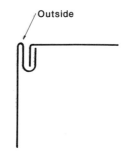

Outside

Fig. 4-5 Sectional View of Coffin Lock.

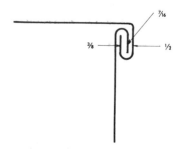

Fig. 4-6   Sectional View Showing Scrap of Metal Inserted in Coffin Lock before Smashing Down.

Fig. 4-8   Sectional View of Slip Lock.

that require invisible seams. The coffin lock seam is soldered on the inside, and then the outside is skim soldered. The outside is then filed off until the seam is hidden. Since this seam takes more time to make than a Pittsburgh seam, it is not used often.

All the bends for forming this seam are made on the brake. To avoid the extra work of opening up the seam, and also to eliminate some of the possibility of denting the metal, a scrap piece of metal is inserted into the double part of the seam before it is smashed completely in the brake. This is shown in Fig. 4-6. This scrap of metal is left in the seam during all the forming operations until the two pieces of metal are ready to be joined. It is then pulled out with a pair of pliers, leaving a gap in the lock large enough to insert the edge.

The usual size for a coffin lock is ¼ in, although 5/16-in and ⅜-in locks are used occasionally. The rule of allowance for metal clearance is the same as that used for the double seam. Figure 4-7 shows the dimensions for a ¼-in coffin lock. Other sizes of locks require the same amount of clearance.

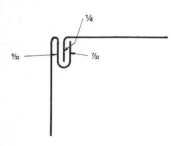

Fig. 4-7   Dimensions of a ¼-inch Coffin Lock.

Slip lock

The *slip lock* has different names in different parts of the country. It is sometimes called a *double-seam duct lock,* a *slide lock,* or simply a *duct lock.* In the sectional view, shown in Fig. 4-8, it has the

same shape as a double seam. However, this lock is formed completely on the brake, and then the two pieces are slid together. Because bends are formed in the brake, the slip lock can only be used on straight corners. It could not be used for the corner seam of a round can, for instance.

This lock is still used occasionally, but its use has been greatly curtailed since the development of the lockforming machines for forming Pittsburgh seams. However, some shops have specially designed lockforming machines that form the edges for the slip lock. In these shops it is felt that this lock is faster to assemble than the Pittsburgh seam.

In forming the edges for the slip lock, great care must be taken that the bends are accurate and that none of the locks are smashed so tightly that they will not slide together easily.

The allowances for the slip lock usually differ from those for the double seam and the coffin lock. Since the slip lock is often slid together in 8-foot lengths, the clearance must be large enough to ensure that it will slide easily. Figure 4-8 shows the allowances for a ½-in slip lock, which is a common size, but these dimensions may be varied.

Pittsburgh seam

One of the most common locks in the sheet metal trade is the Pittsburgh seam. It is sometimes known as the *hobo lock, hammer lock,* or *Irish lock.* The Pittsburgh seam is a corner seam that can be used on either straight or curved edges. The most important seam for duct work, it is used more than 90 percent of the time.

The Pittsburgh seam can be formed either on the brake or by a lockforming machine, such as is

Fig. 4-9 Lockforming Machine Forming a Pittsburgh Seam. *(Lockformer Company)*

shown in Fig. 4-9. If the seam is formed on the brake, the allowance is 1¼ in; if it is formed in a machine, the allowance will vary from ⅞ to 1⅛ in, depending upon the lockformer. The shape of the Pittsburgh seam is shown in Fig. 4-10. Note that there are two parts to the seam; the Pittsburgh seam, and the ¼-in edge that will fit into it. Typical applications for the Pittsburgh seam are shown in Fig. 4-11.

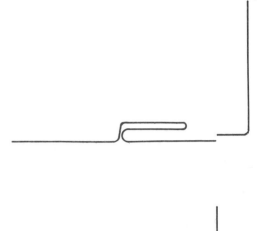

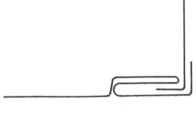

Finished Seam

Fig. 4-10 Sectional View of Pittsburgh Seam.

Fig. 4-11 Fittings Made with Pittsburgh Seams.

Fig. 4-12 Square Duct with a Tap-in. Drawing Shows a Sectional View of the Tap-in Lock.

Fig. 4-13 View from Inside of Duct Showing How the Tap-in Lock Is Locked in Place.

Fig. 4-14 Sweep Tap-in.

Tap-in lock

A very common lock used in duct work is the tap-in lock. This lock is used to connect a small rectangular duct to the side of a larger duct, usually at right angles to it, as shown in Fig. 4-12. This figure also shows the shape of the tap-in lock, and the usual allowance of ¾ in on each bend.

To install the tap-in lock, a hole is cut in the side of the duct into which the tap-in is to be connected. The tail of the tap-in is inserted into the hole and then knocked over against the inside of the main duct to lock it into place, as shown in Fig. 4-13. Notice that in Fig. 4-13 the tail of the tap-in is cut to form small sections. This makes it easier to bend over, especially in places that are hard to reach.

The tap-in lock is used almost exclusively to make right-angle connections in rectangular ducts. It is popular because it is easy to form and because it can be readily used to tap a new duct line into existing ducts.

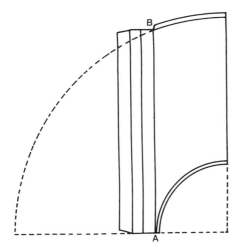

Fig. 4-15 Layout of Check of Sweep Tap-in.

Fig. 4-16 A Tap-in Whose Width Equals That of the Main Duct.

Fig. 4-17 Sectional View Showing Shape of The Top and Bottom of the Tap-in Lock Shown in Fig. 4-16.

Sweep tap-in

An ordinary tap-in lock connects at a 90° angle to the main duct. In order to make a more gradual turn, a sweep tap-in is sometimes used. This is a tap-in with a radius in the throat, as shown in Fig. 4-14. The pattern for the cheek is started just as if a regular elbow cheek were being laid out. After the elbow cheek is laid out, as shown by the dotted lines in Fig. 4-15, a line is squared up from point *A* to form line *AB*. The part of the elbow shown by the solid lines forms the pattern. The seam and tap-in lock allowances are added to this.

S tap-in

Figure 4-16 shows a variation of the tap-in lock, in which the width of the tap-in and the width of the main duct are equal. Since the equal widths leave no room for a tap-in lock on the top and the bottom, a form of S lock is used. The tap-in is formed in the usual way, with the tap-in lock on all four edges. However, after it is formed, hand tongs are used to straighten out the flange and form the lock into the shape shown in the detail in Fig. 4-17. The sides are left in the normal shape and hold the tap-in in place.

Dovetail seam

A dovetail seam is used in the same manner as a tap-in lock, except that it is used for round pipe. In construction it consists of a series of tabs cut into the end of the pipe, with every other tab bent out at a 90° angle. This is shown in Fig. 4-18a.

To connect the dovetail to a duct, a hole of the proper size is cut in the metal and the straight tabs of the dovetail are inserted in the hole as shown in Fig. 4-18b. After the tabs are inserted in the hole, they are knocked over in order to lock the dovetail in place. This results in alternating tabs on opposite sides of the metal, as shown in Fig. 4-18c.

A dovetail seam can be used whenever a round pipe is to be fastened onto a flat piece of metal. The roof jack in Fig. 4-19 shows a typical application of this type of lock. The dovetail seam is popular because it is fast and can be done on the job without any special equipment.

The usual procedure for marking the hole for the dovetail is to set the pipe on the spot it is to fit before the tabs are cut; then the pipe is scribed around to mark the hole. The cuts for the tabs are straight cuts, square to the edge of the pipe. The

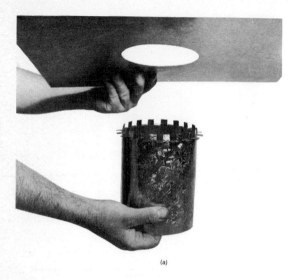

(a)

(b)

(c)

Fig. 4-18   Steps in Making a Dovetail Seam.

Fig. 4-19   Typical Application of Dovetail Seam.

usual size for these cuts is about ⅜ in wide and ⅜ in deep. However, the size of the tabs will vary with the size of the pipe; a very large pipe will have larger tabs. Tab size is governed by appearance and by the speed with which they can be cut.

On pipes of normal size, the natural tendency of the pipe to retain its round shape will hold the tabs in place. On very large pipes of light gauge, the pipe is liable to sag, allowing the tabs to slip away from the plate. In cases where this is a danger, the tabs are soldered or spot welded in place at intervals.

Elbow lock

The elbow lock, like many other seams, has lost much of its importance. However, it is still necessary for the sheet metal worker to know it. It is usually used to join sections of round pipe together. One of its most common uses is on round elbows, such as the one shown in the right foreground of Fig. 4-20, to connect the gores. Another frequent use is for fastening round collars onto fittings like those shown in Fig. 4-20.

The elbow lock is formed by a special elbow machine, illustrated in Fig. 4-21. There are many machines similar to the elbow machine. In fact, changing the wheels on the elbow machine converts it into a different machine.

Fig. 4-20 Typical Applications of the Elbow Lock.

Fig. 4-21 Elbow Machine.

The allowance for the elbow lock is $^3/_{16}$ in on both edges that are to be joined. Many times the allowance for the elbow lock is completely omitted, since the only difference it will make is in the length of the fitting, which in many cases is not critical.

PRACTICE PROBLEMS

Problem 4-1

Purpose. To study the shape and allowance for each seam.

Study. All of Chapter 4, with emphasis on the sectional view and allowance of each seam.

Assignment.

1. On a sheet of 12-by-18-in drawing paper, make a sectional view to the scale indicated of all the seams and locks listed under 2.

2. Make a full-scale pattern, with dimensions, of all allowances of the following seams and locks. Make each side of each seam finish 2 in wide.
   a. Double seam (double scale)
   b. Coffin lock (double scale)
   c. Slip lock (double scale)
   d. Hand Pittsburgh seam (full scale)
   e. Groove seam (full scale)
   f. Tap-in lock (full scale)

Problem 4-2

Purpose. To study the practical uses of the groove seam.

Study. *Groove seam.*

Assignment. Cut two pieces of 26-gauge galvanized iron, 4 by 6 in, and seam them together on the 6-in side, using a ¼-in groove seam.

Problem 4-3

Purpose. To learn how to use the double seam in practical application.

Study. *Double seam.*

Assignment.

1. Lay out the patterns for a rectangular box, as shown in Fig. 4-22. Make it in three pieces, setting in the ends with a ¼-in double seam. Lay it out full size. Include all dimensions.

2. Make the box out of 26-gauge galvanized iron.

Problem 4-4

Purpose. To study another practical application of the double seam.

Study. *Double seam.*

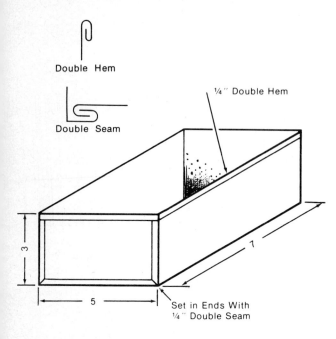

Double Hem

¼" Double Hem

Double Seam

3

7

5

Set in Ends With
¼" Double Seam

Make in Three Pieces

Fig. 4-22   Problems 4-3 and 4-6.

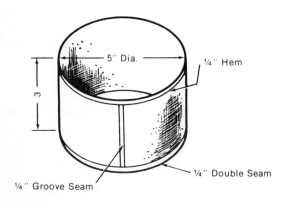

5" Dia.

¼" Hem

3

¼" Double Seam

¼" Groove Seam

Fig. 4-23   Problem 4-4, Using Double Seams on Round Cans.

Assignment.

1. Lay out the patterns for the round can shown in Fig. 4-23. Lay out all the patterns full size. Include all dimensions. Indicate all necessary notches.

2. Make the can out of 26-gauge galvanized iron.

Problem 4-5

Purpose. To study practical applications of the coffin lock.

Study. *Coffin lock.*

Assignment. Cut two pieces of 26-gauge iron, 4 by 6 in, and seam them together on the 6-in side, using a ¼-in coffin lock on the corner.

Problem 4-6

Purpose. To study practical applications of the coffin lock.

Study. *Coffin lock.*

Assignment. Make the box shown in Fig. 4-22. All the dimensions and specifications will be the same as shown in the drawing, except that a ¼-in coffin lock will be substituted for the double seam.

Problem 4-7

Purpose. To study practical applications of the slip lock.

Study. *Slip lock.*

Assignment.

1. Lay out the patterns for two adjacent sides of the rectangular duct shown in Fig. 4-24. Lay them out full size and include all dimensions. Indicate all notches.

2. Form up the complete pipe.

Problem 4-8

Purpose. To study practical applications of the Pittsburgh seam.

Study. *Pittsburgh seam.*

Assignment. Cut two pieces of 26-gauge iron, 4 by 6 in, and join them with a hand Pittsburgh seam along the 6-in side.

Problem 4-9

Purpose. To study practical applications of the Pittsburgh seam.

Study. *Pittsburgh seam.*

Assignment.

1. Lay out the pipe shown in Fig. 4-24, and join each corner with a hand Pittsburgh seam instead of with a slip lock.

2. Form up the complete fitting.

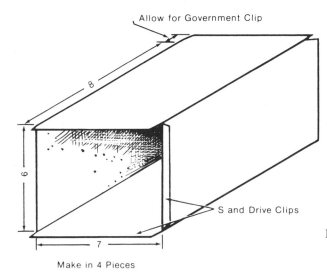

Allow for Government Clip

8

6

7

S and Drive Clips

Make in 4 Pieces

5⁄16″ Slip Lock on All 4 Corners

Fig. 4-24   Problems 4-7 and 4-9.

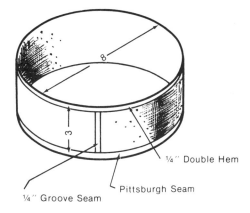

8

3

¼″ Double Hem

Pittsburgh Seam

¼″ Groove Seam

Fig. 4-25   Problem 4-10, Using the Pittsburgh Seam.

Problem 4-10

Purpose. To study practical applications of the Pittsburgh seam on curve corners.

Study. *Pittsburgh seam.*

Assignment.

1. Lay out the patterns for the pan shown in Fig. 4-25. These patterns must be very accurate because it is very difficult to fit in the bottom of a round pan with a Pittsburgh seam if the stretchout of the rim is not exact.

2. Make the complete pan and solder it on the inside.

Problem 4-11

Purpose. To study practical application of a tap-in lock.

Study. *Tap-in lock.*

Assignment.

1. Make the pattern for the tap-in shown in Fig. 4-26.
2. Make the complete fitting.

Problem 4-12

Purpose. To study practical applications of the S tap-in.

Study. *S tap-in.*

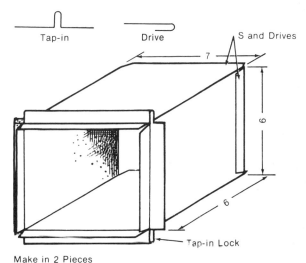

Tap-in

Drive

S and Drives

7

6

6

Tap-in Lock

Make in 2 Pieces
Pittsburgh Seam on Corners

Fig. 4-26   Problem 4-11, Using the Tap-in.

Assignment.

1. Take the tap-in made in problem 4-11 and form the top and bottom into S locks, using hand tongs.

2. Cut a hole to the proper size in the duct made in problem 4-9 and connect the tap-in.

Problem 4-13

Purpose. To study the use of the sweep tap-in.

Study. *Sweep tap-in.*

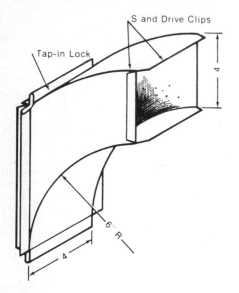

Fig. 4-27   Problem 4-13, Making a Sweep Tap-in.

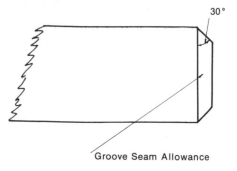

Groove Seam Allowance

Fig. 4-28   Notching for Elbow Lock.

Assignment.

1. Lay out the patterns needed for the sweep tap-in shown in Fig. 4-27.

2. Make the sweep tap-in and connect it into the side of the duct from problem 4-7.

Problem 4-14

Purpose. To study the practical applications of the elbow lock.

Study. *Elbow lock.*

Assignment. Make six pieces of round pipe 5 in in diameter and long enough so that all the sections are of equal length and total finished length is 24 in when they are joined by elbow locks. Pay particular attention to the notching of the elbow lock, as this is important for a neat job. When an elbow lock and a groove seam are used on pipe, the notch is made as shown in Fig. 4-28. The 30° angle is not measured but is estimated when notching. Remember to allow for the metal used by the elbow lock.

Problem 4-15

Purpose. To practice using the dovetail lock.

Study. *Dovetail seam.*

Assignment. Take the collars joined in problem 4-14 and dovetail one end of the pipe into the top of the duct made in problem 4-7. Make the hole in the duct close to one end so that it will be convenient to hammer over the tabs.

Duct Offsets

Whenever a square or rectangular duct is used, transitions and offsets are needed. A student learning the fundamentals of pattern drafting usually works on problems involving rectangular offsets and transitions. However, these problems are generally made in one piece for practice in triangulation. In shop practice offsets and transitions are usually made in two or four pieces, because this is generally the most economical method of cutting them out of the metal.

The purpose of this chapter is to discuss the layout and fabrication of transitions and offsets. It is assumed that the student has learned the fundamental principles of triangulation and true lengths.

Two-piece transitions

Whenever duct work is used, it is usually necessary to change size at some point in the system. The fittings that change size are usually called *transitions*. They are also offsets because they also usually move the side of the duct over one way or another.

A common type of transition is shown in Fig. 5-1; the change is only in the height, and therefore the bottom or top can be flat. This type of fitting is often made in two pieces because it can be cut out of the sheet economically and also saves time by eliminating two corner seams. The bottom and the two parallel sides are made in one piece, and the slanted top is made separately.

The bottom and sides are laid out as shown in Fig. 5-2a. The fourth side is separate, as shown in Fig. 5-2b. Note that the length of this pattern is the

length of the slant of the sides of the first pattern, as indicated by *x*. No allowances are shown on these patterns for seams and edges.

Four-piece transitions

Transitions are often made in four pieces with Pittsburgh seams on the corners. Technically, this is a very simple layout that only involves simple true lengths, but in actual practice mistakes are easily made. Therefore, it is necessary for the student to follow certain set practices when laying these fittings out so as to avoid the common errors.

Figure 5-3 shows a common transition fitting that will serve to illustrate recommended practices. This fitting changes from 9 by 11 in to 6 by 7 in. It is not a centered fitting; the plan view shows two sides slanting in a horizontal distance of 1 in. The other sides slant in enough to make up the proper size opening.

In laying out the patterns for a fitting of this type, it is important that the patterns be laid out with the inside up and that they be marked "inside" as soon as each pattern is completed. If this practice is followed, much confusion will be eliminated.

It may at first seem easier to lay out each side from the center line, but actually it will be easier to learn to lay each side out by measuring from a squared line on the left side of the pattern.

Figure 5-4a shows the plan view of the fitting with the corners lettered and the sides numbered. In the actual layout of the fitting only a sketch is

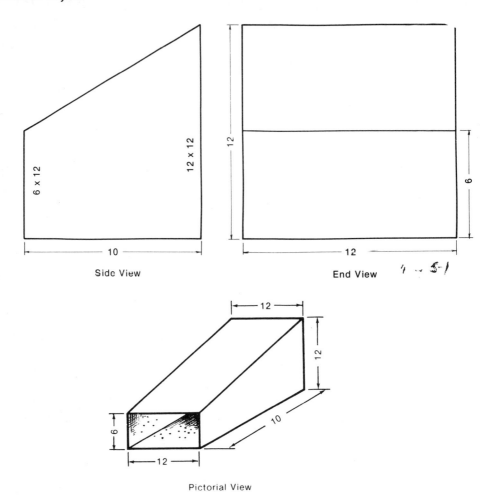

6 x 12

12 x 12

Side View

12

6

End View   4 ~ 5-1

12

12

6

10

12

Pictorial View

Fig. 5-1   Duct Transition with Slant on One Side.

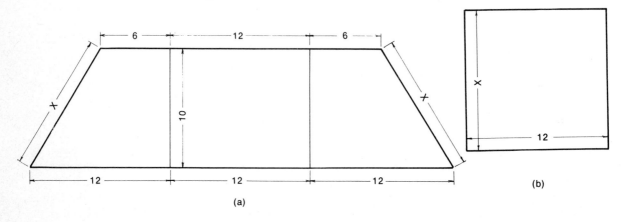

6

12

6

X

10

X

X

12

12

12

12

12

(a)

(b)

Fig. 5-2   Patterns for Fig. 5-1.

Plan View

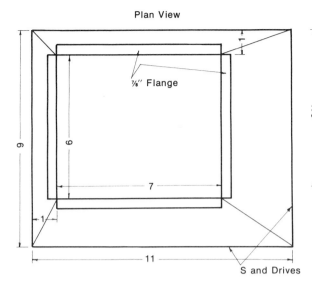

⅞″ Flange

9

6

7

11

1

1

⅞″ Flange

S and Drives

Elevation View

⅞″ Flange

6½

S and Drives

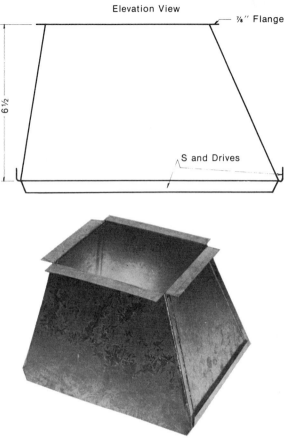

Fig. 5-3 Four-piece Transition.

needed; the plan view is shown here only to make the explanation clearer.

To lay out side 1, first find the true length of its center line. The center line is shown as line *KL*. Since the fitting is to be 6½ in high and this particular side slants in 1 in, the true length of *KL* will be found by drawing a 6½-on-1-in triangle, as shown in Fig. 5-4b. This gives the true length of *KL* as 6⁹/₁₆ in. Once the length of the center line is determined, the side can be laid out.

To start the side, first draw a line 11 in long, which is the length of line DC in Fig. 5-4a. Mark the ends with the proper letters, as shown in Fig. 5-4b, being careful to locate them so the pattern will have the inside up. The best method of doing this is to try to picture yourself inside the fitting. Looking at this side, Point *D* is on your left. Therefore, *D* must also be on the left on the pattern if it is to be inside up.

After line *DC* is drawn, square up a line from point *D*. This will give a reference line to measure from. Draw the top line of the pattern parallel to

DC and 6⁹/₁₆ in up from it, which is the true length found for the center line. These steps are also shown in Fig. 5-4b.

The next step is to locate points *H* and *G*. Since side 3 slants in 1 in also, point *H* must be in 1 in over from *D*. Therefore, measure 1 in over from the squared line to locate point *H*, as shown in Fig. 5-4b. Since the top of the fitting is 7 in wide on this side, measuring 7 in from *H* will establish point *G*.

Connect points *H* and *D* with a straight line, and do the same with points *G* and *C*. This finishes the pattern for side 1, except for seam allowances. Mark the pattern "inside" and add any other markings necessary for forming.

To lay out side 2, first find the true length of the center line *NM*. This side must also rise a vertical distance of 6½ in, but the horizontal measurement is not given. However, this can be found by adding

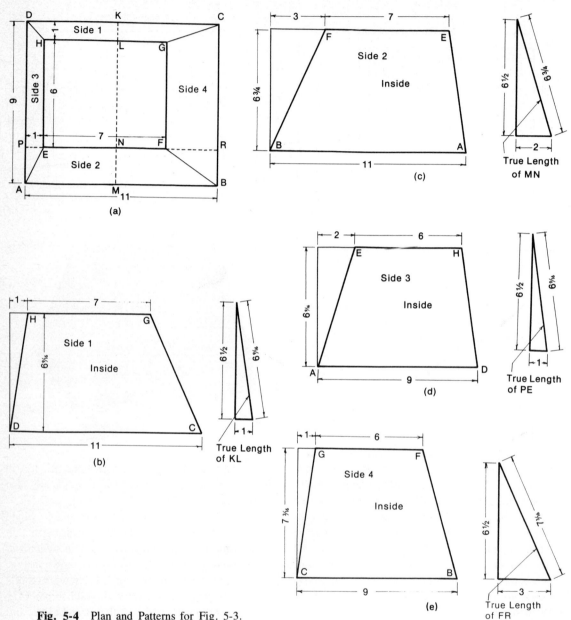

Fig. 5-4   Plan and Patterns for Fig. 5-3.

and subtracting measurements. In the plan view in Fig. 5-4*a, KL* is 1 in and the distance from *L* to *N* is shown to be 6 in. Therefore, the distance from *K* to *N* is a total of 7 in. The overall distance from *D* to *A* is given as 9 in so the distance from *N* to *M* is 9 minus 7, or 2 in. Therefore the true length of *NM* will be found on a 6½-on-2-in triangle, as shown in Fig. 5-4*c*.

To start the pattern for the side, first draw a line 11 in long for line *AB,* as shown in Fig. 5-4*c.* Since the inside should be up, point *B* must be on the left-hand end of the line. Next, draw a line parallel to *AB* and 6¾ in away, since this is the true length just found. Also, draw a line square to line *AB* from point *B.*

The next step is to determine how much point *F* is slanted in from the square line. This is again done by adding and subtracting dimensions from the plan view in Fig. 5-4*a.* The distance from point *P* to point *F* on the plan is a total of 8 in. The distance from *A* to *B* is 11 in. Therefore the distance from *F* to *R* is 11 minus 8, or 3 in. Point *F* can be located on the pattern, therefore, by measuring in 3 in from the square line. Point *E* can then be located 7 in over from point *F.* Draw in the lines to connect the points to complete the pattern, as shown in Fig. 5-4*c,* and add the necessary allowances for seams and edges. Mark the pattern "inside" to avoid confusion later on.

To lay out side 3, first find the true length of *PE,* which will be a 6½-on-1-in triangle. This is shown in Fig. 5-4*d.* Since this side slants 1 in, which is the same amount that side 1 slants, the true length will be the same—$6^9/_{16}$ in.

To start the layout of the pattern, first draw the line *AD,* which will be 9 in long. To have the inside up, point *A* should be on the left. Next, draw a line parallel to *AD* and $6^9/_{16}$ in away from it. Also draw the square line up from point *A.* To locate point *E* along the upper line, measure from the square line the distance of *MN,* which was previously figured to be 2 in. Connect the proper points with straight lines to complete the pattern.

To lay out side 4, the true length of *FR* is first found. On the plan view, *FR* was figured to be 3 in when side 2 was laid out. Therefore, the true-length triangle for the length of side 4 will be 6½ on 3 in as shown in Fig. 5-4*e.* To have the inside up, draw line *CB* with point *C* on the left. Draw the top line $7^3/_{16}$ in up from *CB,* and square up the reference line from point *C.*

Point *G* is located by measuring the distance of *KL* over from the squared line. This distance is 1 in. By measuring 6 in from point *G,* point *F* is found. Draw in the corner lines to finish the pattern.

Checking the accuracy of the layout

As can be seen, the principles involved in the layout of these patterns are comparatively simple. However, in the process of figuring dimensions and finding true lengths, it is easy to make mistakes. Therefore, it is wise to check the accuracy of the patterns before cutting them out. Checking patterns for this type of fitting is done by checking the matching corners to see whether they are the same length. This means that *DH* of side 1 has to be the same length as *DH* of side 3. In the same way, the other three corner lines have to be the same length on the two patterns. If any of the corner lines do not match, one of the patterns is wrong.

If *DH,* for instance, does not match in the two patterns, either side 3 or side 1 is wrong. Checking *GC,* the other corner of side 1, will show whether side 1 is right or wrong. If *GC* matches the length of *GC* in side 4, then side 1 is correct. If it does not match, then side 1 is probably wrong. The same process can be followed for side 3.

If a pattern is wrong, check the true length of the center line. If it is correct, the error is probably in the slant of the corner lines and these should be checked. Although the opposite sides of this pattern are different, they differ only in the length of the center line. In order for the fitting to be square, the opposite sides must have the same amount of slant in on the corners. If they do not, one of the patterns is wrong.

S offsets

An important class of fittings in duct work is S offsets. A typical S offset is shown in Fig. 5-5. These fittings are used in place of transitional fittings where the amount of offset is so great that a straight-sided offset is too abrupt. S offsets can make a very great offset and still provide a smooth curve for the air to follow, which cannot be done with a straight transition. As with plain offsets, these fittings can also be made as transitional offsets.

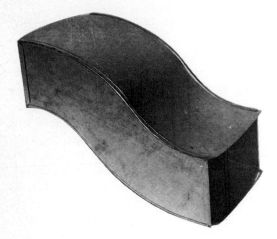

Fig. 5-5 S Offset.

Pittsburgh Seams on All 4 Corners

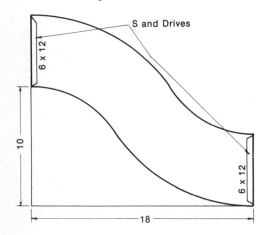

Fig. 5-6 Standard S Offset.

Standard S offset. Figure 5-6 is a drawing of what is usually called a *regular S,* or a *straight S,* offset. "Straight" refers to the fact that the size of the duct does not change on either end. The layout for this S offset is basic because other, more complicated S offsets are based upon it.

To lay out an S offset, four basic steps are always followed. There are variations in more complicated fittings, but these steps are always necessary.

Step 1. Locate the four corners of the offset and the center point of each end.

Step 2. Draw the center line and divide it into four equal parts.

Step 3. Draw lines square to the center line through the quarter points.

Step 4. Swing the arcs, using the intersection of the squared lines and the end lines as center.

A detailed explanation of the four steps is shown in Fig. 5-7, as the pattern for the cheek of the fitting shown in Fig. 5-6 is laid out. In step 1, first measure a line 18 in long, the length of the offset shown in Fig. 5-6. Next, square up lines at each end of this line. On one of the squared-up lines measure off 6 in, the width of the fitting. This locates the corner points C and D. On the other end, first measure 10 in, the amount of the offset, and then measure up 6 in, the width of the fitting. Point F is then located midway between points A and B, and point E is located midway between points D and C. Points F and E are the center points of the ends.

In step 2, connect points E and F with a center line. Then step off the center line into four equal spaces. In any S offset, the center lines are always divided into four equal spaces. This is never changed.

In step 3, lines are drawn square to the center line, through the quarter points K and L.

In step 4, use points H and G, which are the points of intersection of the squared lines and the end lines, as centers; swing arcs through the corner points of the fitting. Point H is the center for the arcs through points A and B. Point G is the center for the arcs through points D and C. If the layout is exact, the curve through B and the curve through D will meet perfectly. The same applies for the curve through A and C. In actual shop practice, these arcs may miss each other. Even if they miss by as much as ½ in, the usual practice is to ignore the error and sketch in a smooth curve to fill in the gap, rather than to take the time to do the fitting over.

S offset that changes size in the cheek. Another common S offset is one that changes size in the

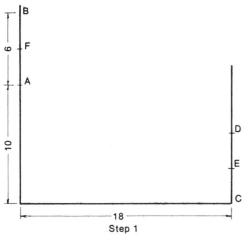

Step 1

Locate the Four Corners and the Center Points

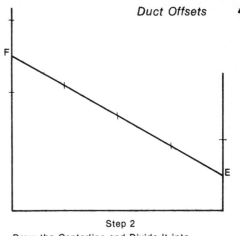

Step 2

Draw the Centerline and Divide It Into
4 Equal Spaces

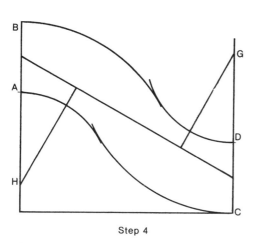

Step 4

Swing the Arcs

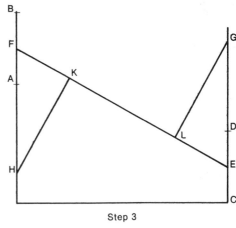

Step 3

Draw Lines Square to the Centerline
and Through the Quarter Points

Fig. 5-7 The Four Steps in Laying Out a Standard S Offset.

cheeks but not in the heel and throat. Figure 5-8 shows a shop drawing of such a fitting. In shop work usually only a rough drawing such as this is given for the mechanic to work from. On a shop drawing, it is understood that the first dimension is the dimension of the side shown. Thus, in Fig. 5-8, in the dimension "6 by 12," 6 is the dimension of the cheek shown and 12 is the width of the heel and throat.

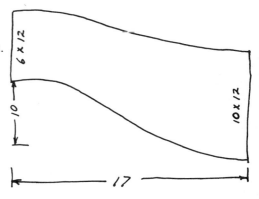

Fig. 5-8 Shop Sketch of an S Offset That Changes Size in the Cheek.

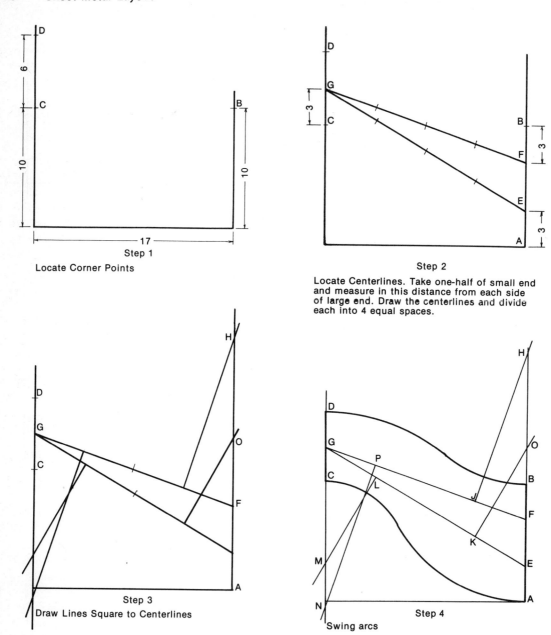

Fig. 5-9 The Four Steps in Laying Out an S Offset That Changes Size in the Cheek.

To lay out the cheek of this fitting, the four basic steps given in the previous problem are still followed. The only difference is that two "center lines" are used.

Step 1. Locate the corner points of the offset. Figure 5-9, step 1, shows the dimensions used to locate the corner points of the offset. This is the same procedure as for a straight offset.

Step 2. Locate the center lines of the fitting. Figure 5-9, step 2, shows the procedure for locating the center lines of the fitting. When the offset changes size in the cheek, two center lines are used. The object is to find the difference between the two ends and add this to the middle of the large end. This is done by first marking the center *G* of the small end, as shown in step 2. Then take one-half the width of the small end (in this case 3 inches) and measure this distance in from each side of the large end. This gives the distances *AE* and *BF*, both of which are 3 in. The distance *EF* is the difference between the two ends. Two center lines, *GF* and *GE*, are then drawn in.

Step 3. Draw lines square to the center line quarter points. The two center lines are next divided into four equal spaces, and lines are squared up from the quarter points just as in a straight offset.

Step 4. Swing the arcs. The arcs for this offset are swung in the same manner as for any offset. In an offset that changes size in the cheek, care must be taken to use the correct center for each arc. In step 4, point *M* is the center for the arc through *C*. Point *N* is the center for the arc through *D*. Point *H* is the center for the arc through *B*. Point *O* is the center for the arc through *A*. A simple way to determine which center is for which arc is to remember that the top center line determines the centers for the top arcs, and the bottom center line determines the centers for the bottom arcs. Thus, the lines squared from center line *GF* determine the centers for the top arcs that pass through points *D* and *B*. In the same manner, the lines squared from the center line *GE* determine the centers for the bottom arcs that pass through points *C* and *A*.

The curves should meet exactly, but in actual practice they may miss by as much as ½ in. However, if the arcs miss by a large amount which makes it apparent that a mistake has been made, the probable cause is that the arcs have been swung from the wrong center.

S offset that changes size in the heel and throat. Laying out the cheek for the standard S offset and for the offset that changes size in the cheek requires only the two methods previously explained. All possible types of these S-offset cheeks can be laid out by these two methods. However, Fig. 5-10 shows an S offset that changes size in the heel and throat. This type of fitting uses the same principles of layout as any other S offset, but there are several new methods to determine true lengths that must be learned.

Figure 5-10 shows that the fitting changes from a 6-by-12-in to a 6-by-6-in opening, and that one side is flat. This means that the slanted side must slant in the difference between 12 and 6, or 6 in. Figure 5-10 also shows a plan view of the fitting, illustrating the amount of the slant of the sides. The length of the flat cheek, *CD*, is the length of the fitting. The length of the slanted cheek is *AB*. These lengths are the actual lengths of the cheeks of the fitting.

The length of the slanted cheek can be found without drawing the plan view by drawing a true-length triangle. Use the length of the fitting as the base and the amount of the slant of the cheek as the height, as shown in Fig. 5-10. The length of the slanted cheek is found to be 17⅛ in.

Once the length of each cheek is found, they are laid out in the regular manner. The only difference between developing the pattern for this fitting and the previous two is that the lengths of the two cheeks are different. The layout for both cheeks is shown in Fig. 5-11.

Figure 5-11*a* shows the layout of the flat side. It is made 16 in long, the length of the fitting. Note that the pattern is turned with the inside up. It is important that the cheeks of any S offset be marked "inside." It is possible to turn the edges "inside out" so the two cheeks will not match up.

Figure 5-11*b* shows the layout for the slanted cheek. The length of this cheek will be 17⅛ in, the true length found in Fig. 5-10*a*. Except for the difference in length, the procedure for laying out this cheek is the same as that for the flat cheek. Note that it is also turned with the inside up and marked "inside" as soon as it is laid out.

Figure 5-12 shows the pattern for the heel and throat for the fitting. The length from *C* to *D* is found by measuring around the curve of the flat

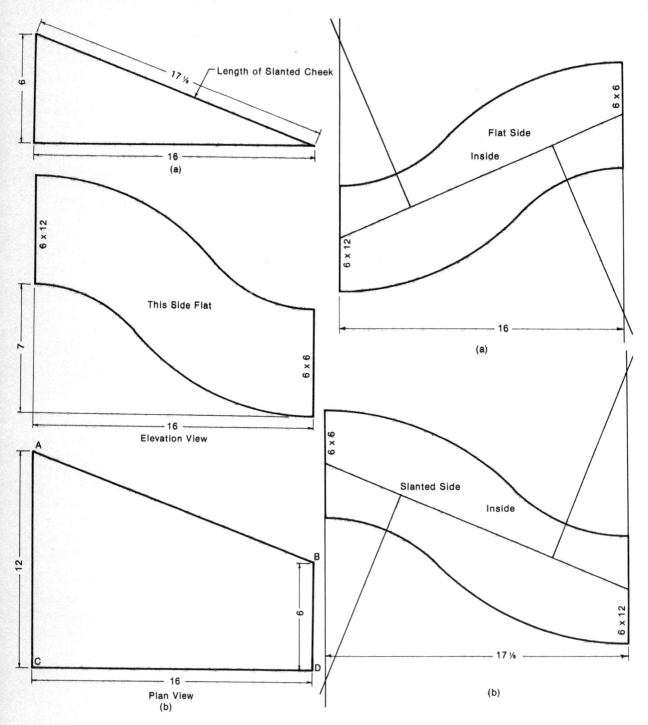

Fig. 5-10   S Offset That Changes Size in the Heel and Throat.

Fig. 5-11   Patterns for Cheeks of Offset in Fig. 5-10.

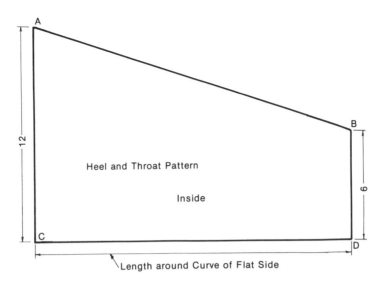

Fig. 5-12 Pattern for Heel and Throat of Offset in Fig. 5-10.

side cheek with a flexible rule. After *CD* is drawn, the ends are squared up and the proper widths measured. In this fitting, one end must be 12 in and the other 6 in. Points *A* and *B* are then connected to complete the basic pattern. If the length of *CD* is made equal to the curve of the flat cheek, the length of *AB* will automatically fit the curve of the slanted cheek. In this fitting, since both ends of the cheeks are the same width, both heel and throat patterns are exactly the same. However, when the cheek changes size also, the lengths of the curves on both sides of the check are different, and two separate patterns must be laid out for the heel and throat. In either case, care must be taken that the inside of every pattern is marked, as they will fit in only one position.

S offset that changes size in both cheek and heel. Figure 5-13 shows a typical shop sketch of an S offset, such as is commonly handed the sheet metal layout worker. It is crude and not to scale, but the worker is expected to interpret it correctly and make the fitting accurately. This S offset embodies most of the principles covered in this chapter. The student should try to lay out all the patterns without reference to the drawings and the

explanations that follow so that the student's understanding of S offsets can be checked. After all the patterns are laid out, they can be checked against those in the book for accuracy. A good check for accuracy on fittings of this type is to check the lengths of the slanted sides of the heel and throat pattern against the length of the curve it is to fit. If they are not the same length, or within an ⅛ in, there is a mistake in the pattern.

The layout for the cheeks is shown in Fig. 5-14 and is similar to that of the previous problem.

The layout for the heel and throat patterns is shown in Fig. 5-15*a* and *b*. Since there is no flat cheek on this fitting, the length of the heel and throat pattern is found in a slightly different manner. Measuring the curve *AB* in Fig. 5-14*a* shows that it is $17^{13}/_{16}$ in long. Note that the inside curve is measured—not the outside one—because the inside one is the outline of the basic pattern. Since it is $17^{13}/_{16}$ in, the edge of the heel and throat pattern for that particular side must also be $17^{13}/_{16}$ in. In addition, the edge of this side must slant in 3 in. To start this heel and throat pattern, first draw line *EB* in Fig. 5-15*a* and then draw line *AF* parallel to it and 3 in above. Then, holding the end of the rule on point *A,* move the rule until the

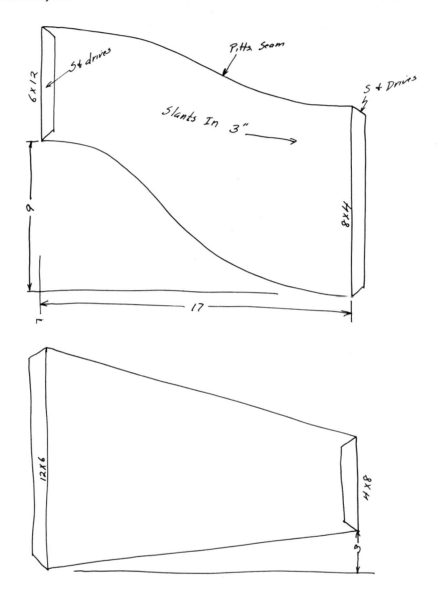

Fig. 5-13   Shop Sketch of an S Offset That Changes Size in Both Heel and Cheek.

$17^{13}/_{16}$-in mark hits line *EB*. This point is shown as *B*. This establishes the side line of the fitting at the proper length and at the proper slant. Draw lines square to *AF* through *A* and *B*, and measure the proper width of the side on each end, as shown in the same drawing. Then draw in the lines to complete the pattern and add the allowances for seams and edges. The length of the other edge of this pattern will automatically be the proper length to fit the curve of the 5 in slanted cheek, if everything has been done correctly.

The pattern for the opposite heel and throat pattern is found in the same manner. Measurement of the curve *CD* in Fig. 5-14*a* shows that it

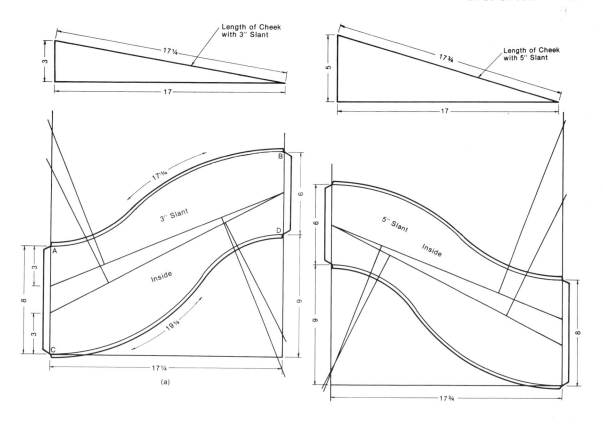

Fig. 5-14 Layout of Cheek Pattern for Fig. 5-13.

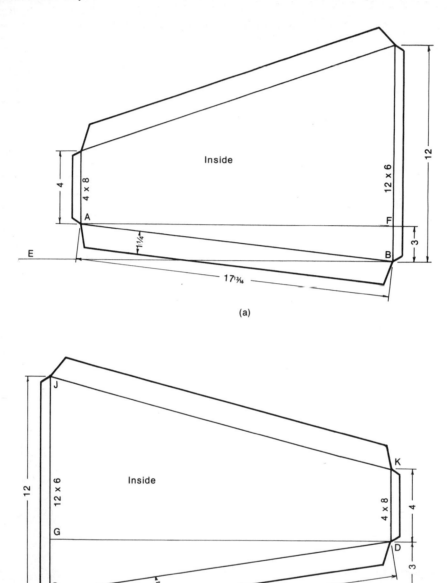

Fig. 5-15 Layout of Heel and Throat Pattern for Fig. 5-13.

measures 19⅝ in. To start the pattern, draw line *CH*, as shown in Fig. 5-15*b* and then draw line *GD* parallel to it and 3 in up. Measure a line from *C* that is 19⅝ in long at the point where it strikes line *GD*. Draw square lines through points *C* and *D* to measure the proper width of the sides. Connect points *J* and *K* with a line, and add all the necessary allowances for the Pittsburgh seam and for the S-and-drive clips, as shown in Fig. 5-15*b*.

PRACTICE PROBLEMS

Problem 5-1

Purpose. To study the layout of the four-piece transition.

Study. *Four-piece transition.*

Assignment.

1. Make patterns for all four sides of the transition shown in Fig. 5-16. Lay them out with the inside up.

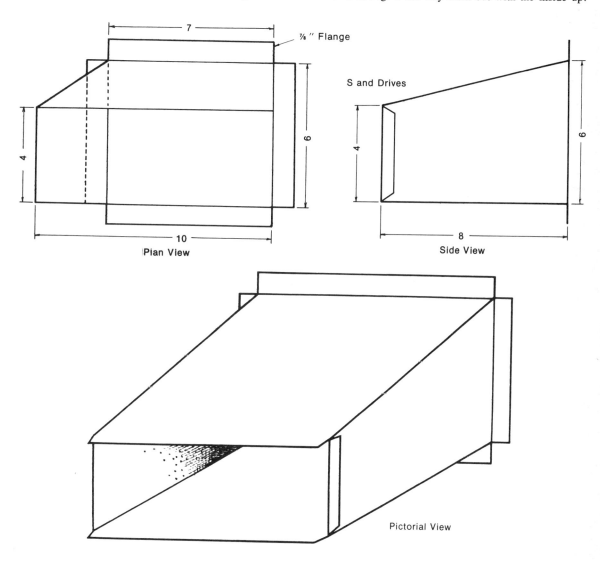

Fig. 5-16 Problem 5-1, Making a Four-piece Transition.

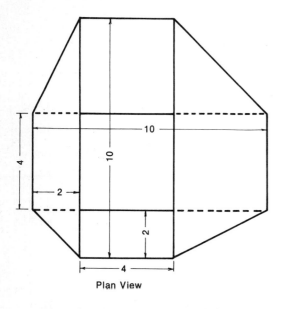

Plan View

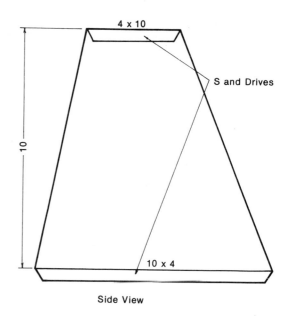

4 x 10

S and Drives

10 x 4

Side View

Fig. 5-17 Problem 5-2, Making a Four-piece Transition.

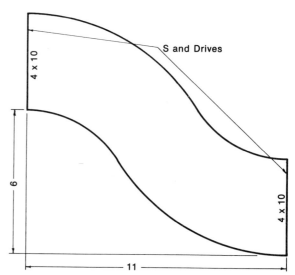

4 x 10

S and Drives

4 x 10

Fig. 5-18 Problem 5-3, Making a Standard S Offset.

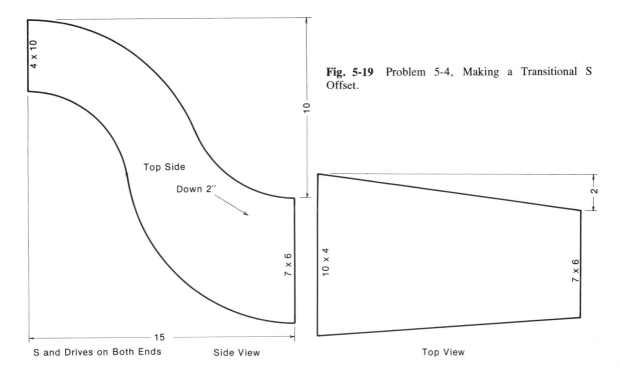

4 x 10

Top Side

Down 2″

7 x 6

10

15

S and Drives on Both Ends   Side View

Fig. 5-19 Problem 5-4, Making a Transitional S Offset.

10 x 4

2

7 x 6

Top View

Add all the allowances for seams and edges. Note that the dotted lines in the plan view indicate that the 4-by-10-in side is the top.

2. Make up the fitting out of 26-gauge galvanized iron.

Problem 5-2

Purpose. To practice making four-piece transitional offsets.

Study. *Four-piece transition. Checking the accuracy of the layout.*

Assignment.

1. Lay out the patterns for the offset shown in Fig. 5-17. Add all allowances for seams and edges, and lay out each pattern with the inside up. Note the dotted lines in the plan view that indicate which end is the top. If the other end is regarded as the top, the fitting will be made inside out.

2. Make up the offset out of metal.

Problem 5-3

Purpose. To practice making standard S offset.

Study. *S offsets, Standard S offset.*

Assignment.

1. Lay out all the patterns for the fitting shown in Fig. 5-18.

2. Make up the fitting out of 26-gauge galvanized iron.

Problem 5-4

Purpose. To practice making a transitional S offset.

Study. *S offset that changes size in the cheek; S offset that changes size in the heel and throat; S offset that changes size in both cheek and heel.*

Assignment.

1. Lay out patterns for the fitting shown in Fig. 5-19.

2. Make up the fitting from the patterns.

Duct Elbows

One of the most common fittings in the sheet metal trade is the rectangular duct elbow.

Because these fittings are so common, many methods are used to lay them out. A good layout worker should be familiar with several different methods, since each has special advantages. Although these methods differ, they are all based upon the same principle. Therefore, the best way to learn them is first to learn the method upon which they are based. After the basic method is thoroughly understood, the others can be explained in a few words.

Before the basic method is studied, the parts of the elbow should be learned. Figure 6-1 illustrates the parts given below.

Cheeks. The two flat sides of the elbow.

Heel. The large piece that forms the outside curve of the elbow.

Throat. The small piece that forms the inside curve of the elbow.

Radius-throat elbows

Locating centers. The first thing to learn about elbows is how to locate the centers from which to swing the arcs of the cheek.

For cheeks not changing size. If the cheek is the same width on each end, as in Fig. 6-2, it is called a *straight* cheek. On a straight cheek both the center for the throat radius and the center for the heel radius are at the same point, as shown in Fig. 6-2.

For cheeks changing size. If the ends of the cheek are of different widths, as in Fig. 6-3, it is called a *transitional* cheek. In such cheeks, the centers for the throat and for the heel will be in different locations. Figure 6-4 illustrates the steps in a layout for cheeks changing size.

Step 1. Draw a square corner. Measure out from the corner *B* the amount of the throat radius, and swing the arc for the throat using *B* as a center. This gives the arc through points *C* and *D*, as shown in Fig. 6-4a.

Step 2. From the ends of the throat radius, points *D* and *C* in Fig. 6-4a, measure the widths of the cheek (*CE* and *DA*).

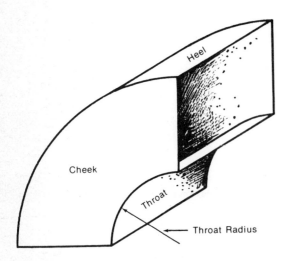

Fig. 6-1 The Parts of a Duct Elbow.

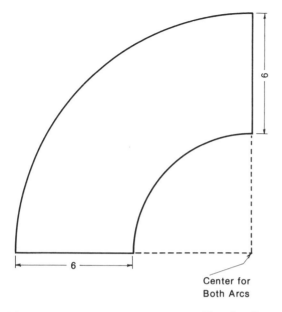

Fig. 6-2 Heel Center for Cheeks Not Changing Size.

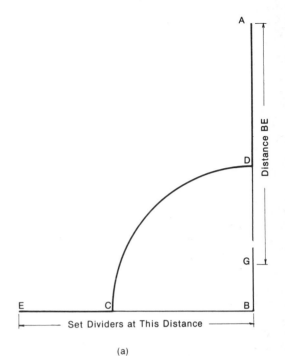

(a)

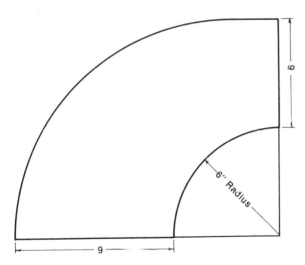

Fig. 6-3 Transitional Cheek.

Step 3. Set dividers from the throat-radius center *B* to the heel of the smallest end (distance *BE*).

Step 4. Measure this distance from the heel of the large end (point *A*). This point *(G)* is the center for the heel radius, as shown in Fig. 6-4*b*.

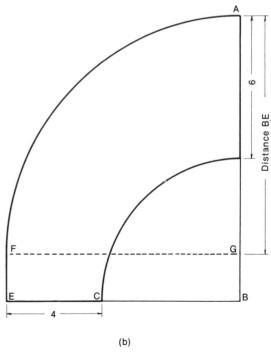

(b)

Fig. 6-4 Finding Heel Center of Transitional Cheek.

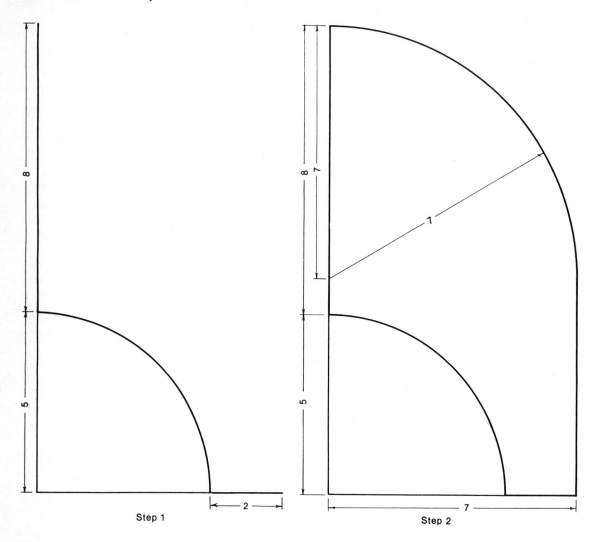

Step 1   Step 2

Fig. 6-5 Example of Finding Heel Center for Transitional Cheek.

Step 5. Swing in the heel arc and complete the heel as shown in Fig. 6-4*b* by drawing a straight line from point *E* and tangent to the heel arc. This is shown by line *EF*.

Figure 6-5 shows another cheek laid out in this manner. In this problem, dimensions are given in order to show practical relationships.

Basic layout for transitional elbow. The basic method just discussed for laying out a rectangular elbow cheek is used when only the cheek changes size. When the elbow changes size in both the heel and throat, additional methods must be used because the pattern must allow for the extra metal used by the slanted side. For a slanted cheek on a 90° angle, the pattern must be less than a 90° angle so that it forms a 90° angle when the elbow is made.

An elbow that changes size in the heel and throat, causing the cheek to slant in or out, is called a *transitional elbow* or a *drop-cheek elbow*. This is different from the transitional cheek of an elbow.

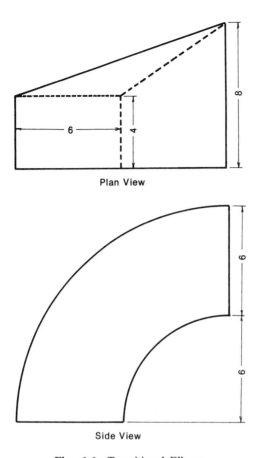

Plan View

Side View

Fig. 6-6 Transitional Elbow.

Figure 6-6 is the plan and side view of a typical transitional elbow. This elbow is made so that one cheek is flat and the other slants.

To lay out this elbow, draw a pattern for the flat cheek as in Fig. 6-7a. From this pattern, the pattern of the slanted cheek can be developed.

After the flat cheek is drawn, divide both the heel and the throat curves into an equal number of spaces, as shown in Fig. 6-7b. In this drawing the curves are divided into six spaces; however, it could be more or less spaces depending upon the job. An extreme slant on the cheek would require six or more spaces. Less slant would need fewer spaces.

To lay out this cheek, find the true lengths of the dotted lines shown in Fig. 6-7c and triangulate,

starting from line 1-2. To find the true lengths of the dotted lines, it is first necessary to find the rise of each line. To do this, draw the patterns for the heel and throat of the elbow. In Fig. 6-7d the two patterns of the heel and throat are shown drawn over one another to clarify the explanation. The dotted lines show the pattern for the throat. In actual practice, the two would be laid out separately so that they could be cut out and used.

To find the true length of line 1-3 in Fig. 6-7c, it is necessary to find how much the line drops. This drop can be obtained by measurement, from Fig. 6-7d.

In Fig. 6-7c, line 1-3 is drawn from point 1 to point 3. To find the drop of line 1-3, it is necessary to learn how high point 1 is and how high point 3 is. The difference in these two heights is the drop. In Fig. 6-7d, distance 1-1' is the height of point 1. Distance 3-3' is the height of point 3. The drop of line 1-3 is the difference between these heights, which is shown by dimension x in Fig. 6-7d. Figure 6-7e shows the true-length triangle for line 1-3.

In another example, the drop of line 9-4, in Fig. 6-7c is found in Fig. 6-7d as the difference between lines 9-9' and 4-4'. The drop is shown as distance Z in Fig. 6-7d. Notice that this drop is the same as the drop of line 1-3 (Fig. 6-7e).

Notice also that points 9' and 3' are even. This means that line 9-3 in Fig. 6-7c is level and, therefore, is already a true length on the cheek in Fig. 6-7c.

After starting the pattern with line 1-2, the true length of line 1-3 is swung from point 1, as in Fig. 6-8a. Then the true length of 2-3 (2'-3' in Fig. 6-7d) is swung from point 2. The intersection of these two arcs is point 3. Point 9 is located next, by measuring from points 1 and 3. Examination of Fig. 6-7d will show that 3' and 9' are at the same level. Therefore, line 3-9 in Fig. 6-7c is not dropping and is a true length on the drawing.

The complete layout of the cheek is shown in Fig. 6-8b.

Three-point method. All shortcut methods of laying out duct elbows are based upon the triangu-

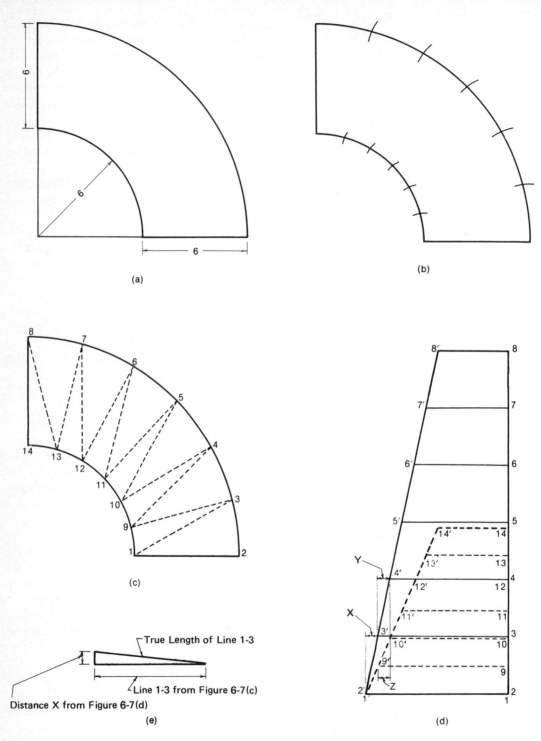

Fig. 6-7   Layout of Cheek for Fig. 6-6.

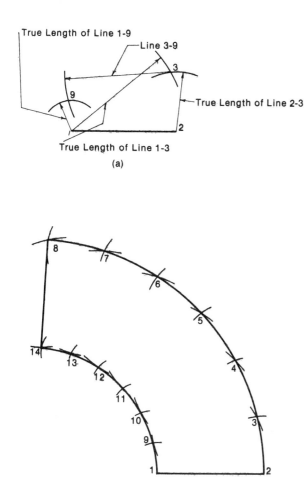

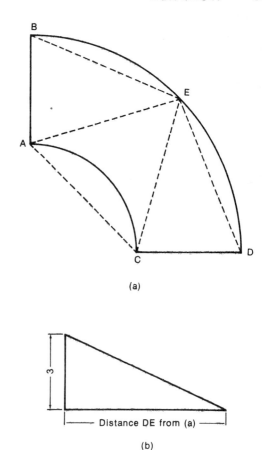

True Length of Line 1-9

Line 3-9

True Length of Line 2-3

True Length of Line 1-3

(a)

(b)

Fig. 6-8 Complete Layout of Cheek for Fig. 6-6.

Distance DE from (a)

(b)

Fig. 6-9 Lines for Three-point Method of Laying Out a Transitional Cheek.

lation method just described. The most common method of laying out a transitional elbow is shown in Fig. 6-9. This method is accurate in almost all cases except those in which the cheek has a very extreme slant; in such cases, more points should be used.

The dotted lines in Fig. 6-9a show the layout lines used in the three-point method. By measuring point E halfway around the curve BD, the drop of line DE can easily be established.

For instance, assume that the elbow cheek in Fig. 6-9a must be laid out for a slant of 6 in. This

means that points A and B are 6 in lower than points C and D. Since point E is halfway between D and B, point E must be half of 6 in, or 3 in, lower than D.

The true length of line DE is shown in Fig. 6-9b. Using the same method, the true lengths of lines CE, AE, and BE may be found.

Line AC can also be found by this method. However, remember that line AC is drawn from one end of the elbow to the other, which means that line AC is dropping 6 in. Therefore, when finding the true length of AC, instead of the 3 in in Fig. 6-9b, the rise is 6 in.

In actual layout, lay the cheek out first as if it were flat. Then establish the midpoint of the heel

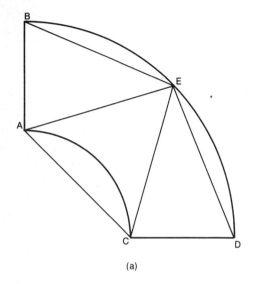

(a)

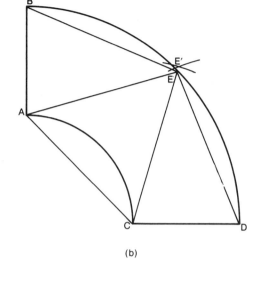

(b)

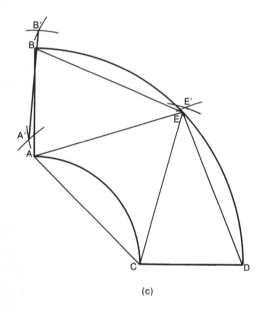

(c)

Fig. 6-10 Layout of Transitional Cheek by Three-point Method.

and draw in the construction lines. Figure 6-10*a* shows these first steps.

After this is done, find the true lengths of the construction lines, as shown and explained previously in Fig. 6-9.

To start the actual layout, set the dividers to the true length of line *DE*. Use point *D* as the center and swing an arc near point *E*, as shown in Fig.

6-10*b*. Next, set the dividers to the true length of *CE* and swing an arc using *C* as center. The intersection of this arc with the previous one establishes the location of point *E'*. Figure 6-10*b* shows these steps.

Next, establish the new location of point *A*. Do this by swinging the true length of *AC* from point *C*. Remember that line *AC* drops the full drop of the cheek. Next, swing the true length of *AE* from point *E'* (not point *E*). The intersection of these arcs is point *A*, as shown in Fig. 6-10*c*.

Relocate point *B* by swinging line *AB* from point *A'* (note that *AB* is already a true length on the drawing) and by swinging the true length of *BE* from *E'*. This is also illustrated in Fig. 6-10*c*.

After the new end points have been located, a common method of establishing the new curve for

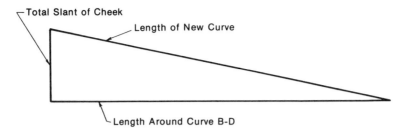

Fig. 6-11 Finding the Length of the Heel on a Transitional Cheek.

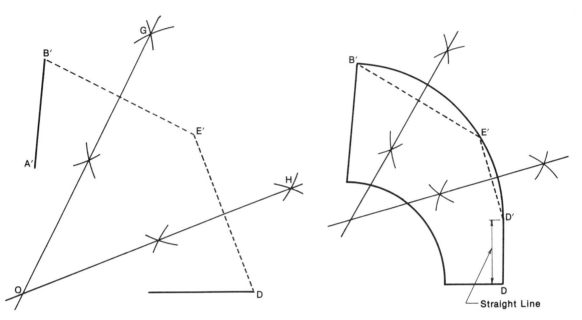

Fig. 6-12 Finding the Heel Center on a Transitional Cheek.

Fig. 6-13 Allowing for Straight Lines on the Heel Curve.

the heel and the throat is to hold a flexible rule at the proper length and draw around it. The easiest way to find the proper length is to measure the distance of the original flat curve and find the true length of it, as shown in Fig. 6-11. After finding the length of the new curve, hold a flexible rule through points B', E', and D so that it is the exact length of the new curve, and scribe a line around it. Both the heel and throat curves can be found by the same method.

Determining curves by locating centers.
Another method of determining the heel curve

is shown in Fig. 6-12. After the new points A', B' and E' are located, draw lines $B'E'$ and $E'D$. Erect perpendicular bisectors to these lines. The point of intersection of these bisectors (point O) is the center of the arc that will be the right length to fit the heel pattern.

One point should be remembered. If the heel of the cheek consists partly of a straight line, as in a cheek that changes size (see Fig. 6-4), lines $B'E'$ and $E'D'$ are drawn from the ends of the arc—not from the ends of the elbow. See Fig. 6-13.

This method can also be used to swing the throat curve, if the midpoint of the throat is first located

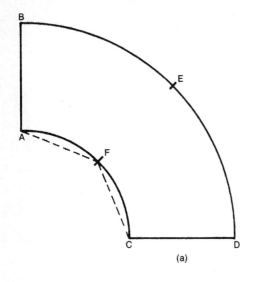

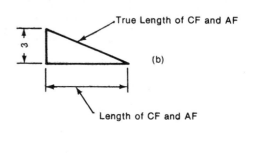

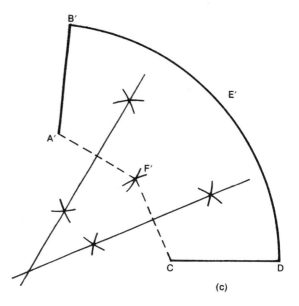

Fig. 6-14   Finding the Throat Center.

as shown in Fig. 6-14. To locate the midpoint, set the dividers to the true length of lines *CF* and *AF*, as shown in Fig. 6-14*b,* and swing this distance from the end points *C* and *A'* of the throat curve. The intersection of these two arcs locates the midpoint *F* in Fig. 6-14*c*. Draw in the base lines *CF'* and *A'F'*; then erect perpendicular bisectors to them. The intersection of these two arcs locates the center point in the same manner as for the heel.

Shortcut for true lengths. A shortcut for finding true lengths for a slanted cheek elbow layout is shown in Fig. 6-15. Instead of drawing true-length triangles, as shown before, one can save time by using the lines already drawn on the cheek pattern. Thus, in Fig. 6-15, if line *EF* is equal to one-half the rise and is square to line *DE*, the distance from

D to *F* is the true length of *DE*. In like manner, *CH* is the true length of *CA*, and *CG* is the true length of *CE*. By drawing the lines on the cheek and squaring up the height, time is saved and the true lengths are handy for use. Note that the dotted lines in Fig. 6-15 are for purposes of explanation and need not be drawn in. Another timesaver is to set the dividers at one-half the rise and swing a circle, using *E* as center. This marks half the rise on all the squared-up rise lines and eliminates the need to measure each line separately. This is a small item, but it is such small items that make the expert mechanic.

Three-line method. A variation of the three-point method is to eliminate the middle point on the heel. This method is the same as described before,

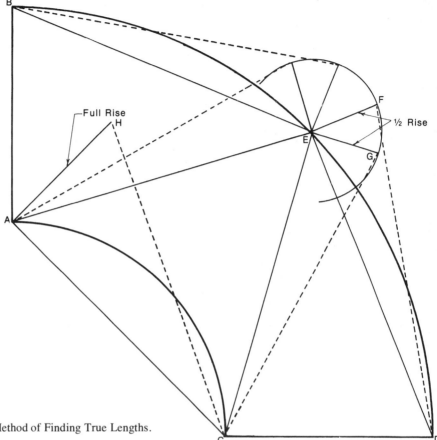

Fig. 6-15   Short-cut Method of Finding True Lengths.

except that there are fewer lines making it less accurate. This method works for elbows with little slant. Figure 6-16*a* illustrates the start of the three-line method. The true lengths are found and the arcs are located–the same as in the three-point method. Figures 6-16*b* and *c* show the new steps. Points *A'* and *B'* are the new points. The new arcs on the heel and throat are found by the methods previously described.

Guessing the pattern. When the elbow cheek has only a slight slant, it is practical to *guess* the pattern. This means simply to figure the amount the heel and the throat of the slanted side will grow to add this growth at one end of the cheek pattern. By the *growth* of the heel or throat is meant the difference between the straight side and the slanted

side of the pattern. Figure 6-17 illustrates this method. The first step is to lay out the flat cheek, and the heel and throat patterns; the growth is then figured and added to the end of the cheek pattern. This method is not accurate; in fact, it is very inaccurate, but it is fast, and for small growths is accurate enough.

Slipping the pattern. Another shortcut method of layout based upon growth is *slipping* the pattern. This method is practical only if one cheek of the elbow is flat. It is very accurate and can be depended upon on all but the most extreme elbows.

The purpose of this method is to add the growth of the slanted side into the center of each curve of the slanted cheek. First, lay out the pattern for the flat cheek, adding all allowances for seams and

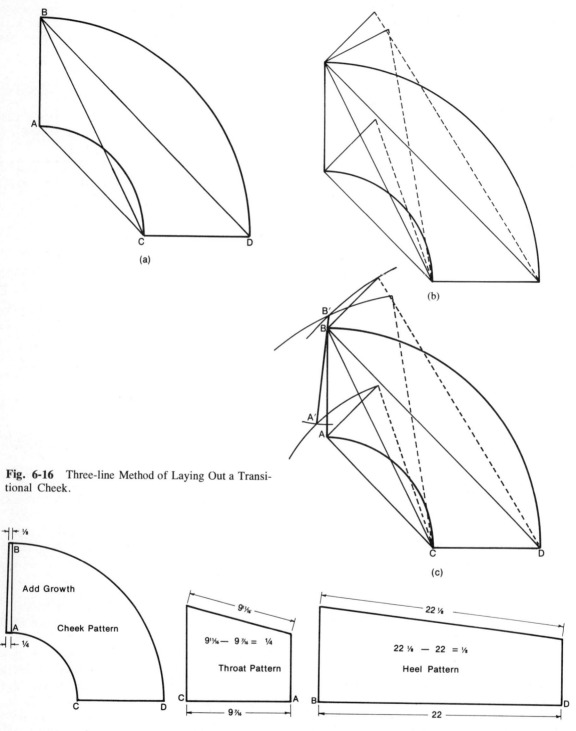

(a)

(b)

(c)

Fig. 6-16 Three-line Method of Laying Out a Transitional Cheek.

Add Growth

Cheek Pattern

Throat Pattern

$9^{11}/_{16}$ — $9^{7}/_{16}$ = $^{1}/_{4}$

$9^{11}/_{16}$

$9^{7}/_{16}$

Heel Pattern

$22^{1}/_{8}$ — 22 = $^{1}/_{8}$

$22^{1}/_{8}$

22

Fig. 6-17 ''Guessing'' the Pattern for a Transitional Cheek.

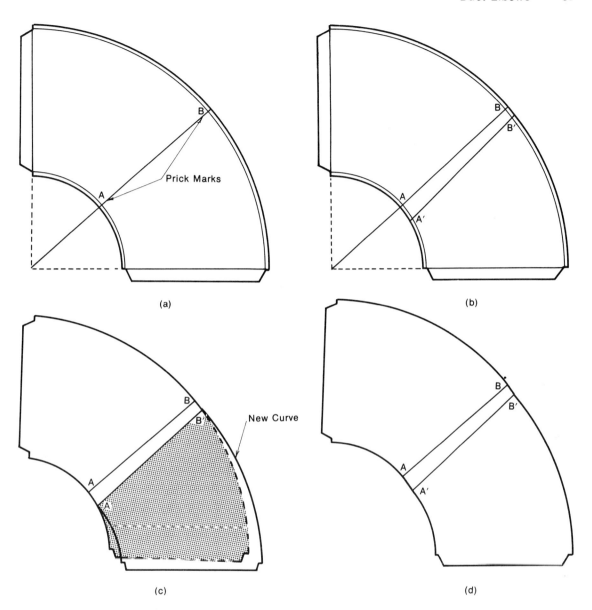

Fig. 6-18 "Slipping" the Pattern for a Transitional Cheek.

clips. On this cheek draw a line—*AB* in Fig. 6-18a—from the center point of the throat and through the approximate center of the heel. Prick mark it as shown in Fig. 6-18a. Cut this pattern out and mark another pattern from it, being sure to prick mark line *AB*. Now figure the growth of the heel and of the throat, as described in Fig. 6-17. Figure 6-19 also illustrates this method of finding

the growth. The quickest method of figuring growth is to lay out the heel and throat patterns, adding all the needed allowances, and figure the growth from these, instead of making special calculations.

After the growth is determined, measure it on the second cheek, as shown in Fig. 6-18b by the distances *BB'* and *AA'*. Note that the growth of the

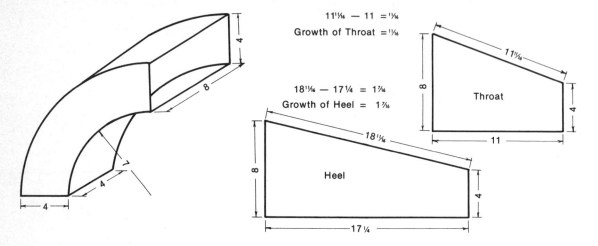

$$11^{11}\!/_{16} - 11 = {}^{11}\!/_{16}$$
Growth of Throat $= {}^{11}\!/_{16}$

$$18^{11}\!/_{16} - 17\tfrac{1}{4} = 1\tfrac{7}{16}$$
Growth of Heel $= 1\tfrac{7}{16}$

Throat

Heel

Fig. 6-19   Figuring the Growth of the Heel and Throat.

throat is always greater than the growth of the heel. Draw another line through the new points *A'* and *B'*. Now lay the original cheek pattern over the second cheek so that line *AB* of the original cheek matches line *A'B'* of the second cheek. This throws half the original pattern out of line with the second pattern. Re-mark this half of the pattern to obtain the new curve shown in Fig. 6-18c. This completes the slanted-cheek pattern.

After the curves are drawn in, the pattern will look like Fig. 6-18d. The lines between *B'B* and *A'A* will not match exactly. Redraw this rough area freehand in order to make a smooth, flowing curve. After this is done, the cheek may be cut out for the slanted cheek of the elbow. With this method, all the allowances are added automatically, and there is no need to sketch in any of the allowances around the curve.

Paneling the cheeks. In order to put an elbow together easily, a slanted cheek must be creased in the brake. These bend lines are shown in Fig. 6-19. Point *B* is the midpoint used in laying out the pattern. If no midpoint is used in laying out the cheek, then point *B* should be the approximate center of the heel.

Bend the two lines in opposite directions. Starting from line *AD,* if the cheek is slanting

down, bend line *AB* down. If the cheek slants up from *AD,* bend *AB* up. Bend line *CB* opposite to *AB.*

Square-throat elbow

The layout of *square-throat* elbows involves a slightly different problem than other elbows. The principles involved are the same, but the triangulation lines are drawn differently.

Before one studies the layout of the slanted cheek, it is first necessary to learn how to locate the center for the arc of the heel. When both ends of the cheek are the same, the center for the heel arc must always be at point *A* in Fig. 6-21. If it is swung from anywhere except this corner, the distance from *A* to *B* will either be choked down too small or made so oversized that the elbow will look out of proportion.

Square-throat transitional cheek. In the case of a square-throat elbow that changes size in the cheek, the procedure is much the same as that for a curved-throat elbow. The distance from the center to the back of the small end (*AB* in Fig. 6-22) is measured from point *C.* This gives the center of the arc, as shown.

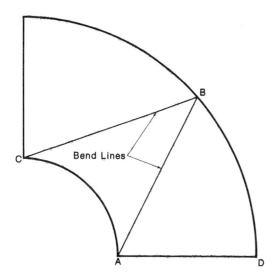

Fig. 6-20 Bend Lines for Paneling a Transitional Cheek.

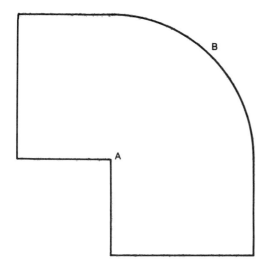

Fig. 6-21 Center Point for Straight Square-throat Cheek.

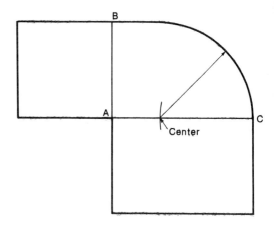

Fig. 6-22 Center Point for Transitional Square-throat Cheek.

Square-throat transitional elbow. In laying out a square-throat elbow with a slanted cheek, the triangulation lines are drawn as shown in Fig. 6-23a. The true lengths are found in the same manner as before. Point F' in (b) is located first by using the true lengths of CF and DF; then point E' is found by using the true lengths of line EF and line CE. Point A' is found next by using the true lengths of AE and AF. The last point (B') is found by using the true length of BF and the actual length of AB. Note that point E and point F are both halfway between the end points and, therefore, are dropping one-half the rise. Since both of these points have dropped one-half the rise, they are on the same level. It follows, therefore, that the line from points E to F is a level line. In other words, line EF is a true length on the drawing and can be taken from the drawing.

Figure 6-23b shows the complete layout for the cheek. The arc of the heel can either be drawn in with a flexible rule or swung from a new center in the same manner as the curve of the heel of any slanted-cheek pattern.

Unequal square throat. In the special case where the sides of a square throat are unequal, as in Fig. 6-24a, the throat pattern must be laid out to find how much point A is above point C. Figure 6-24b shows the pattern of the elbow throat. Dimension X is the drop of line CA, and $C'A'$ is the true length of CA. In like manner, $B'A'$ is the true length of BA.

The true length of line AF is found as shown in Fig. 6-24c. When the throat sides are unequal, line AF is no longer level because point A is not

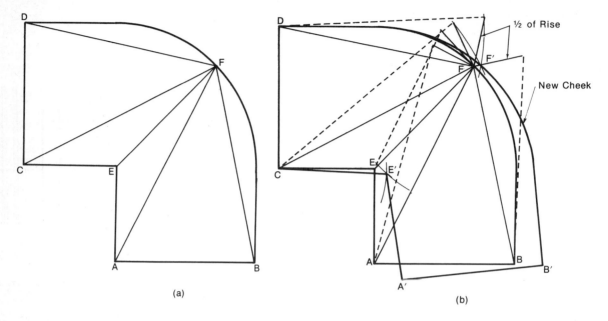

Fig. 6-23 Triangulation Lines for Square-throat Transitional Elbow.

halfway between the ends; therefore, it is not one-half the rise below point *C*. In order to find the amount that line *AF* drops, it is necessary to subtract the amount that point *F* drops from the amount that point *A* drops. Since *F* is halfway around the heel curve, it drops half the rise (Fig. 6-24*d*). The drop of *A* is distance *x* in Fig. 6-24*b*. This is drawn to complete the true length triangle in Fig. 6-24*c*. The difference between the two vertical heights is the rise on line *AF*. Figure 6-24*c* shows this process. The other true lengths and the completed pattern for the slanted cheek are shown in Fig. 6-24*e*.

Choosing the proper method

In this chapter, different methods of laying out duct elbows were discussed. It remains for the layout worker to choose the proper method to fit a particular job. In general, the faster the layout, the more inaccurate it is. A good method to determine the accuracy needed in a layout is to check the growth of the throat. This is illustrated by the transitional elbow in Fig. 6-25. Assuming that both cheeks slant in the same amount, each one slants in 4 in. The throat radius of the elbow is 6 in, which means that the stretchout of the throat is $9^{7}/_{16}$ in. By drawing $9^{7}/_{16}$ in on a 4-in rise, as shown in Fig. 6-25*b*, the exact amount of the growth can be found. If this growth is about ⅛ in, then the elbow can be guessed out. If the growth is around ¼ in, the pattern can be guessed out, or it can be laid out by one of the short triangulation methods. The choice depends upon whether the elbow is to be installed where appearance is important or where it will not be seen. Another factor in choice of method is whether 1 or 100 elbows of that size are to be made. If a great number of elbows are to be marked from one pattern, it is important to spend enough time on the pattern to ensure accuracy.

If the growth on the throat is 1 in or more, one of the more accurate layouts is required. The exact choice again depends upon the factors already mentioned.

One of the qualities of a good mechanic is the ability to choose quickly the fastest method of layout consistent with the requirements of the job.

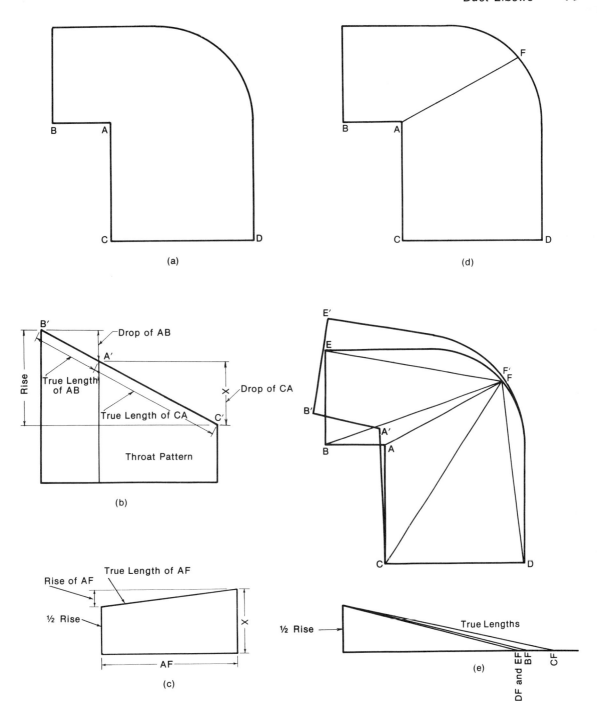

Fig. 6-24 Layout of Square-throat Transitional Elbow with Unequal Throat.

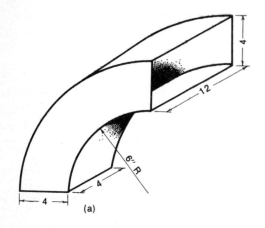

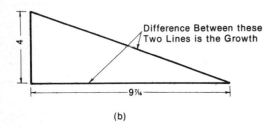

Fig. 6-25   Finding the Growth of an Elbow.

For this reason it is important that the mechanic be familiar with all the methods described in this chapter and be able to choose the correct one for each job.

PRACTICE PROBLEMS

Problem 6-1

Purpose. To learn the names of the parts of a duct elbow.

Study. The introduction to Chapter 6.

Assignment. On a sheet of notebook paper, make a pictorial sketch of a duct elbow as neatly as possible. Label each of the three parts with the proper name.

Problem 6-2

Purpose. To learn how to locate the centers for swinging the arcs of a straight elbow cheek, how to draw the heel and throat pattern for an elbow, and how to allow for Pittsburgh seams on an elbow.

Study. *Locating centers, for cheeks not changing size.*

Assignment.

1. Draw the patterns for the cheek, heel, and throat of an elbow, 7 (cheek) by 6 in (heel and throat), with a 5-in throat radius. Allow for Pittsburgh seams and S-and-drive clips.

2. Make up the elbow out of 26-gauge iron.

Problem 6-3

Purpose. To learn how to locate the centers for the arcs of an elbow cheek that changes size.

Study. *For cheeks changing size and First method.*

Assignment.

1. Lay out the patterns for the cheek, heel, and throat for the elbow shown in Fig. 6-26. Allow for Pittsburgh seams; indicate notches in red pencil. NOTE: In shop sketches, the first dimension given is for the side shown in the drawing. In Fig. 6-26, the cheek would be 8 in on one end and 4 in on the other.

2. Make up the fitting out of metal.

Problem 6-4

Purpose. To learn how to panel a transitional elbow cheek.

Study. *Paneling the cheeks.*

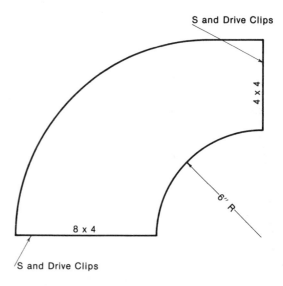

Fig. 6-26   Problem 6-3.

Assignment. Make an approximate sketch of the slanted cheek for Figs. 6-19, 6-25, 6-26, 6-27 and 6-28. Draw the cheeks with the inside up and give dimensions for each end. Draw in the bend lines for paneling, if they are needed, and mark them for the directions of the bend (either "in" or "out").

Problem 6-5

Purpose. To learn how to lay out the patterns for an elbow that is changing size in the heel and throat, by use of the basic method. Though this method is seldom used because in most cases shortcut methods are accurate enough, it is important to learn it because all shortcuts are based upon it.

Study. *Basic layout for transitional elbows, Allowances for government clips.*

Assignment.

1. Lay out all patterns for the elbow shown in Fig. 6-27. Note that one side is flat. Allow for seams and edges; indicate the notches with red pencil. Lay out the patterns with the inside up and mark them "in." Save the patterns for reference in problem 6-6.

2. Make up the fitting out of metal.

Problem 6-6

Purpose. To learn how the basic method is shortened for use in practical shop layout.

Study. *Three-point method.*

Assignment.

1. Lay out the patterns for the elbow shown in Fig. 6-27.

2. If the fitting in problem 6-5 was not made up, make up problem 6-6.

3. Compare the pattern for shape with the pattern of problem 6-5. Save both patterns for comparison with those of later methods.

Problem 6-7

Purpose. To learn how to swing in the arcs of a transitional elbow instead of drawing them in.

Study. *Determining curves by locating centers.*

Assignment. Lay out the patterns for the elbow in Fig. 6-28. Locate the centers for the new curves for both the heel and throat and swing them in. Check the length of these curves against the length of the slant of the heel and throat patterns.

Problem 6-8

Purpose. To learn the shortcuts used in shop layout to find the true-length lines on a transitional elbow cheek.

Study. *Shortcuts in true lengths.*

Assignment. Lay out the patterns for the elbow in Fig. 6-29, using the shortcut methods of finding true lengths.

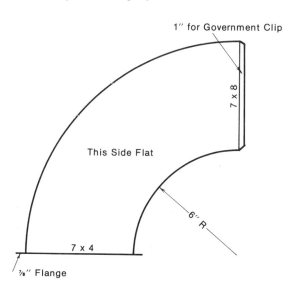

Fig. 6-27 Problems 6-5, 6-6, 6-9, 6-10, and 6-11, Transitional Elbow.

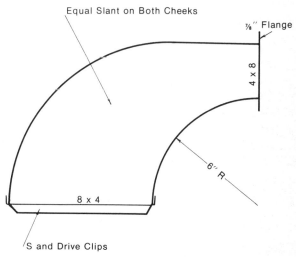

Fig. 6-28 Problem 6-7, Swinging in the Heel Arcs for a Transitional Elbow Cheek.

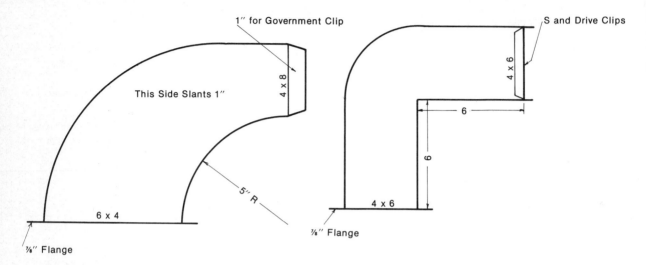

Fig. 6-29 Problem 6-8, Using Short Cuts for Finding True Lengths of a Transitional Elbow Cheek.

Fig. 6-30 Problem 6-12, Laying Out the Patterns for a Square-throat Elbow.

Problem 6-9

Purpose. To learn a shorter method of laying out for a transitional elbow.

Study. *Three-line method.*

Assignment. Lay out the patterns for the same elbow in Fig. 6-27, using the three-line method. Compare it for shape with the patterns of problems 6-5 and 6-6. Save the patterns for comparison with those of other methods.

Problem 6-10

Purpose. To learn how to lay out the patterns for a transitional elbow by guessing it.

Study. *Guessing the pattern.*

Assignment. Lay out the pattern for Fig. 6-27 by guessing. Check it against those of problems 6-5 and 6-6 to see how it differs. This method is the least accurate; that of problem 6-5 should be the most accurate. Save the patterns for comparison with those of other methods.

Problem 6-11

Purpose. To learn how to slip a pattern on a transitional elbow that has one side flat.

Study. *Slipping the pattern.*

Assignment. Lay out the patterns for Fig. 6-27 by slipping the patterns. Compare them with the patterns in Problems 6-5, 6-6, and 6-10 for accuracy.

Problem 6-12

Purpose. To learn how to locate the center for swinging the heel curve on the flat cheek of a square-throat elbow.

Study. *Square-throat elbow.*

Assignment. Lay out the complete patterns for Fig. 6-30.

Problem 6-13

Purpose. To learn how to locate the center for the heel of a transitional elbow cheek with square throat.

Study. *Square-throat transitional cheek.*

Assignment.

1. Lay out the patterns for the elbow in Fig. 6-31.
2. Make up the fitting out of galvanized iron.

Problem 6-14

Purpose. To learn how to lay out the patterns for a transitional square-throat elbow.

Study. *Square-throat transitional elbow.*

Assignment. Lay out the patterns for the elbow shown in Fig. 6-32.

Problem 6-15

Purpose. To learn how to lay out the patterns for a square-throat transitional elbow that has unequal lengths on the throat.

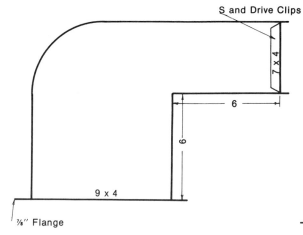

Fig. 6-31 Problem 6-13, Locating the Center for the Heel of a Square-throat Transitional Elbow.

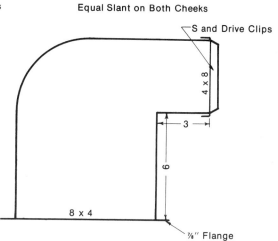

Fig. 6-33 Problem 6-15, Laying Out the Patterns for a Square-throat Transitional Cheek with Unequal Throat.

Study. *Unequal square throat.*

Assignment. Lay out the patterns for the elbow shown in Fig. 6-33.

Problem 6-16

Purpose. To gain an understanding of factors in choosing the proper method of elbow layout.

Study. *Choosing the proper method.*

Assignment.

1. In general, how is the speed of a layout method related to its accuracy?

2. Sketch how the growth is determined on the throat of the elbow in Fig. 6-27.

3. In determining the growth of an elbow, why is the throat used instead of the heel?

4. List the factors that have to be considered in choosing the method of layout to be used on a job.

5. Do you think that a journeyman should know more than one method of elbow layout? Give your reasons.

6. Do you think that a journeyman should know all the layouts in this chapter? Give your reasons.

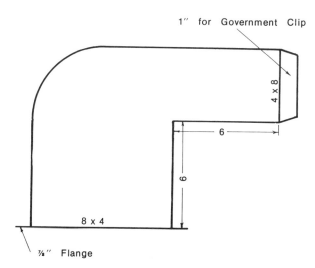

Fig. 6-32 Problem 6-14, Laying Out the Patterns for a Transitional Square-throat Elbow.

7

Duct Work

Rectangular duct work makes up such a large portion of the work done in the average sheet metal shop that any book on shop practices should include a chapter on the subject. Many pattern-drafting books devote much space to showing how to lay out fittings of such an unusual nature that they would not be encountered once in twenty years. In fact, the kinds of unusual duct fittings possible are limited only by the imagination of the drafter. Unusual fittings help the beginner to gain experience in applying the principles of triangulation and parallel lines. However, this chapter assumes that the student knows the elementary principles of pattern drafting, and discusses the practical shop methods of making and assembling modern duct runs. Like all other shop methods, duct work has been reduced to the simplest, most practical form that will do the job.

At first glance, the prints of a large duct job make it seem to be an intricate system made up of many difficult fittings. However, any large duct job is merely a large number of small duct runs grouped into one building and made up of the common basic fittings made daily in the shop. Figure 7-1 illustrates how this is done. The drawings on the left (a) show how a branch fitting appears on the plans and how it is usually solved in pattern-drafting texts. The drawings on the right (b) show how the fitting is normally made in the shop. Note that the double-line drawing in (a) would require a layout that is not routine. Even more important, it would be difficult to turn the edges for the Pittsburgh seam on the heel. None of the edging machines in the shop could turn the heel edge all the way to the crotch of the Y, and the last portion would have to be turned by hand and

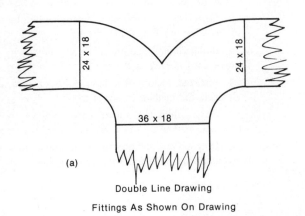

(a)

Double Line Drawing

Fittings As Shown On Drawing

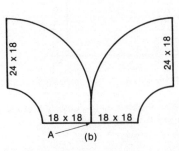

Shop Method of Making 2 Elbows
Back to Back

Fig. 7-1 Duct-branch Fittings.

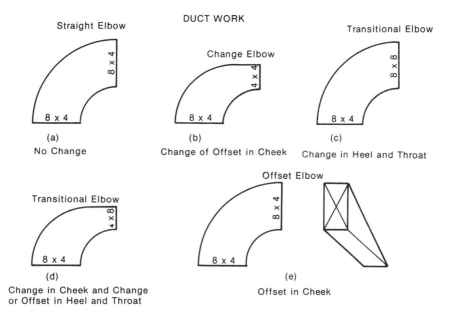

DUCT WORK

Straight Elbow
(a)
No Change

Change Elbow
(b)
Change of Offset in Cheek

Transitional Elbow
(c)
Change in Heel and Throat

Transitional Elbow
(d)
Change in Cheek and Change
or Offset in Heel and Throat

Offset Elbow
(e)
Offset in Cheek

ELBOWS

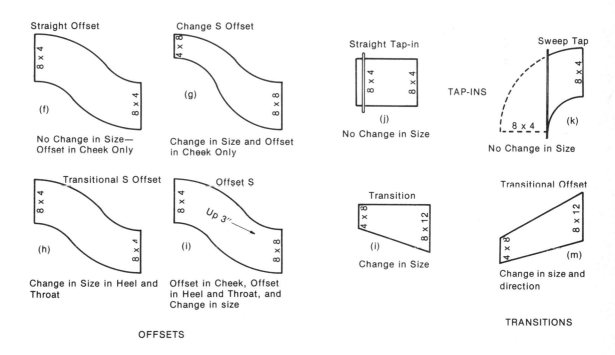

Straight Offset
(f)
No Change in Size—
Offset in Cheek Only

Change S Offset
(g)
Change in Size and Offset
in Cheek Only

Transitional S Offset
(h)
Change in Size in Heel and
Throat

Offset S
(i)
Offset in Cheek, Offset
in Heel and Throat, and
Change in size

OFFSETS

Straight Tap-in
(j)
No Change in Size

TAP-INS

Sweep Tap
(k)
No Change in Size

Transition
(i)
Change in Size

Transitional Offset
(m)
Change in size and
direction

TRANSITIONS

Fig. 7-2 Basic Rectangular Duct Fittings.

dollied into place. In contrast with *(a)*, the method shown in *(b)* would consist of two standard elbows connected back to back; since these involve standard layout methods and fabrication procedures, there would be no time lost on the fitting.

Almost all the "complicated" fittings in duct runs are made in the same manner as the one in Fig. 7-1*b*. In most duct runs, about a dozen basic fittings comprise all the many Ys and branches in the entire system. Figure 7-2 shows all the basic rectangular fittings. The layout of all these has been discussed in previous chapters, and only a sketch is included here in order to identify them. If the worker can lay out all these fittings efficiently, workers can make almost any fitting required for any duct run, since these fittings are the building blocks that are combined in different ways to make a limitless number of fittings.

Note that the fittings shown in Fig. 7-2 are basic fittings and that one form can be combined with another form to make more complicated fittings; the more complicated fittings can be combined again to make yet more complex branch fittings. For instance, the change elbow shown in Fig. 7-2*b* can be combined with the transitional elbow shown in Fig. 7-2*c* to make a transitional-change elbow that changes size in the cheek and also in the heel and throat as shown in Fig. 7-2*d*. Even more combinations can be made by combining more than two basic forms. For instance, an offset-transitional-change elbow can be made that changes size in the cheek and in the heel and throat, and also offset in the cheek. This elbow combines the forms in Fig. 7-2*b, c,* and *e*.

It should be noted that the names given for these basic fittings may vary from book to book. There is also great variation in the names of the fittings in actual shop practice. No sheet metal worker ever bothers to say "offset-transitional-change elbow." The worker merely says "offset elbow" or "transitional elbow"; if workers must be more specific, the term may be "transitional elbow offsetting in the cheek." The important thing is not to remember the exact technical names of the fittings, but to know their shapes and recognize them when they are described.

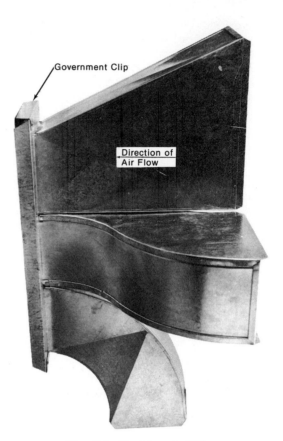

Fig. 7-3   Duct-branch Fitting.

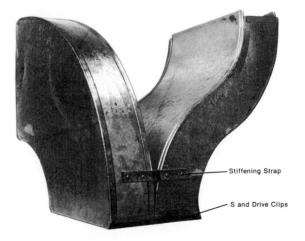

Fig. 7-4   Duct-branch Fitting.

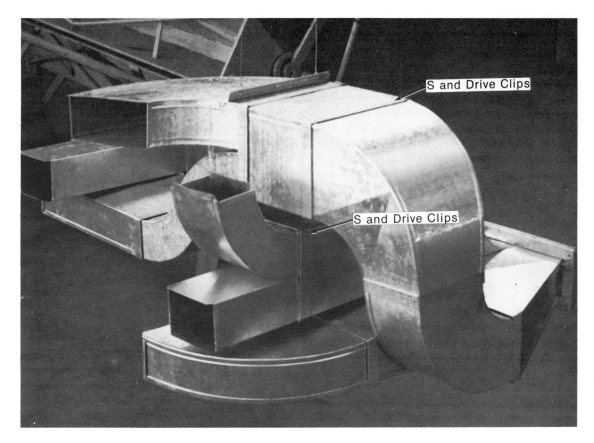

Fig. 7-5 Basic Fittings in a Variety of Combinations.

Since the number of ways in which the basic fittings can be combined to form more complex fittings is limitless, it is not possible to show even the beginning of all these combinations. Figures 7-3 and 7-4 show two forms that they may take, and suggests other combinations that can be made. Figure 7-5 is a photograph of a complex run of duct that was made to illustrate how duct runs can be turned to any direction and size by use of the basic fittings. All the fittings used in this duct run are the basic fittings shown in Fig. 7-2.

Joining the basic fittings

Similar techniques have been developed, and are practiced by most shops to combine basic fittings to form branches and other complex fittings. Most of these techniques are based upon the utilization of a standard clip or bend, so there is little new to learn to join these fittings. It is only necessary to study the illustrations given and understand how they are used.

Referring back to Fig. 7-1*b*, where two straight elbows join to form a branch fitting, one can easily see that at point *A*, indicated by the arrow, there would be a gap between the two elbows where air would leak out of the duct. In order to seal this off, a *hook edge,* shown in Fig. 7-6, is used. This is simply a ¾- or ⅞-in flange bent out square on one fitting and then bent around with tongs to hook over the raw edge of the other fitting. After the hook edge is flattened down in place, it is usually

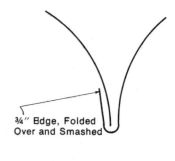

¾" Edge, Folded
Over and Smashed

METHOD OF JOINING FITTINGS

Fig. 7-6 Hook Edge.

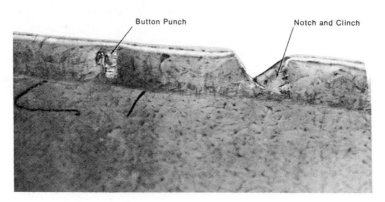

Button Punch

Notch and Clinch

Fig. 7-7 Methods of Clinching a Hook Edge.

fastened with the same button punch used to fasten government clips. If such a punch is not available, the hook edge is riveted or notched and clinched over. Figure 7-7 shows a hooked edge and illustrates both the clip punch and the notched-and-clinched method of fastening.

Sometimes the basic fittings are assembled on the job, and it is found that the hook edge has not been provided for. In such cases, the usual solution is to make both edges raw by cutting off any clip allowance that may be on them and then setting a cap strip over them, as shown in Fig. 7-8. The cap strip is fastened in the same manner as a hooked edge. Often an S clip is used in place of a cap strip, since they are handy on the job.

Tying the fittings together. After the backs of the fittings have been hooked in some manner, the completed fitting often is still too flexible because the hooked edge only holds the basic fittings to-

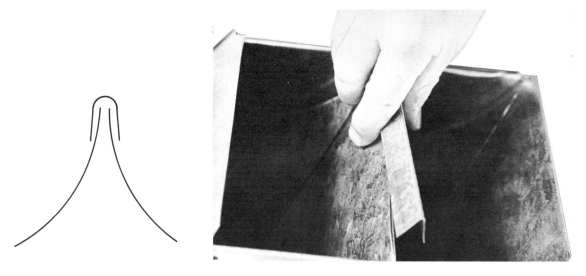

Fig. 7-8 Using a Cap Strip in Place of a Hook Edge.

gether and does not keep them from swaying back and forth. The government clip is usually used to stiffen the complete fitting, as shown in Fig. 7-3. On this particular fitting, the government clip is connected to the fitting and clipped in place to stiffen it. In other cases a ⅞-in flange may be turned on all edges of the fittings, then the flange fit into a government clip from the adjoining fitting or straight duct. Whether the clip is attached to the fitting or the fitting fits into an adjoining clip depends upon the direction of the flow of air in the run. In Fig. 7-3, the air is flowing from the small openings to the large opening as it would in an exhaust system.

The government clip is the most common method of tying the fitting together, but another common procedure is the use of S-and-drive clips. The choice between a government clip or S-and-drive clips depends on the worker's preference, on the type of clip specified for the system, and on the size of the fitting. In general, S-and-drive clips are used on the smaller sized ducts, while the government clip is used on larger sizes since it provides a more rigid connection.

Figures 7-4 and 7-5 show how the S-and-drive clip is used to tie the fittings together. Note that

this is one case where the drive clip is sometimes used on the long side of the duct. The drive clip is generally used on the side of the fitting that is a common side for two or more different fittings, because the drive will keep them from moving. If the S clip is used on this kind of side, there is nothing to prevent the fitting from bending and pulling out of the clip. In some cases, where the flexible side is much too long to use a drive clip, the S is used and then sheet metal screws are driven through the S and the duct to stiffen the fitting and prevent it from pulling out of the clip.

Reinforcing straps. In addition to stiffening by clips, larger fittings are sometimes stiffened by straps that tie all the fittings together. Figure 7-4 illustrates the use of a reinforcing strap. The strap is usually a heavy piece of sheet metal, hemmed on both edges for additional stiffness. It is metal-screwed to the fittings at strategic spots so that there is no danger of the fitting bending or folding out of position. Reinforcing straps may not be necessary after the fitting is completely installed, but they are needed to stiffen the fitting while it is being set in place. These straps are especially useful on a large, complex fitting to save installa-

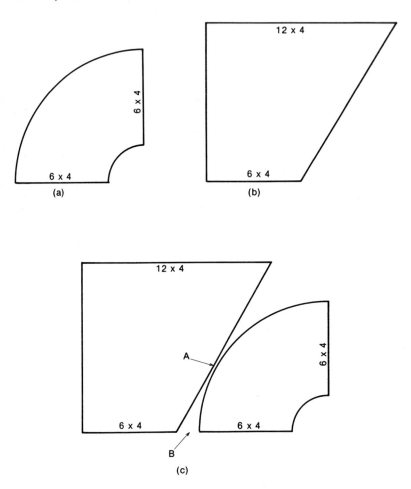

Fig. 7-9   Interference between Fittings.

tion time because the workers do not have the additional problem of fighting flexibility while installing the fitting.

Interference between fittings. To build complex fittings from basic ones, the sheet metal worker must design the fittings to allow for the sides of fittings that interfere with one another and make them impossible to assemble. Figure 7-9 shows how this may happen. If the two fittings shown in Fig. 7-9a and b are assembled into a branch, the side of b indicated by the arrow A has a slant that would hit the heel of the elbow before the two ends

of the fittings could be joined. Fig. 7-9c shows how the fittings would hit at A, making it impossible for them to come together at B. Interference of fittings can easily be avoided if considered while the fittings are being designed. To correct the design in Fig. 7-9, refer to the fittings shown in Fig. 7-15. The transition is attached to the straight pipe *(A)* after it is clear of the elbow heel; or the slant is made on the side away from the elbow *(B)*.

Dampers for fittings

When making any type of branch fitting, it is always necessary to provide some type of damper

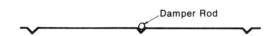

Fig. 7-10 Edge for Stiffening Dampers.

Fig. 7-11 Method of Stiffening Large Volume-control Dampers.

Fig. 7-12 Damper Quadrant. (Courtesy Duro-Dyne Co.)

to guide the air and control its volume. Theoretically, if the take-offs for each fitting were proportioned properly, there would be no need for dampers because the air would be divided into the required amounts. However, in actual practice, there are so many variables that it is impossible to balance the system correctly without dampers.

To construct duct runs, the sheet metal worker uses four basic types of shop-made dampers: the *splitter damper,* the *volume-control damper,* and the *slide damper.* These three are single-blade dampers. The fourth type is the *multi-blade damper.* Multi-blade dampers may be made in the shop or purchased from suppliers. Of course, there are variations of these basic types; however, if the sheet metal worker knows these four types and how to use them, workers are equipped to handle almost all the damper problems that will arise.

Damper construction. Usually multi-blade dampers are used in very large jobs that call for automatic dampers controlled by air motors. These dampers automatically adjust and mix the air according to preset temperatures. Automatic dampers are outside the scope of this book. If the student learns and understands the vaious types of shop-made dampers, workers can easily master the automatic dampers so far as their construction in sheet metal ducts is concerned.

Shop-made dampers are most often single-blade dampers and are used on ducts of normal size. The damper is usually a piece of 16-gauge iron, sometimes with raw edges and sometimes hemmed, depending upon its size. If the damper is very large or the velocity of the air is fast enough to vibrate the damper, the edges of the metal are bent

to the shape shown in Fig. 7-10 in order to provide additional stiffness. Large volume-control dampers can also be formed as shown in Fig. 7-11, again to provide additional stiffness. Care must be taken to make the damper slightly smaller than the duct size to eliminate any danger of the damper rubbing on the duct and jamming. On all damper blades, the corners are slanted in about ½ in so that there will be less chance of them hitting the corners of the duct and jamming the damper.

The usual way to install a damper is to use a damper-quadrant set, such as the one shown in Fig. 7-12. This set usually consists of the damper-quadrant dial, a round shaft (often called a "bearing"), and a square shaft that fits the damper quadrant. The shafts are first riveted or spot welded onto the sheet metal damper; the damper is then inserted in holes punched in the proper place in the duct.

Fig. 7-13 Blade-direction Mark on Damper Quadrant. (Courtesy Duro-Dyne Co.)

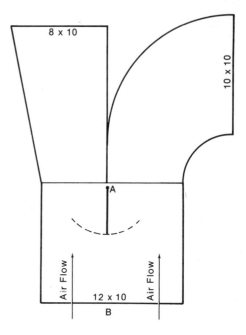

Fig. 7-14 Splitter Damper.

On most damper-quadrant sets, the round shaft is made so it can be slid back to set the damper in place and then slid forward and locked in place to hold the damper in position. If the round shaft is not of this type, the damper is usually installed before the duct is assembled.

After the damper is in place, the damper quadrant is screwed on the outside of the duct. Care must be taken with the direction in which it is installed. Every damper quadrant is marked "open" and "shut," but it is not always possible to make these markings read correctly. Of course, whenever it is possible, the damper quadrant should be turned so that it will read correctly, but if that cannot be done, always follow the standard procedure of keeping the damper-quadrant handle in line with the blade. Remember that once the duct is closed up, the damper quadrant is the only clue to a stranger as to which way to turn the damper. Always put a hacksaw cut or a chisel mark on the end of the square shaft in line with the damper blade so that it shows the blade direction. (See Fig. 7-13.) Some damper quadrants come with this mark already on the shaft, to guarantee that there will be no confusion.

Splitter dampers. A splitter damper is used to balance the air that enters two branches of a fitting, as shown in Fig. 7-14. The pivot point of the damper is at *A* and is located as close to the start of the branch as possible. The purpose of the splitter damper is to vary the amount of air that enters each branch. Since most damper quadrants allow a swing of 90°, the splitter damper is usually set so that the damper will swing 45° in either direction, as shown by the dotted arc.

It should be pointed out that the splitter damper only balances the amount of air that enters the two branches. It will not shut off either branch completely, nor will it control the total amount of air that enters the two branches.

The whole purpose of the splitter damper is to adjust the flow of air into each branch to the designed amount. Without a damper, the volume of air in each branch is usually not correct because of the many variables that enter into the situation. For instance, in the branch shown in Fig. 7-14, if the two take-offs are equal in area, there will probably be a slightly larger amount of air passing through the straight branch than through the elbow branch because there is more friction in an elbow than in a straight run. On the other hand, if the elbow branch is connected to a very short run of duct and the straight run is very long and complex, the increased friction from the long run might result in more air entering the elbow branch.

Volume-control dampers. The purpose of a volume-control damper is to control the volume of air in a line. It is not designed to shut off the air in the line completely, but to help balance out the system. The volume damper can be opened completely and usually can shut off the line to about 90 percent.

Volume-control dampers are often used in the lines 3 or 4 ft in front of the registers to provide a means of shutting off some of the air to the register. Most registers have a damper of some sort built into them, but shutting off the air at this point is an unsatisfactory means of balancing the system, since it destroys the air distribution in the room, usually causes air noise, and, most importantly, can be changed by anyone passing by. A volume damper in the duct, however, can be used to balance the system with some assurance that the correct setting will remain untouched.

Volume dampers are often used in conjunction with splitter dampers to control the flow of air into the various branches. In Fig. 7-14, if the amount of air entering the large pipe at point *B* is too great, no matter how the splitter damper is adjusted, both small branches will have too much air. However, if a volume damper is installed in the large pipe, as shown in Fig. 7-15, the volume of air in the large pipe can be adjusted properly and the splitter damper can be used to balance the flow into the branches.

Volume dampers are often installed after a splitter damper for further control of the system. The amount of air that a splitter damper can divert is

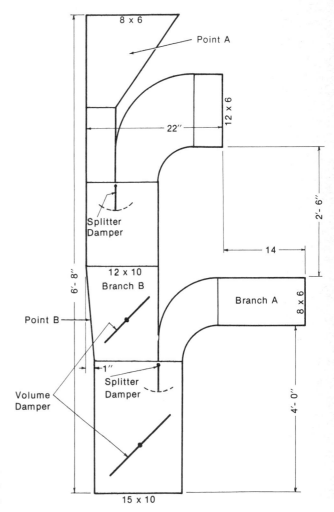

Fig. 7-15 Duct Branches and Location of Dampers.

limited, and a volume damper located in the branch after a splitter can be used to increase the pressure in the line and aid the splitter in controlling the air. In Fig. 7-15, note that there is a volume damper in the small branch after the first splitter damper. If the first splitter damper is used and too much air is still entering the straight pipe, the volume damper can be used to shut down the flow of air still more. Note also that the splitter damper in the second branch is located after the volume damper and can be used to balance the air for the second branch.

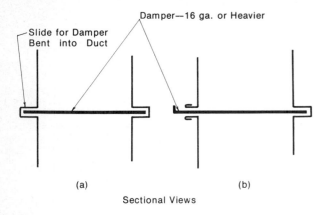

Damper—16 ga. or Heavier

Slide for Damper
Bent into Duct

(a)   (b)

Sectional Views

Fig. 7-16   Construction of Slide Damper.

Using a damper in this manner is common when the length of the lines of the two branches varies a great deal. In Fig. 7-15, if branch *A* is connected to a long run with many turns and branch *B* is a very short and comparatively straight run, the increased pressure in branch *A* will make it hard to divert enough air into that line. Then the volume damper in branch *B* can be shut down, equalizing the pressure in the two lines and allowing the splitter to balance them.

Slide dampers. A slide damper is a damper that slides across the duct, completely shutting it off. Its purpose is to provide 100 percent manual shutoff of a line. The usual way to install a slide damper is to make a special section of pipe, such as is shown in Fig. 7-16. A slide is bent into three sides of the duct (Fig. 7-16*a*) for the damper to be slid in; the fourth side is left open (Fig. 7-16*b*) to allow the damper to be slid in. This type of damper is removed from the duct completely when the duct is open, and is slid into place when the duct needs to be closed. Slide dampers are most commonly installed in duct systems used for heating in the winter and cooling in the summer. They shut off the furnace from the duct when the cooling unit is being used and do the reverse when the furnace is in use.

PRACTICE PROBLEMS

Problem 7-1

Purpose. To practice picking off and sketching fittings for a duct run.

Study. All of Chapter 7.

Assignment. Figure the dimensions for the four take-offs in Fig. 7-15. Make a sketch of each fitting and each section of straight duct needed. Each sketch should be a freehand shop sketch, giving all information necessary for a journeyman to make the fitting. Indicate the sides where the drive clip must be, and also the raw edges and hooked edges where fittings connect together. List the exact number of S-and-drive clips needed in the following manner: "1 set for 15-by-10-in duct."

Problem 7-2

Purpose. To study dampers and their uses.

Study. *Dampers for fittings.*

Assignment. Make a rough sketch of the plan view of Fig. 7-17 and on it locate all the necessary splitter and volume-control dampers for complete control of the air.

Problem 7-3

Purpose. To practice picking off fittings from a duct run.

Study. All of Chapter 7 and problem 7-2.

Assignment. From Fig. 7-17, pick off all the items for the complete run just as you would have to do if you were sketching it for someone else in the shop to make up.

1. Show on each fitting the clips, edges, radii, and any other information needed.

2. Make a list of each straight duct, showing exact size and length.

3. Number each duct and fitting and sketch a plan view showing the location of each number.

4. Make a list of dampers needed, showing their type, size, and location (by numbering the plan view).

5. Make a list of S-and-drive clips needed, as in problem 1.

6. There is no one correct way of running the duct, and each student will have different fittings sketched. The instructor will judge the sketches on the following basis.

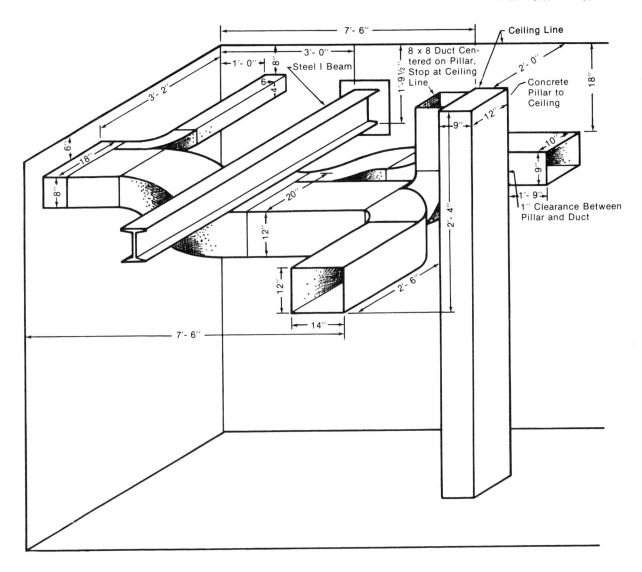

Fig. 7-17 Typical Duct Run.

a. Does each sketch give all the information the layout worker needs?

b. Are the fittings designed as simply as possible so that there will be no unnecessary layout?

c. Where basic fittings join for a branch, will they fit one another?

d. Will the fittings all fit together to make the complete run to the correct dimensions?

8

Square to Rounds

An important class of fittings is known by the general term *square to round*. When a fitting is designated as square to round, it does not necessarily mean that one end is square and the other round; it means that one end is formed by straight lines and the other is in some circular or elliptical form. A square to round could be rectangular to round, triangular to round, or even triangular to elliptical.

Layout by triangulation

All square to rounds are laid out by triangulation. The basic layout principles are always used, but specific techniques may apply. If a very unusual and complex fitting is being formed, one of the longer methods of layout may be employed. If it is a centered fitting of a common type, shortcut methods will probably be used.

Figure 8-1*a* shows the plan and elevation view of a common square to round. Although many shortcut methods could be employed on this fitting, we will lay it out by basic triangulation to illustrate the basic techniques used in square-to-round layouts.

The first step is to try to divide the fitting into symmetrical halves. If this can be done, then only half the fitting need be laid out because the other half will be identical.

After the fitting is divided into halves, the half circle is divided into equal spaces, as shown in the plan view of Fig. 8-1*b*. Unless it is a very large fitting, it is common trade practice to divide the half circle into six equal spaces.

After the half circle is divided into equal spaces, lines are drawn from the corners to the spaces of the nearest quarter circle, as shown in the plan view in Fig. 8-1*b*. The spaces and the corners of the fitting are numbered and lettered as shown. This facilitates greater speed and convenience in locating points and lines when laying out the pattern. Many beginners try to save time by eliminating the identifying numbers, but if the points are not numbered or lettered, layout is slower and the chances for error are greatly increased.

The next step is to find the true lengths of all layout lines. Since all layout lines are drawn from the bottom of the fitting to the top, all of them are rising the height of the fitting, which is indicated as H on the elevation view of Fig. 8-1*a*. The true lengths of the layout lines are shown in Fig. 8-1*c*. The height of the fitting is marked on the vertical line as shown by H. The length of each layout line is taken directly from the plan view (Fig. 8-1*b*) and marked out on the horizontal line of the triangle. For example, the distance $A4$ is taken from Fig. 8-1*b* and measured from point X on the true-length triangle (Fig. 8-1*c*) to locate point $A4$. The line drawn from Y to $A4$ is the true length of $A4$. All other true lengths are found in a similar manner.

After all the true lengths are found, the pattern for the square to round can be started. It is standard practice to start by drawing the longest side on the metal and then locating the midpoint of the curve. This practice is varied on special jobs, but normally it is the easiest way to start the layout.

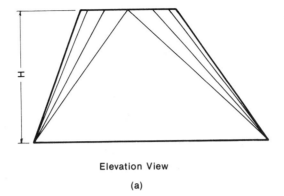

Elevation View

(a)

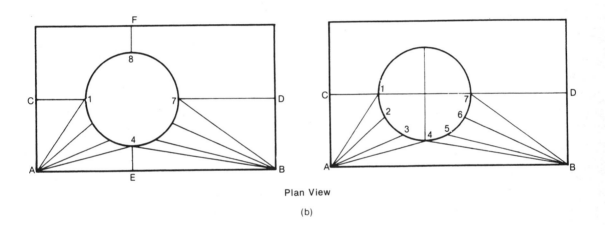

Plan View

(b)

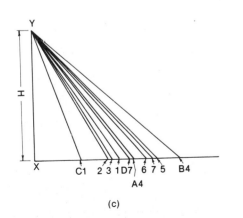

(c)

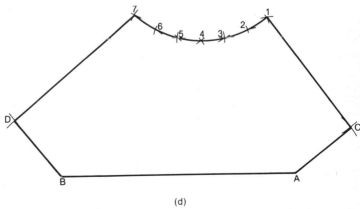

(d)

Fig. 8-1 Square to Round.

Figure 8-1*d* shows the pattern, which is started by drawing out line *BA* to the proper length. Then the true length of *A*4 is swung from point *A* and the true length of *B*4 is swung from point *B*. The intersection of these two arcs will give point 4.

After point 4 is located, all other points on the circle are located in a similar manner until points 1 through 7 are located. Point 5, for instance, is found by swinging the true length of *B*5 from point *B* and by swinging the distance of 4 to 5 from point 4. The intersection of these two arcs will give point 5. Note that the distance that is swung from point 4 to point 5 is taken directly from the plan view without finding a true length for it. This is because the distances from point to point of the circle are actual lengths on the drawing, since they are horizontal lines and therefore not rising.

All other points will be located in the same manner as point 5. Point 3 is found by swinging the true length of *A*3 from *A* and by swinging the distance of 4 to 3 from point 4.

After points 1 to 7 are found, half the circle is located on the pattern. In order to have a half pattern, points *D* and *C* must next be located.

Point *D* is located by measuring from point *B* and from point 7. This is done by swinging the true length of 7*D* from 7 and by swinging the distance of *BD* from *B*. The intersection of these two arcs gives point *D*. Note that the distance *BD* is a horizontal line and is taken directly from the drawing. Point *C* is found in the same manner. The distance from *A* to *C* is swung from *A* and the true length of 1*C* is swung from 1.

After points *C* and *D* are located, the basic pattern is completed. Lines are drawn connecting the points, and the curve is drawn through the points of the circle. If the mechanic has developed the ability to draw a smooth curve, it can be drawn in freehand. If not, a steel rule is held on edge and bowed to pass through the points, and a curve is drawn around it.

Shortcut methods

Although no square to round can be laid out without using these basic methods, the actual system used by experienced layout workers may employ many different shortcuts. The next few sections of this chapter will show some of the common ones. Since time is one of the most expensive items in a sheet metal shop, it is essential that the layout worker make the best use of it by employing every shortcut possible.

Shortcut methods of finding true lengths. Figure 8-2 shows half the plan view of the fitting from Fig. 8-1, as it would be drawn by a layout worker. Since the circle is centered in one direction with the square, only half the plan needs to be drawn; the other half is symmetrical, and drawing the other half would be a duplication of lines.

The important points of the fitting are identified with a letter or number. Some labeling system is necessary so that the layout worker will know the general location of each point by the way it is labeled. One common method is to letter the points on the square in the manner shown in Fig. 8-2 and to number the points on the circle starting with 1 on the left end. If this method is followed, the layout worker always knows that he or she first will draw line *AB* and then locate point 4. It is details such as a systematic method of identifying points that make one journeyman faster and more accurate than another.

After the plan view is drawn, the true lengths must be found. Instead of drawing a separate true-length triangle and transferring distances from the plan, it is faster to determine the true lengths right on the plan view. Because this method makes a confusion of lines on the plan view, it is important that the layout worker thoroughly understands the principles involved so that there will be no errors made by picking off the wrong line.

The basic idea of this shortcut is to use the square corner of the plan view for the true-length triangle. Figure 8-3 is a duplicate of the plan view of Fig. 8-2, except that only one layout line and its true length are drawn in so that the method may be more clearly seen.

After the plan view is drawn, line *AC* is extended and the distance *AE* is marked off equal to the height of the fitting. This makes *AE* the height of the true-length triangle and *AB* the base line.

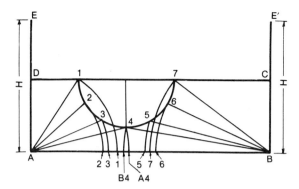

Fig. 8-2 Plan View for Finding True Lengths.

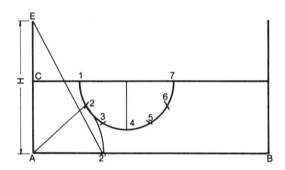

Fig. 8-3 Short Cut in Finding True Lengths.

their true lengths are found by measuring from point E'. For instance, the true length of line $A4$ is measured from point E to point $A4$, but the true length of $B4$ is measured from point E' to point $B4$.

Finding the wings by means of a square. In Fig. 8-1*a*, the parts of the pattern outlined by $1AC$ and $7BD$ are known as the *wings* of the pattern. Many times it is easier to lay out the wings of the pattern by a square rather than by swinging the arcs.

The method of using a square to lay out the wings can be used whenever the angles $AC1$ and $BD7$ in Fig. 8-1*b* are 90° angles. If these angles are other than 90°, this method cannot be used.

When all the points of the circle have been found on the pattern, instead of laying out point C by swinging the arcs, a square is held so that the blades of the square run through point 1 and point A, as shown in Fig. 8-4. The blade that runs through point A should be held so that the exact length of AC is held at A. In other words, if AC is 6 in long in the plan view, then the 6-in mark of the square must be held on point A. If this is done, the distance from A to C is the proper measurement, and corner $AC1$ is a 90° angle—the two requirements for a correct wing. The wing on the other side of the pattern is found in the same manner.

The first step in finding the true length of $A2$ is to set the dividers to the distance $A2$. Then, without moving the dividers, swing the arc 2-2', using point A as the center. This makes the distance $A2'$ on line AB the same length as the layout line $A2$. The distance $E2'$ is then the true length of $A2$. In actual practice, it is not necessary to draw in line $E2'$. It is enough to know that setting the dividers from E to 2' will give the true lengths of $A2$.

Figure 8-2 shows the arcs swung for all the true lengths. It is best to swing the arcs in completely, as shown, so it is easily seen which point they come from; and it is best to number the points on line AB for quick reference. Note that the lines drawn from point B are swung from point B, and

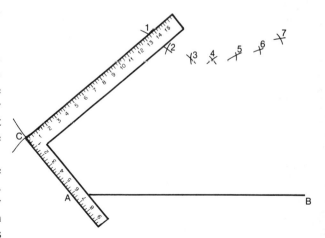

Fig. 8-4 Layout of Wings with Square.

Checking a square to round for accuracy.
Because there are two different methods for laying
out the wings, a square to round may be easily
checked for accuracy.

If the wings are laid out by swinging the arcs,
the accuracy of the layout can be checked by
holding a square up to the angles of the wings. In
Fig. 8-1c, if the angles AC1 and BD7 are both 90°,
the layout of the pattern is correct. If one of them is
not 90°, that side of the pattern is wrong in some
manner.

If the wings are laid out by using the square, the
accuracy of the layout can be checked by finding
the true lengths of D7 and C1 in Fig. 8-1b and
checking them against the same lines on the
pattern. If these lines on the pattern are the same as
their true length, the pattern is correct; if either of
the lines do not check out, that side of the pattern is
wrong.

It is always good practice to check the patterns
for a square to round, since it takes very little time
and ensures against wasted time and material. It is
possible that the pattern for the square to round
appears correct but actually is not.

Layout by means of a square. A square to round
can be laid out by use of a square only, if the layout
need not be accurate. This method is a shortcut that
can be used only if the height of the fitting does not
have to be exact. It results in an approximate
pattern that has to be trimmed down after it is
formed.

Figure 8-5 shows the layout of a fitting similar
to that in Fig. 8-1, except that the circle is
centered. To start the layout, draw line *AB*. Next,
locate the midpoint *F* of line *AB* and square up line
F 4, which will be equal to the height of the fitting.
If the circle is not centered in the square, point *F*
will be located off center the proper amount. Line
1-7 is then drawn through point 4 and parallel to
AB. The distances 1-4 and 4-7 are both marked off
equal to one-fourth the circumference of the circle,
so line 1-7 is equal to half the circumference.

After points 1 and 7 are located, the wings are
found by a square in the same manner as described
for Fig. 8-4. Next, lines *D* 1 and *C* 7 are extended

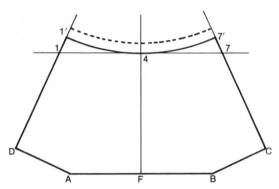

Fig. 8-5 Layout of Square to Round with Rule and
Square Only.

and points 1' and 7' are located by guess. Whatever the distance of 1 to 1' is, the distance of 7 to
7' will be the same. The distance from 1 to 1' is
found by guessing and by experience. It is possible, however, to figure what the true length of *D* 1'
should be and measure this distance from *D*. After
points 1' and 7' are found, the curve from 1' to 7'
is drawn in freehand so that it passes through point
4. Drawing in the curve completes the pattern
except for the addition of necessary seams and
edges.

This shortcut method is very approximate, and
after the fitting is formed up it will be necessary to
trim the round end to the proper size and level it
up. Because of this, an extra ¾ in should be added
around 1'-7', as shown by the dotted lines. It
should be remembered that this shortcut is best
when the circle is centered in the square or
rectangular end.

Locating the seams on the square to round. At
the start, it is important to locate the seam lines in
the best way for laying out the pattern. If the seams
are located in the wrong position, it can mean that
both halves of the pattern will have to be laid out
instead of only one half.

In Fig. 8-1, the seam lines on the plan view
should be located on line *C* 1 and line *D* 7. If they
are located thus, the plan view is divided into two
symmetrical halves and only a half pattern need be
laid out because the other half can be marked from

it. However, if the seam lines are located on lines $F8$ and $E4$, the pattern is divided into two dissimilar portions and both patterns have to be laid out separately.

Whenever possible, the seam line should be made to form a 90° angle with the bottom line of the square. In other words, in Fig. 8-1, angle $AC1$ should be a 90° angle. If this angle and the corresponding one on the other side of the pattern are kept to 90°, the method of laying out the wings by a square can be used and the accuracy of the pattern can be checked.

When a square to round is off center in both directions, both half patterns have to be laid out. In such a case, the usual practice is to maintain the 90° angle between the seam line and the bottom line. This is illustrated in Fig. 8-6. The seam lines of this square to round should be located on line $D1$ and $C7$. The seams could be located on lines $G10$ and $H4$, but this would divide the fitting into unequal proportions.

Note that $D1$ and $C7$ are still made square to the bottom lines AF and BE, even though this does not divide the bottom line in half. Again, this is done because it is easier to form up the fitting when the seam line is at a square angle; it is also easier to check the accuracy of the pattern.

Layout of centered square to round. When the circle of a square to round is centered in the square or rectangle, only a few true lengths of the layout lines need be found, because many of the lines are of equal length.

Fig. 8-7 is a plan view of a square to round in which the circle is exactly centered in the square. When the end of the fitting is an actual square, only three true lengths need be found. In Fig. 8-7, lines $A1$, $A4$, $B4$, and $B7$ are all the same length and, therefore, have the same true length. Only one true length need be found for lines $A2$, $A3$, $B5$, and $B6$ because these lines are all the same length. The only other true length that need be found is the seam line $C1$. The other seam line $D7$ is the same length. When a square to round can be centered, the time spent in laying out the fitting is reduced.

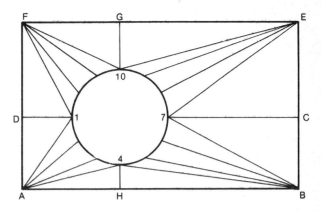

Fig. 8-6 Square to Round Off-center in Two Directions.

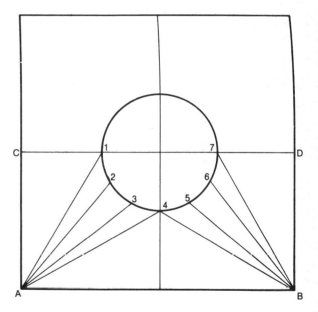

Fig. 8-7 Centered Square to Round.

When the bottom of the square to round is rectangular, as is shown in the plan view in Fig. 8-8, and the circle is centered in the rectangle, all four layout lines will be different, but time will still be saved because the lines of the other quarter plan view will be duplicates. In Fig. 8-8, $A1$, $A2$, $A3$, and $A4$ are all of different lengths, but $A1$ and $B7$ are the same length, as are all other similar lines.

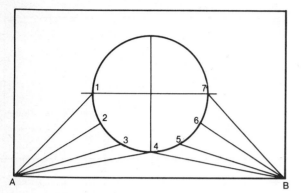

Fig. 8-8 Centered Square to Round.

This means that, although a rectangular-to-round requires more true lengths than a square-to-round fitting, it is still easier to lay out than a fitting that is off center in one or both directions.

Drawing the plan views of a square to round. As in every other phase of layout work, in the layout of square to rounds all unnecessary lines are eliminated. This means that in most cases a full plan view of the fitting is not drawn.

In the fitting shown in Fig. 8-6, the circle is off center in both directions and, therefore, is different in all four quarters. In this case, the full plan view must be drawn.

However, in Fig. 8-1, the circle is off center in only one direction, making it possible to divide the plan view into identical halves. In this case, the plan view would be drawn as shown in Fig. 8-2; any more of the plan view would merely be a duplication of lines.

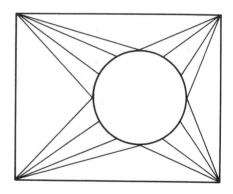

Plan View

Elevation View

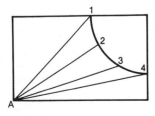

Fig. 8-9 Quarter Plan for Centered Square to Round.

◀ **Fig. 8-10** Square to Round on a Pitch.

When the circle is centered in the square or in the rectangle, such as in Figs. 8-7 and 8-8, only one-fourth of the plan view need be drawn, as shown in Fig. 8-9. Any more of the plan view would be duplication of lines.

Square to round on a pitch

Often square to rounds must be laid out with one end on a pitch. Figure 8-10 illustrates a typical

square to round of this type. Though the basic principles of layout are the same, the method of finding the true lengths is different.

Though the true lengths could be found from a side view, it is usually easier to use a plan view. This is done in the same manner as for a regular square to round, except that two different heights for the true-length triangles are used. In the plan view in Fig. 8-11, all the layout lines drawn from points B and E will be found with a true-length triangle the height of which is the distance X in the elevation view. All the lines that are drawn from

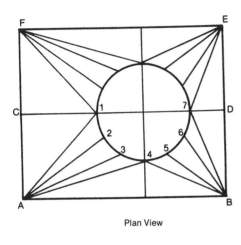

Plan View

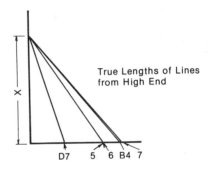

True Lengths of Lines from High End

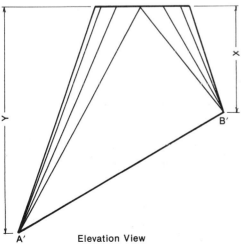

Elevation View

Fig. 8-11 Layout Procedure for Square to Round on a Pitch.

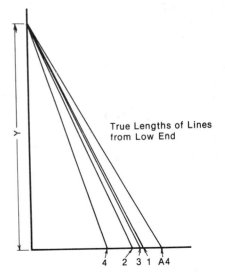

True Lengths of Lines from Low End

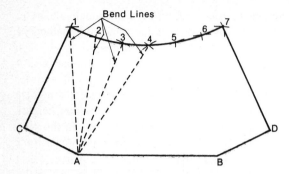

Fig. 8-12 Pattern for Fig. 8-11.

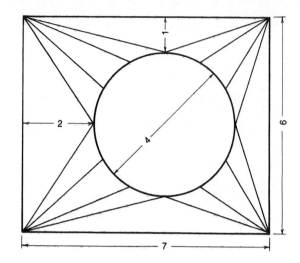

points *A* and *F* will be found on a true-length triangle of a height equal to the distance *Y*.

After the true lengths are found, the pattern is laid out in the usual manner, as shown in Fig. 8-12. Note that to start the pattern, the proper length of line *AB* must be used. The distance of *AB* in the plan view of Fig. 8-11 is not a true length because it is slanting upward. The true length of *AB* is taken from the distance *A'B'* in the elevation view. This is the length of line *AB* when it is drawn to start the pattern.

After line *AB* is drawn in Fig. 8-12, the square to round is laid out in the regular manner. Point 4 is found first, and then all other points are found in the proper order. If the plan view is drawn so that the seam lines are square to the bottom line, points *C* and *D* of the wings can be located by means of a square, as described previously, or they can be laid out by swinging arcs.

Except for the use of the two different heights to find the true lengths, the layout of the pattern is the same as for any square to round. No other special consideration for the pitch of the bottom need be made; it will take care of itself as the pattern is laid out.

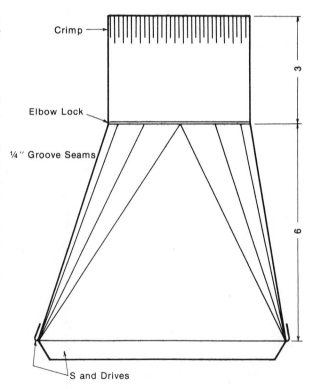

Fig. 8-13 Problem 8-1, Laying Out a Square to Round by Technically Correct Method.

PRACTICE PROBLEMS

Problem 8-1

Purpose. To learn how to lay out a square to round by the technically correct method.

Study. Introductory paragraphs of Chapter 8 and *Layout by triangulation.*

Assignment.

1. Lay out the half pattern for the square to round shown in Fig. 8-13 by using the methods described under *Layout by triangulation.* Allow for all seams indicated.

2. Make up the fitting, including the collar, out of metal.

Problem 8-2

Purpose. To learn how to use the shortcuts for a centered square to round, how to lay out the wings with a square, and how to use only the necessary parts of the plan view.

Study. *Finding the wings by means of a square, Checking a square to round for accuracy, Locating the seams on the square to round, Layout of centered square to round, Drawing the plan views of a square to round.*

Assignment.

1. Lay out the square to round shown in Fig. 8-14. Lay out the wings by using the square, and check the accuracy of the layout by checking the lengths of the seam lines. Find only the necessary true lengths, and draw only the part of the plan view that is needed. The purpose of this assignment is to give practice in using shortcuts. Learning to apply these is as important in this assignment as being able to lay out the fitting. Save the pattern for comparison with the pattern to be made in problem 8-3.

2. Make this fitting up completely, including the collar.

Problem 8-3

Purpose. To learn how to lay out an approximate pattern for a square to round by means of a square and rule only.

Study. *Layout by means of a square, Locating the seams on the square to round.*

Assignment.

1. Lay out the pattern for the fitting shown in Fig. 8-14, using a square and rule only. Compare it for

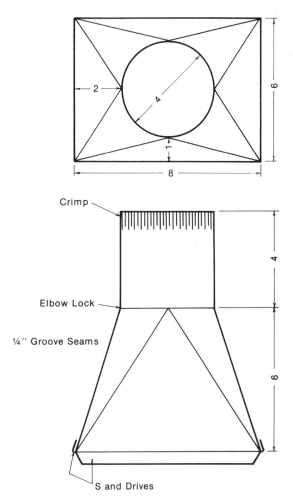

Fig. 8-14 Problem 8-2, Laying Out an Off-center square to Round Using Short Cuts.

accuracy with the same pattern laid out in problem 8-2.

2. Form the fitting out of metal; trim it to size and add the collar.

Problem 8-4

Purpose. To practice using all the shortcut methods for laying out a square to round and to learn how to use a shortcut method for finding true lengths.

Study. All of Chapter 8, with special emphasis on *Shortcut methods of finding true lengths, Locating the seams on a square to round, Drawing the plan views of a square to round.*

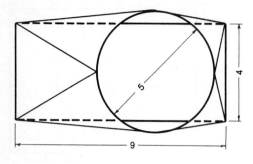

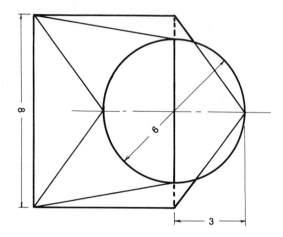

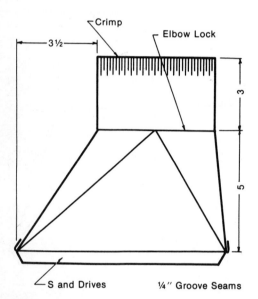

Fig. 8-15 Problem 8-4, Laying Out an Off-center Square to Round.

Assignment.

1. Lay out the pattern for the fitting shown in Fig. 8-15. Use the shortcut method of finding the true lengths. Draw only the necessary part of the plan view, and eliminate all unnecessary lines on the layout. Have your layout checked by the instructor to see if all possible shortcuts are used.

2. Make up the pattern out of metal, including the collar.

Problem 8-5

Purpose. To learn how to lay out the pattern for a square to round on a pitch.

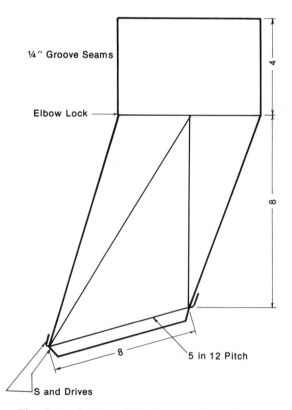

Fig. 8-16 Problem 8-5, Laying Out a Square to Round on a Pitch.

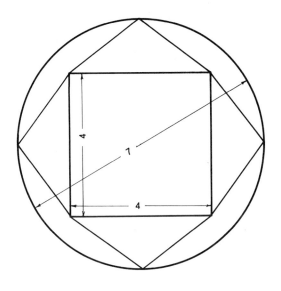

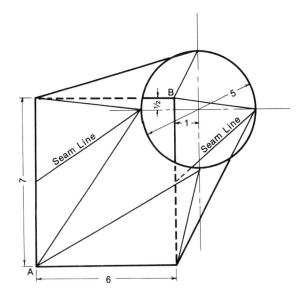

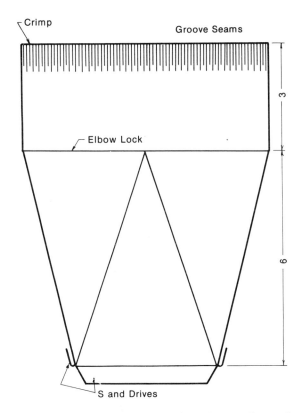

Fig. 8-17 Problem 8-6, Laying Out a Centered Square to Round.

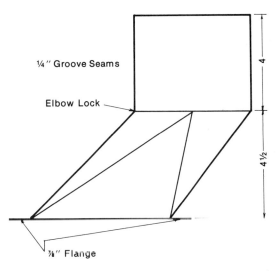

Fig. 8-18 Problem 8-7, Laying Out a Square to Round That is Off-center in Two Directions.

Study. All of Chapter 8, with special emphasis on *Square to round on a pitch*.

Assignment.

1. Lay out the pattern for the fitting shown in Fig. 8-16, using all possible shortcuts. Note that the 8-in side that is on a pitch is not shown in its true length on this plan view.

2. Make up the fitting, including the collar.

Problem 8-6

Purpose. To gain experience in laying out centered square to rounds.

Study. All of Chapter 8, with special emphasis on *Layout of centered square to round.*

Assignment.

1. Make the pattern for the square to round shown in Fig. 8-17, using all the shortcuts possible, and the minimum of lines.

2. Make up the fitting, including the collar.

Problem 8-7

Purpose. To gain experience in laying out square to rounds that are off center in both directions.

Study. All of Chapter 8.

Assignment. Lay out the patterns needed for the fitting shown in Fig. 8-18. Use any methods you desire.

Problem 8-8

Purpose. To gain experience in laying out unusual square to rounds.

Study. All of Chapter 8.

Assignment. On the plan view of Fig. 8-18, draw a line from corner *A* to corner *B*. Assume that the square end of this fitting is on a 4-in-12 pitch along this line and that *B* is the high corner. The fitting height will be 4½ in, as shown in the elevation view. Since this fitting is pitched from corner to corner, it is a slightly different problem than Fig. 8-16, in which the pitch is parallel to the side. Lay out the patterns for the altered fitting using any methods desired.

9
Round Tapers

Round tapers are a class of fittings that involve the same basic principles as square to rounds. Like square to rounds, tapers are basically a triangulation problem. They are also like square to rounds in that many shortcut layout methods have been developed. There are several ways to lay out round tapers, and the layout worker should be able to choose the best one for any particular job.

Sweeping a taper

One of the most common ways to lay out a round taper is by *sweeping* it out. This method is really nothing more than simplified radial-line layout. For simple tapers, it has the advantage of being fast and accurate.

Sweeping is a simple, four-step procedure that is the same for any centered taper, that is, a taper whose top and bottom circles are on the same center so that the side is slanted at the same angle all around. Sweeping is limited to tapers that are centered and have a fairly sharp slant. Step 2 of Fig. 9-1 shows how the sides of the taper are extended to locate a center point. If the taper is slight, this center point may be 10 or 20 ft away. Since arcs are swung from this center point, a 10 or 20 ft radius would be very difficult to swing. The tapered sides must be slanted enough so they will intersect within 2 or 3 ft for this method to be conveniently used.

The steps in sweeping out a round taper are shown in Fig. 9-1.

Step 1. Draw an exact side view of the fitting.

Step 2. Extend the side lines until they intersect. After the side view is drawn, continue the side lines until they intersect. If the side view is drawn accurately, the two side lines will intersect at the center line of the fitting, as shown by point *A* in step 2.

Step 3. Swing the arcs. Using the apex (point *A*) as center, swing arcs through the corner points *C* and *D* in step 3. These arcs are swung to an indefinite length at this time.

Step 4. Measure the circumference. After the two arcs are swung, measure the circumference of the large diameter around the large arc. Actually, the pattern may be started at any point along the arc. Line *AG* in step 4 may be drawn at any convenient angle. The circumference of a circle of diameter *DH* is then measured around the large arc by using a flexible rule. This measurement locates point *E* in step 4. A line is then drawn from point *E* back to the center point *A*. This completes the pattern, which is the shaded area outlined by the points *FGEB*. The circumference of the top arc is not measured, since drawing the lines from the large arc up to the center line will give the proper circumference around the top. A good check on the accuracy of the pattern is to check the length of the small arc. It should be the same length as the circumference of a circle with a diameter equal to that of the top of the taper.

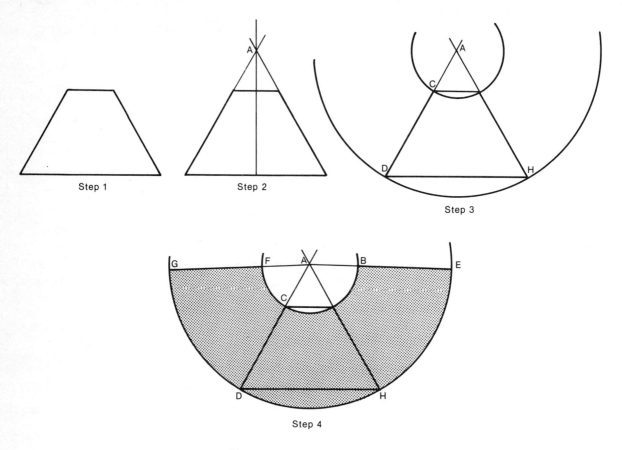

Fig. 9-1 Sweeping a Taper.

Shortcuts in sweeping a taper

As in other types of layout, the shortcuts in sweeping a taper involve understanding the principles of the layout and then eliminating all unnecessary lines. To illustrate these shortcuts, Fig. 9-2 shows a funnel and the layout of its pattern.

The first shortcut is to draw only half the side view; this eliminates duplication. In Fig. 9-2, step 1, only the part of the side view that is shaded is necessary.

Another shortcut is that the side view need not be drawn over the spot where the pattern is to be located. Since the only purpose of the side view is to find the length of the radius *AB* and of *AC,* as shown in step 1, the side view may be drawn

anywhere and on any handy piece of scrap metal. This eliminates having to place the side view so that the pattern will be located economically on the sheet of metal. After the half side view is drawn and distances *AB* and *AC* found, the pattern is laid out as shown in step 2 of Fig. 9-2.

To lay out the pattern in step 2, first set the dividers at the length of *AC* from step 1 and swing the large arc of the pattern. Locate the center point so that the arc may be swung in the corner of the sheet of metal without waste. Then swing the small arc with the radius of *AB* in the side view, using the same center point.

After the two arcs are swung, draw line *AC* to position the pattern most economically on the

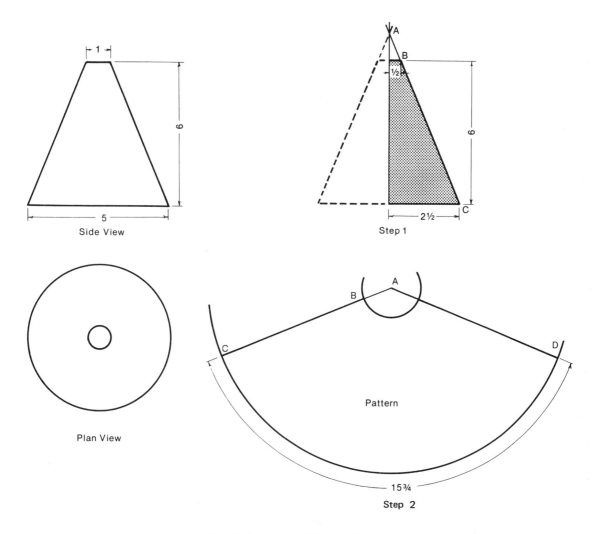

Fig. 9-2 Layout of Funnel Pattern.

sheet. Since the diameter of the large end is 5 in, measure the circumference of 15¾ in around the large arc; then draw a line from this point *(D)* up to the center point *(A)* to complete the pattern.

Standard funnel pattern

If height is not important in a required funnel or short taper, the *standard funnel* method is quickest. Like all shortcuts, it has limitations. The limitation in this case is that the height of the taper cannot be controlled.

The principle behind this method is that, if a half circle is drawn with a *radius* of 5 in, for instance, the distance around this half circle is equal to the circumference of a 5-in-*diameter* circle.

If the height of the funnel shown in Fig. 9-2 does not matter, then the pattern may be laid out by the standard funnel method. Figure 9-3*a* shows the pattern for this funnel. The large radius *R* will be

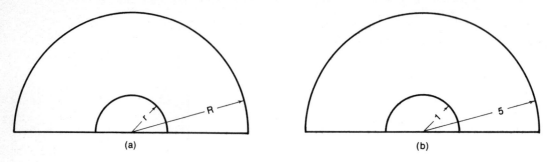

Fig. 9-3 Layout of Standard Funnel.

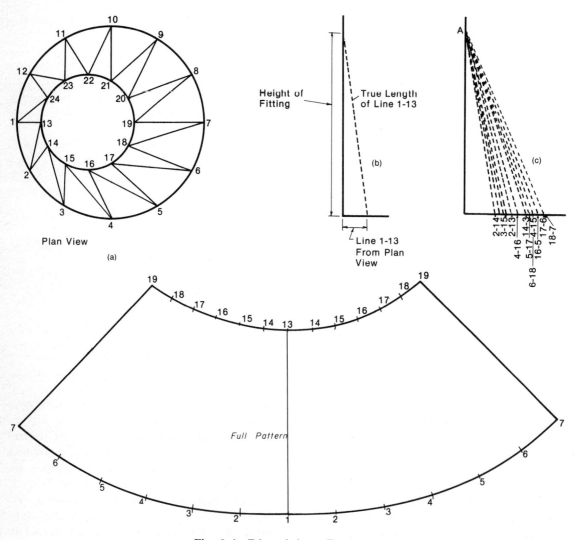

Fig. 9-4 Triangulating a Taper.

equal to the diameter of the top of the funnel, and the small radius *r* will be equal to the diameter of the small end of the funnel. The dimensions for the pattern are shown in Fig. 9-3*b*.

In this method, the pattern will always be a half circle, and the radii of the two arcs will always be equal to the diameters desired.

Triangulation of a round taper

Whenever a round taper is off center, neither sweeping nor the half-circle method can be used. To obtain an accurate pattern, it must be triangulated by the conventional method. Triangulation of a round taper is a basic method that must be familiar to every layout worker.

An off-centered fitting is shown in Fig. 9-4*a*. To lay out the pattern, first divide the plan view into equal spaces as shown. Usually each circle is divided into twelve equal spaces.

After the circles are divided, draw lines to connect the points. Then find the true length for each line. Since all these lines are rising the same distance, the true length of each line is found as in the example in Fig. 9-4*b*. The distance 1-13 is taken directly from the plan view, and the height of the true-length triangle is the height of the fitting. All other true lengths are found in the same manner. It is usual to draw the lengths in the manner shown in Fig. 9-4*b*. All distances from the plan view are set off on the bottom line and marked. The true length of each line, as shown by the dotted lines in Fig. 9-4*c*, is usually not drawn. The true length of each line is measured by setting the dividers from point *A* to the proper point on the bottom line.

After all true lengths are found, the pattern can be laid out. To start the layout, draw the true length of line 1-13; then, taking the true length of line 1-14, swing an arc on the pattern using point 1 as center. Next, set the dividers the distance from 13 to 14 on the plan and swing this distance from point 13 on the pattern. The intersection of these two arcs is point 14, as shown on the pattern.

After point 14 is located, point 2 is found by measuring from point 14 and from point 1. The true length of 14-2 is swung from point 14, and the distance from 1 to 2 in the plan view is swung from point 1. The intersection of these two arcs is point 2.

All other points on the pattern are found in the same manner. Point 15 is found next by swinging the true length of 2-15 from point 2 and by swinging the distance from 14 to 15 from point 14.

After point 15 is located, point 3 is found next. All other points on the pattern are located in the same manner until points 7 and 19 are found.

At the same time as these points are found, the pattern is also developed in the other direction from line 1-13. For instance, a duplicate of point 14 is located on the other side of line 1-13. This point is actually point 24 on the plan, but since the two halves of the plan are the same, the points are numbered the same. If the pattern is worked in both directions simultaneously, the whole pattern will be developed as shown.

In actual practice, only half the plan view is necessary, since the other half is a duplicate. On a round taper, no matter how the circles are offset, it is always possible to draw a center line that will cut the plan view into two symmetrical halves and thus eliminate the need for a complete plan view.

Except for eliminating half the plan view, there are no shortcuts for triangulating a taper. The only shortcut would be to make fewer points around the circles and thus make a quick, approximate pattern.

Taper from three side views

Since triangulating a taper pattern is a long process, and sweeping can be used only on tapers with sufficiently sharp slants, the layout worker must know other methods of developing the pattern. A fast, accurate method that works on gradual tapers is the three-side-views method. It works on any centered taper, no matter how gradually the sides slant.

Figure 9-5 shows a taper laid out by the three-side-views method. Since this taper is centered, the fitting could also be laid out by sweeping. However, if sweeping were used, the radius

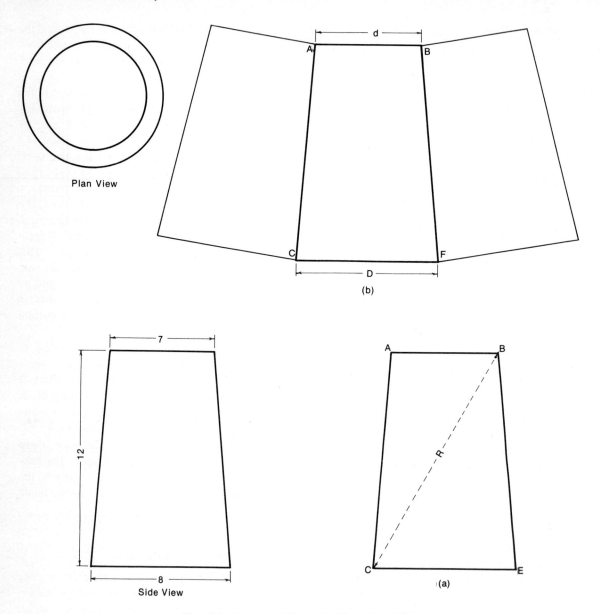

Plan View

(b)

Side View

(a)

Fig. 9-5 Layout of Taper by Three Side Views.

needed for the large arc would be 8 ft, which would be very awkward to handle.

To lay out this fitting by the three-side-views method, first draw an exact side view, as shown in Fig. 9-5a. Next, draw two other side views attached to each side of the original view, as shown in Fig. 9-5b. These two side views must be

duplicates of the first in *angles* as well as in *lengths*. It is not possible to square a line from the side of the first view to draw the other views because this makes a 90° angle on one corner.

To duplicate the sides, first set the dividers at the distance of the diagonal indicated by *R* in Fig. 9-5a. Since both diagonal lines of the first side

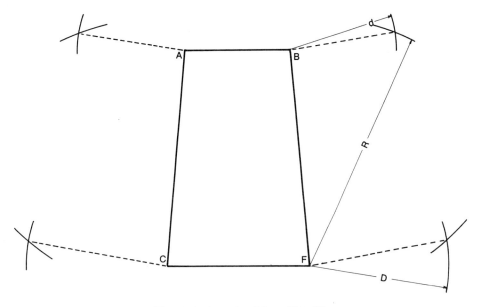

Fig. 9-6 Drawing Three Side Views.

view will be the same length, the distance R must be the length of all the diagonals on the other two side views. Swing the radius R from points A, B, C, and F, in Fig. 9-6.

After these arcs are swung, the distances of the top and bottom of the side views are located. To do this, first set the dividers to the distance AB. This radius, shown by d in Fig. 9-6, is swung from point A and from point B. The intersection of this arc with arc R gives the location of the top corners of the side view. Next, the dividers are set to the distance CF and swung from point C and point F, as shown by D in Fig. 9-6. The intersection of this arc with arc R gives the location of the bottom corners of the side views. When these points are connected, the construction of the side views is complete.

After the three side views are completed, draw arcs by bowing a steel rule through the corner points as shown by A', A'', C', and C'' in Fig. 9-7. When drawing these arcs, extend them beyond the end lines of the side view because material will be added to make the stretchout of the fitting correct.

Refer back to Fig. 9-5. The diameter of the top of the fitting is to be 7 in. The circumference of a 7-in diameter circle is 22 in. Since the distance around the top of the three side views in Fig. 9-7 is approximately 3×7, or 21 in, the difference between 21 and 22 in will have to be added to the pattern. To be exact, the distance from A' to A'' in Fig. 9-7 should be measured with a steel rule, since the curve may measure slightly more than the straight-line measurement of 21 in.

If the distance from A' to A'' is 21 in, the stretchout of the top curve of the fitting is 1 in short. Half this difference is added to each end of the pattern, which means that ½ in is added to each end of the top curve, as is shown by $A''G$ and $A'H$ in Fig. 9-7.

On the bottom of the pattern, the finished diameter is 8 in, which means that the bottom curve of the pattern must measure 25⅛ in. Since the bottom curve will measure 8×3, or 24 in, the bottom curve will be 1⅛ in short. Half this difference, ⁹/₁₆ in, is added to each end of the curve. This is shown by $C''J$ and $C'I$. Lines are

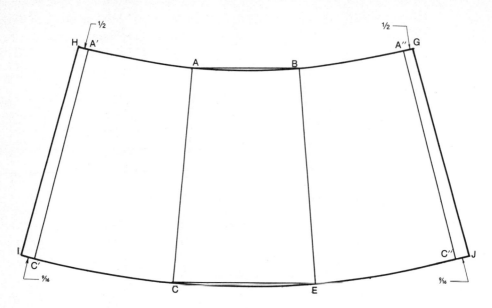

Fig. 9-7 Correcting Stretchout in Three-side Views Method.

drawn to the new points on the curve to finish the pattern. The completed pattern is outlined by the corner points *HIJG* in Fig. 9-7. Necessary allowances for seams and edges will have to be added to the pattern.

Approximate pattern by square and rule

The approximate pattern by square and rule is a "jump" method of laying out a round taper that is fast but comparatively inaccurate. It results in an approximate pattern that can be trimmed to size after it is formed.

To lay out the pattern for the fitting in Fig. 9-5 by this method refer to Fig. 9-8. Draw a line equal to the circumference of the bottom diameter. This line is 25⅛ in long in Fig. 9-8. Next, square up a line at the center of this base line and make it 12 in long, the height of the fitting. At the end of this 12-in line draw the circumference of the top diameter parallel to the base line, and center it equally on the 12-in center line. This line is shown by the 22-in line in Fig. 9-8. Draw end lines to connect the ends of the top and bottom lines. This is the basic pattern. However, it is good practice to add about 1 in of metal to the top and the bottom so

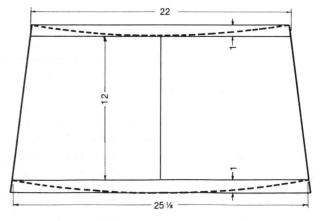

Fig. 9-8 Laying Out an Approximate Taper Pattern.

that the fitting can be trimmed straight and to the right size after it is formed. Make allowances on each end for seams.

Sometimes a steel rule is used to draw an approximate curve into the pattern, as shown by the dotted lines in Fig. 9-8. The amount of the curve is estimated, and the final curve is trimmed to size after the fitting is formed. In some cases,

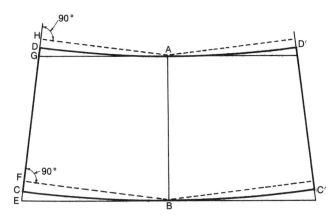

Fig. 9-9 Locating the End Points on an Approximate Pattern.

where appearance is of no importance, very little trimming is done, and the fitting is installed in the shape in which it is formed up. In other cases, a great deal of trimming is done to make the fitting acceptable.

If a more accurate curve is needed, the procedure shown in Fig. 9-9 may be followed. The pattern is laid out as shown in Fig. 9-8, but instead of completely guessing at the curve, points D and D' are located for the top curve and points C and C' for the bottom curve. A rule is then bent through the three points to draw in the curve. To locate point D, draw a line square to the line EH so that it will run through the center point A; then take half the distance from H to G to find D. Points D', C, and C' are located in the same manner.

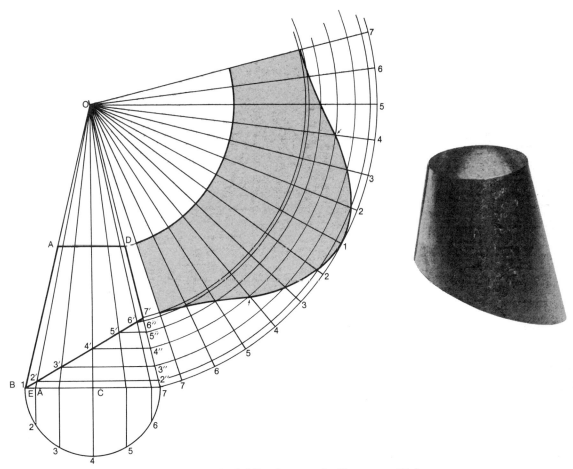

Fig. 9-10 Radial-line Layout of a Taper on a Pitch.

Tapers on a pitch

Round tapers in which the top and bottom are not parallel often have to be made. A round roof jack, such as that in Fig. 4-19, is an example of such a fitting. These fittings may be laid out by triangulation in the manner shown in Chapter 12 for the triangulation of a Y branch. However, a faster method is by *radial lines*. This is the method most often used.

Radial-line layout is actually a more complicated version of the method for sweeping out a funnel. Like sweeping out, it can only be used if the fitting is a centered taper and if the sides are slanted sufficiently to reach an apex in a reasonable distance. Figure 9-10 shows a taper on a pitch and the layout by radial lines.

The first step is to draw an exact side view, as shown in Fig. 9-10 (area *AB*7'*D*), and extend the short side to complete the cone (area *AB*7*D*). Next, draw the profile at the base of the cone. Divide the profile into the usual number of parts, and square lines from these points to the base line 1-7. Find the apex *O* by extending the side lines until they intersect. All points thus obtained on line 1-7 are drawn up to the apex *O*. At the point where these tapering lines cross the pitch line of the taper bottom, draw lines *square to the center line CO* so that they intersect the side line *O*7. On the slanted line *EO*, for instance, a line is drawn square to *CO* and through point 2' until it intersects line *O*7 at point 2''.

After all lines are squared over to *O*7, swing arcs from these points, using point *O* as center. In other words, using *O* as center, swing arcs from points 7', 6'', 5'', 4'', 3'', 2'', and 7.

Next, measure the bottom arc (7-7) equal to the circumference of a circle with a diameter equal to

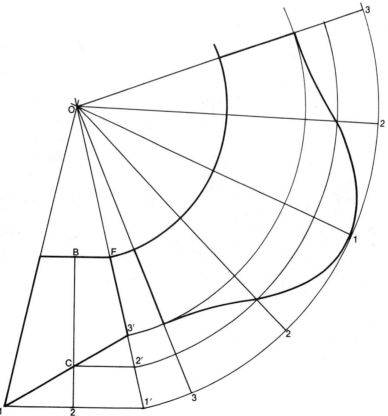

Fig. 9-11 Short Method of Radial Lines.

line 1-7. Divide this distance into twice the number of spaces that are on the profile, and draw lines from these points up to the apex *O*. The points of intersection of the corresponding arcs and lines give the points of the curve of the pattern. For instance, the intersection of line 1-4 and the arc from 4″ gives the points indicated by the arrow. The finished pattern is shown by the grey area in Fig. 9-10.

Short method of radial lines

Many times a round taper on a pitch need not be laid out very accurately, and a shorter method of radial lines can be used which employs only the essential steps.

In the shorter method, only the quarter points of the pattern are found, and the curves are drawn in from these. To start the layout, first draw a side view just as for regular radial lines. Then continue the short side of the taper on down to form a regular cone. This is shown in Fig. 9-11.

After the side view is drawn, draw the center line *2B*. At point *C*, which is the point at which the center line intersects the pitch line of the bottom of the taper, draw a line square to the center line so that it intersects the side line to locate point 2′.

Find the center point *O* by extending the side lines up until they intersect. Using point *O* as a center, swing arcs through the points *F*, 3′, 2′, and 1′. Next, measure the arc from point 1′ equal to the circumference of a circle of diameter equal to the distance 1-1′. Divide this circumference into four equal spaces, and draw lines from these points up to the center point *O*. Number these lines as shown in Fig. 9-11, and locate the quarter points of the curve of the pattern where the lines of corresponding numbers intersect. For example, the first point of the pattern is where line 3-*O* intersects the arc from 3′. The second point is the intersection of line 2-*O* and arc 2′.

It should be remembered that this method will only work if quarter points alone will give the needed accuracy. If more points than this are needed, it is necessary to draw a profile and proceed as for regular radial lines.

PRACTICE PROBLEMS

Problem 9-1

Purpose. To learn how to sweep a taper.

Study. *Sweeping a taper, Shortcuts in sweeping a taper.*

Assignment.

1. Lay out the pattern for the taper shown in Fig. 9-12.

2. Draw only half the side view when laying out the pattern.

3. Lay out the pattern so it is not drawn over the side view.

4. Form up the fitting, using the seams indicated.

Problem 9-2

Purpose. To learn how to lay out a taper by the standard-funnel-pattern method and by sweeping.

Study. *Sweeping a taper, Shortcuts in sweeping a taper, Standard funnel pattern.*

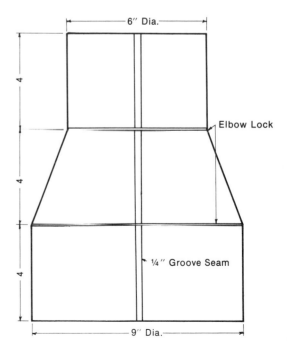

Fig. 9-12 Problem 9-1, Sweeping a Taper.

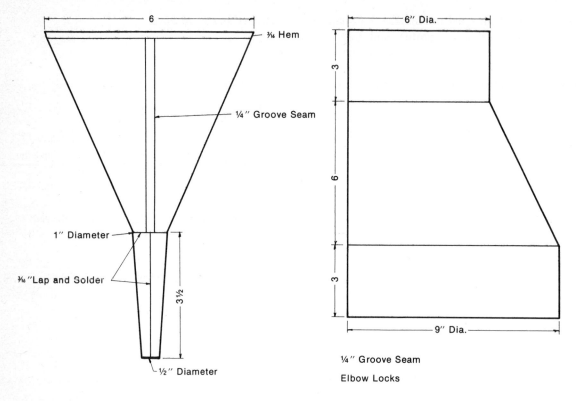

Fig. 9-13 Problem 9-2, Laying Out a Taper by the Standard Funnel Method.

Fig. 9-14 Problem 9-3, Laying Out an Offset Taper by Triangulation.

Assignment.

1. Lay out the pattern for the top part of the funnel shown in Fig. 9-13 by the standard funnel method. Lay out the pattern for the spout of the funnel by sweeping it out.

2. Make up the complete funnel using the seams indicated.

Problem 9-3

Purpose. To practice laying out an offset round taper by triangulation.

Study. *Triangulation of a round taper.*

Assignment.

1. Lay out the full pattern for the fitting shown in Fig. 9-14.

2. Make up the complete fitting from the patterns laid out.

Problem 9-4

Purpose. To study the short method of laying out a round taper by three side views.

Study. *Taper from three side views.*

Assignment.

1. Lay out the pattern for the taper shown in Fig. 9-15, using the three-side-views method.

2. If trammel points are available, lay out the pattern for this same fitting by sweeping and compare the two for accuracy. If there is any difference, the pattern obtained by sweeping is the more accurate.

3. Save the patterns for comparison with the ones to be made in problem 9-5.

Problem 9-5

Purpose. To learn how to make patterns for a taper using only a square and rule.

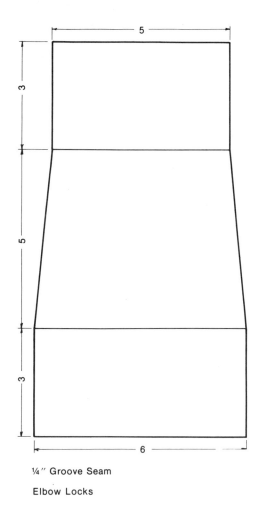

¼" Groove Seam

Elbow Locks

Fig. 9-15 Problem 9-4 and 9-5, Laying Out a Taper by Short-cut Methods.

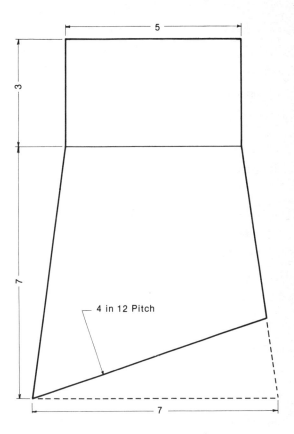

Fig. 9-16 Problem 9-6, Laying Out a Taper on a Pitch by Radial Lines.

Study. *Approximate pattern by square and rule.*

Assignment.

1. Lay out the patterns for the fitting shown in Fig. 9-15, using only a square and rule.

2. Compare this pattern with the patterns for the same fitting that were laid out in problem 9-4.

Problem 9-6

Purpose. To learn how to lay out the patterns for a round taper on a pitch by use of radial lines.

Study. *Tapers on a pitch.*

Assignment.

1. Lay out the patterns for the fitting shown in Fig. 9-16, using the method shown in the study reference.

2. Make up the complete fitting.

3. Save the pattern for comparison with those in problem 9-7.

Problem 9-7

Purpose. To learn how to lay out the patterns for a round taper on a pitch by use of the short method of radial lines.

Study. *Short method of radial lines.*

Assignment.

1. Lay out the pattern for the fitting shown in Fig. 9-16. Use the shortened method of radial lines and locate only the quarter points of the pattern.

2. Compare this pattern with the one for the same fitting that was laid out in problem 9-5. If there is any difference in these patterns, the one laid out in problem 9-6 is more accurate.

Problem 9-8

Purpose. To study all methods of laying out a round taper.

Study. All of Chapter 9.

Assignment. Answer the following questions:

1. List six methods of laying out the pattern for a round taper; under each method list *(a)* the advantages of the method and *(b)* the limitations or disadvantages of the method.

2. Would you class sweeping a funnel pattern as triangulation or radial lines? Why?

3. Would it be possible to sweep out a funnel pattern without drawing a side view? If so, how would it be done?

4. What is the basic principle of laying out a funnel by the standard funnel method?

5. Since triangulating the pattern for a round taper is a comparatively long process, is there any reason why this method should be learned? If so, what is it?

6. What would be the determining factors in deciding to lay out a taper pattern by the three-side-views method rather than with a square and rule only?

Another common class of fittings is round tees (Fig. 10-6). These are laid out by *parallel-line* development. Tees are usually laid out by shortcuts, so once the basic principles are mastered the layout worker must learn all the shortcuts commonly used.

Standard layout

Fig. 10-1 shows the technically correct method of tee layout, which illustrates basic principles. The tee shown is a 90° intersection with both pipes of equal diameter.

The first step in laying out tees is to develop the line of intersection between the two pipes. After this miter line is developed, the pattern for the tee can be laid out by simple parallel-line layout.

To start the layout by the technically correct method, draw the plan view and the elevation view as shown in Fig. 10-1*b*. Next, draw a profile of the intersecting pipe in both plan and elevation views. Both profiles are divided into the same number of equal spaces, as also shown in Fig. 10-1*b*. It is customary to divide the profiles into six equal spaces to the half circle.

Next, draw lines from the profile in the plan view over to the curve of the pipe. At the point where these lines intersect the curve of the pipe, project lines down to the elevation view. For example, the lines that run through points 11 and 3 in the plan-view profile are drawn over to point *A* as shown in the plan view. From point *A*, the line is projected down through the elevation view. The intersection of this line with lines *11* and *3* in the elevation gives points *C* and *D*, which are the points on the miter line. The other points on the miter are found by projecting the other lines in the same way.

After the miter line is located, as shown in Fig. 10-1*b*, the pattern may be laid out by simple parallel-line development. This is also shown in Fig. 10-1*c*. The first step in this layout is to draw line 10-10 equal to the circumference of the tee. Then divide this circumference into twelve equal spaces, and square up lines from each point thus obtained.

After these measuring lines are squared up, mark off the proper length of each line. The proper length for each line is taken from the elevation view and is measured from line *EF* to the miter line. The distance for the line from points 11 and 9, for example, is taken as the distance from *G* to *C* in the elevation view. Similarly, the distance for the line from points 3 and 5 on the pattern is taken as the distance from *H* to *D*.

After all the lines are picked off, draw a smooth curve through the points either freehand or with the aid of a flexible rule. Shape the pattern as shown in Fig. 10-1*c*.

Tee pattern from plan view

The method just described is the proper way to lay out a tee pattern. However, in the shop all possible shortcut methods are used.

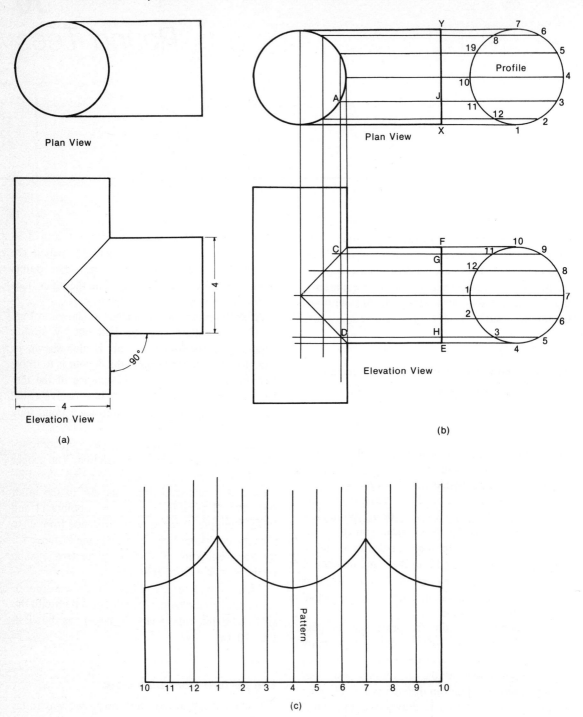

Fig. 10-1   Standard Layout of Round Tee.

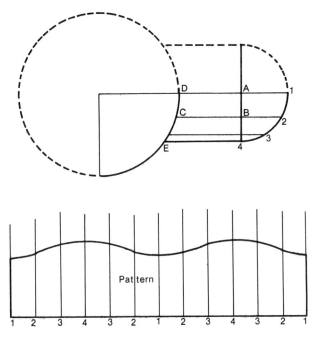

Fig. 10-2 Short-cut Method of Laying Out a 90° Tee.

Whenever the tee is a 90° tee, much time can be saved by eliminating the elevation view and laying out the pattern from the plan view. This method can only be used, however, when the two pipes intersect at a 90° angle. If the tee is anything but a 90° tee, this shortcut cannot be used.

To lay out the tee from the plan view, draw the plan view as shown in Fig. 10-2 but do not draw the elevation view. Draw the profile for the plan view and project the lines over to the curve of the circle in the same manner as in the longer method. However, do not square any lines down to the elevation. Lay out the pattern in the same manner as before, but take the proper lengths for the measuring lines on the pattern from the end line *A* 4 of the plan view over to the point where the line intersects the curve of the pipe. For example, the distance for line 1 on the pattern is taken from the plan view as the distance from point *A* to point *D*. All other distances are taken from corresponding lines in the same way.

From quarter plan

When the tee is 90°, it is usually possible to make the layout even shorter. If the tee is centered so that one half is identical with the other, only a quarter plan view is necessary.

For a 90° tee such as the one shown in Fig. 10-1, the only drawing that is necessary to make the layout is shown by the solid lines in Fig. 10-2. All of the plan view that is indicated by the dotted lines is a repetition of the quarter plan already drawn.

Note in this drawing (Fig. 10-2) of the quarter plan that only one quarter of the profile circle is drawn and that it is attached to the end of the plan view. This is done because only the necessary parts of the plan view are drawn.

To lay out the pattern, use the method described in the previous problems. Since the profile has only four numbered spaces, number the measuring lines on the pattern in the manner shown in Fig. 10-2. The proper lengths for the measuring lines in

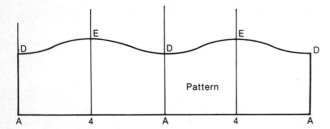

Fig. 10-3   Layout of Tee by Four Quarter Points.

the pattern are taken on the plan view from line *A* 4 to the curve of the pipe. The distance of measuring line 2 on the pattern, for instance, is taken from *B* to *C* on the plan view.

Four points from elevation

In cases where only one of a certain size tee is required, if it is to be installed in a location where it will be unseen it is common practice to lay out only a few points on the pattern and sketch in the rest.

If the tee is a regular 90° tee, the four points needed can be found from a quarter plan view, such as that shown in Fig. 10-3. The only lines necessary for the layout are shown in Fig. 10-3. The profile or the measuring lines need not be drawn. After the quarter plan is drawn, draw the stretchout of the pattern and divide it into four equal spaces, as is shown in Fig. 10-3 by the points marked *A* and 4. Next, square up lines from these quarter spaces, and take the distances *AD* and 4*E* from the quarter plan and mark them off on the proper lines of the pattern. These points on the pattern indicate the key points. Since the curve of a tee pattern always follows the typical shape of the patterns in Figs. 10-1 and 10-2, it can be drawn in with considerable accuracy either freehand or with the aid of a flexible rule (as shown in Fig. 10-3) and then trimmed to exact size after it is formed.

Angle tee

If the tee is an angle other than 90°, as shown in Fig. 10-4, a little more work is involved in developing the line of intersection of the two pipes. This miter line is developed as in a standard layout in the same manner as for the tee in Fig. 10-1. After the miter line is established, the tee may be laid out by the standard layout shown in Fig. 10-4.

Pattern for hole

Thus far, laying out the hole for the pipe of the tee has not been mentioned. Usually the hole pattern is not laid out because it is much easier to form up the tee and the pipe that it intersects and then mark the hole by holding the tee in place and marking around it with a pencil. This procedure is shown in Fig. 10-5. After the hole is marked, it is cut out with airplane snips.

In rare cases where large numbers of the same tee are to be made, the hole pattern might be laid out. If it is necessary to lay out the hole pattern, standard parallel-line layout is used. No shortcuts are employed because the layout is done so seldom that very little time is ever involved.

Seams in a tee

The longitudinal seams on a tee are almost always ¼-in groove seams. The standard location of these seams is shown in Fig. 10-6. Sometimes on a rushed job a tee may be knocked together hurriedly with spot-welded or soldered seams, but this is poor practice and should be avoided whenever possible.

The actual joining of the two pipes to the intersection is accomplished in several different ways, depending on the conditions of the job. The method of connecting the intersection will vary with the use to which the tee is to be put as well as with the gauge of the metal used. The following material illustrates the most common methods of connection.

Dovetail. A tee with a dovetail seam is shown in Fig. 10-7. The dovetail seam is described in detail in Chapter 3. This is one of the easiest and simplest ways to connect the tee, but it is not the strongest or the neatest. Many times the dovetail joint is soldered in order to make it stronger or

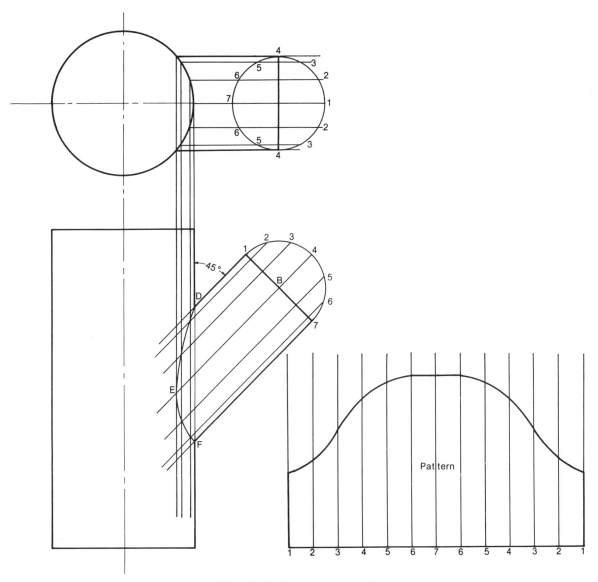

Fig. 10-4 Layout of Angle Tee.

watertight, and on large tees some of the tabs are spot welded.

In order to make a neater-appearing seam, it is important to make the tabs of the dovetail as small as possible while retaining an edge that will not slip out. On pipe of 4 in diameter or less, it is possible to make the tabs as small as $5/16$ in. On larger sizes of pipe, the length of the tabs should vary from $3/8$ to $3/4$ in, depending on the diameter of the pipe. If the tabs are kept short, they will tap down flatter and will make a neater job.

If the tee is to be dovetailed, it is important to remember to use the formed tee to mark the hole in the pipe before the tabs are cut and bent. This

Fig. 10-5   Marking the Hole for the Tee.

Fig. 10-7   Dovetail Seam on Tee.

Fig. 10-6   Location of Seams on a Tee.

makes it easier to mark and results in a more accurate hole. When marking and cutting the hole, it is best to cut it small rather than oversize. When the tee is set in place, it is easy to see whether the hole is slightly small and to trim it out to size with airplane snips; but if the hole is oversize, nothing can be done to make it into a tight, neat job.

To knock over the tabs inside a small tee, a bar of solder is often the best tool. Before all the tabs are knocked over, the tee should be inspected for straightness. Once the tabs are down, there is little chance to adjust the tee.

Notched and riveted lap. A joint that is much stronger but involves more work and skill is the notched and riveted lap shown in Fig. 10-8. This seam is usually used on large tees.

The width of the notches will vary with the diameter of the pipe in the manner described for dovetail notches. In cutting the notches, it is good practice to end the cuts about $1/16$ in away from the line so that, when the tabs are bent and the tee is set over them, the ends of the cut will not show past the tee; thus, the lap will appear from the outside to be a solid lap and not a notched one.

Two-rivet method. A method of riveting the tee that is used almost as often as the dovetail joint is shown in Fig. 10-9. This method is exactly the same as that described for notched and riveted laps, except that after the two rivets are set in the tips of the tee the job is finished; only the two rivets are used to hold the tee in place. This may seem to be a rather flimsy method, but it is actually very strong because the lap bent on the inside keeps the tee from shifting.

Fig. 10-8 Notched and Riveted Lap on Tee.

Welded joint. Tees made out of heavy-gauge iron are often welded. In former times most heavy-gauge tees were riveted; but welding is now almost universally used.

If the tee is to be welded, the patterns are laid out in the same manner as for any tee, except that no allowances are made for laps at the joint. The joint is merely butted and welded.

PRACTICE PROBLEMS

Read all of Chapter 10 before doing the following problems.

Problem 10-1

Purpose. To practice laying out a tee pattern by the standard method.

Study. *Standard layout, Dovetail.*

Assignment.

1. Lay out the pattern for the tee shown in Fig. 10-10.

Fig. 10-9 Lap and Two-rivet Seam on Tee.

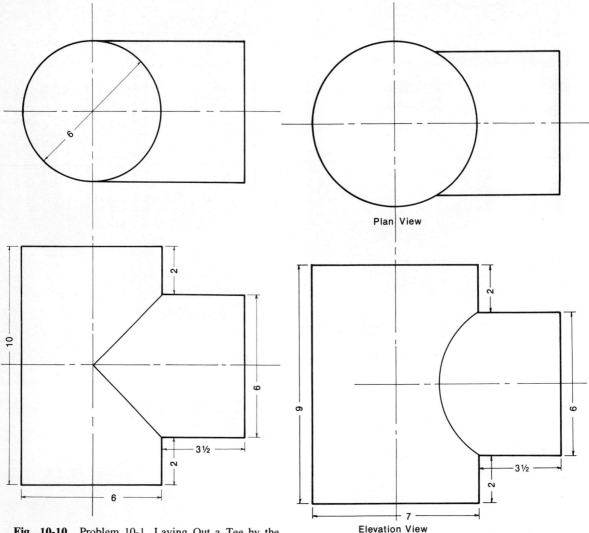

6

10

2

6

3½

2

6

Fig. 10-10   Problem 10-1, Laying Out a Tee by the Standard Method.

Plan View

9

2

6

3½

2

7

Elevation View

Fig. 10-11   Problem 10-2, Laying Out a Tee from the Plan View.

2. Make up the tee pattern and the pipe for the tee, but do not lay out the hole. Mark the hole from the formed tee and make the joint with a dovetail seam.

Problem 10-2

Purpose. To practice laying out a tee from a plan view.

Study. *Tee pattern from a plan view, From quarter plan, Notched and riveted lap, Two-rivet method.*

Assignment.

1. Lay out the tee pattern for the tee shown in Fig. 10-11; lay out the pattern for the pipe but not for the hole. Use only a quarter plan view for laying out the patterns.

2. Make up the tee and join it by means of a notched lap and two rivets.

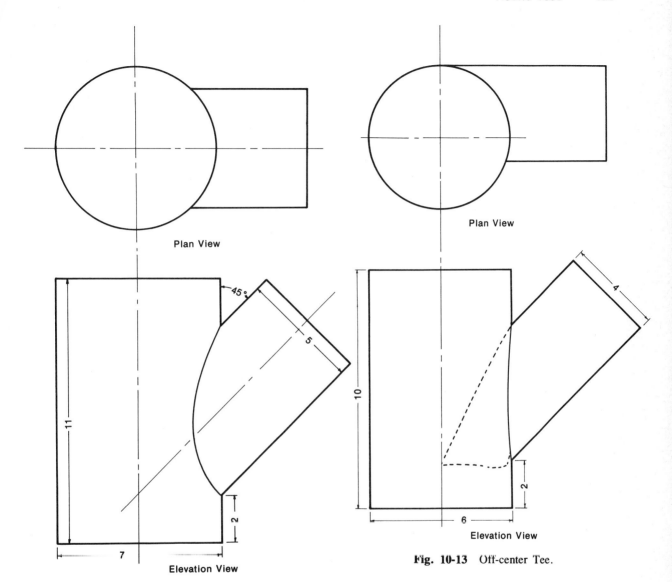

Fig. 10-12 Problem 10-4, Laying Out the Pattern for the Tee Hole.

Fig. 10-13 Off-center Tee.

3. Save the pattern to compare with the one to be made in problem 10-3.

Problem 10-3

Purpose. To learn how to lay out an approximate pattern by laying out four points only.

Study. *Four points from elevation, Dovetail.*

Assignment.

1. Lay out the pattern for the tee in Fig. 10-11, allowing for ¼-in groove seams and a ⅜-in dovetail. Use only quarter points on the pattern.

2. Compare the pattern with the one made in problem 10-2. If there is any difference between the two patterns, the one from problem 10-2 is more accurate.

Problem 10-4

Purpose. To practice laying out the hole for the tee.

Study. *Pattern for hole*.

Assignment.

1. Lay out the tee pattern for the fitting shown in Fig. 10-12, using any accurate method you wish. Lay out the pattern for the hole in the pipe before forming the pipe. Allow for ¼-in groove seams and a ⅜-in dovetail.

2. Make up the complete fitting.

Problem 10-5

Purpose. To study the different methods of joining tees.

Study. Chapter 10, from *Seams on a tee* to end of chapter.

Assignment. List all the methods for joining tees that you know; under each method list *(a)* the advantages and disadvantages and *(b)* what conditions determine whether it is the best seam for the particular job.

Problem 10-6

Purpose. To study the layout methods used in developing tee patterns.

Study. Chapter 10, up to *Seams on a tee*.

Assignment. Answer the following questions:

1. Could the tee in Fig. 10-1 be laid out from a quarter plan only? Give the reasons for your answer.

2. Could the tee in Fig. 10-4 be laid out by a quarter plan? Give the reasons for your answer.

3. For the tee in Fig. 10-11, would a layout from a quarter pattern be more accurate than a layout from the side view? Give your reasons.

4. Why would the pattern for the tee in Fig. 10-13 involve more work than any of the others in this chapter?

11
Round Elbows

There are many different types of layouts for round elbows. All of them are practical if used in the proper circumstances. Some methods are long but extremely accurate. Other methods are very fast but not very exact. The expert layout worker knows several different methods and the proper times to use them. All the methods for round-elbow layout, including shortcuts, are based upon parallel-line development.

Study Fig. 11-1 for the common trade terms for the parts of the elbow. These terms will be used frequently in this chapter, and it is important that the student be familiar with them.

The first problem in elbow layout is to establish the miter line for each gore. Angles 1, 2, 3, 4, 5, and 6 in Fig. 11-2 should be equal because, if all these angles are equal, the pattern for one gore will serve as a pattern for all the gores. This means that the end gores *A* and *B*, in Fig. 11-2, must turn only half as much as the middle gores, because they have only one angle and the middle gores have two. In other words, angles *A'* and *B'* must be one-half of angles *C'* and *D'*.

The common way to determine these angles is to multiply the number of pieces in the elbow by 2 and subtract 2. This gives the number of spaces

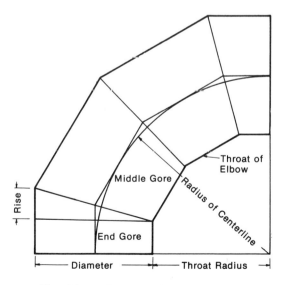

Fig. 11-1 The Parts of a Round Elbow.

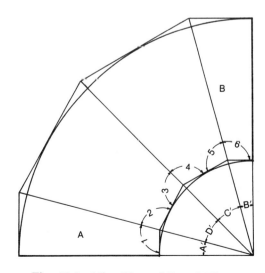

Fig. 11-2 Miter Lines of Round Elbow.

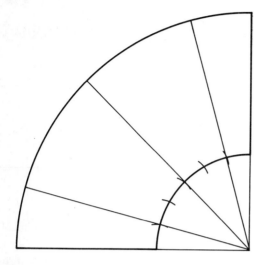

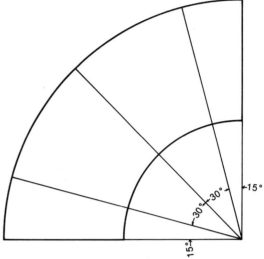

Fig. 11-3 Method of Locating Miter Lines for Four-piece Elbow.

Fig. 11-4 Figuring the Degree of Angle of the Miter Line for a Four-piece 90° Elbow.

N = the number of spaces to divide the throat or heel
$(2 \times N) - 2 = 8$
   Example:
     $2 \times 4 = 8$
     $8 - 2 = 6$ spaces in which to divide the throat of elbow

N = the number of pieces in the elbow
$(2 \times N) - 2 = $ spacing
$(2 \times 4) - 2 = 6$
  $90 \div 6 = 15°$ for first gore

into which the throat or heel of the elbow is divided. Each end piece is made up of one of these spaces, and all the middle gores are made up of two spaces. This is illustrated in Fig. 11-3 for a four-piece elbow.

Sometimes, on very large elbows, the miter lines are determined by calculating the degree of angle on one piece. The rule for this is "multiply the number of gores in the elbow by 2, subtract 2, and divide this number into the total degrees of turn in the elbow." In Fig. 11-4, the calculations are given for a 90°, four-piece elbow.

Allowance for growth

After the miter line on an elbow has been obtained, it is sometimes necessary to allow for a certain amount of error in the fabrication of the elbow. This is known as *allowing for growth.*

When elbow gores are run through an elbow machine, the throat, or narrow part of the gore, is

difficult to hold against the gauge. If each gore of a four-piece elbow is allowed to slip away from the gauge only $^1/_{16}$ in, the pattern is growing $^1/_{16}$ in at each edge. Since there are six edges on a four-piece elbow, the throat of the elbow would grow ⅜ in out of square. Figure 11-5 illustrates this.

This growth can be counteracted by allowing for it when laying out the elbow pattern. This is done by obtaining the miter line in the usual way and then changing it slightly, as shown in Fig. 11-6.

The amount to allow depends upon several things: the thickness of the metal, the radius of the throat, the number of gores in the elbow, and the skill of the worker are all factors that affect the growth. There is no rule by which to determine the amount of allowance. It must be learned by experimentation and experience. If each finished elbow is checked to see how much it has grown, one can soon estimate quite closely how much an elbow will grow.

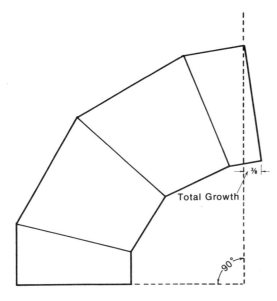

Fig. 11-5 How an Elbow Can "Grow."

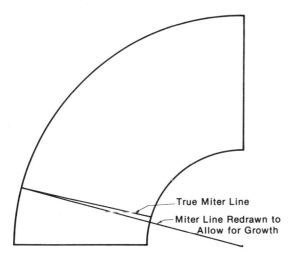

Fig. 11-6 Allowing for Growth.

In general, an elbow of 24 gauge or lighter with four gores or more and with a throat radius of 6 in or more can be put together without allowing for any growth. When the metal is thicker, the gores fewer, or the throat radius smaller, allowance will have to be made. In any case, the allowance is slight—usually $^1/_{16}$ in or less and almost never over ⅛ in.

How to figure the size of the pattern

Often the sheet metal worker must know exactly how much metal an elbow will require. Figure 11-7 shows the pattern for a four-piece, 5-in, 90° elbow for which the exact size of metal needed for the patterns must be known.

One dimension of this pattern will equal the circumference of a 5-in circle, which is easily found. The other dimension (*L* in Fig. 11-7) will equal the center line of a side view of the elbow, as also shown in Fig. 11-7.

This dimension can be measured directly from a side view, or it can be figured mathematically. To figure it mathematically, first determine the radius of the center line (see Fig. 11-1). This would be the sum of the throat radius and one-half the diameter of the elbow. In Fig. 11-7, the center-line radius is 6 + 2½ = 8½ in. By taking half of this number and determining the circumference of a circle of this diameter, the length of dimension *L* is determined. In Fig. 11-7, this is 8½ ÷ 2 = 4¼ in. The circumference of a 4¼-in circle is equal to 4¼ × 3.14 = 13.35 in. Therefore, the length *L* of the pattern is 13⅝₁₆ in long. The metal needed for this elbow should be 15¾ by 13⅝₁₆ in plus allowance for seams. Any elbow with this diameter and throat radius requires a piece of metal this size regardless of the number of gores used.

Standard layout of round elbows

Figure 11-8 shows the standard layout procedure for a round elbow. The standard rules of the trade for making the pattern and the elbow are listed here.

1. Seams should run along the center line of the elbow and not on the heel and throat. This gives a better-looking elbow and one that is easier to fabricate.

2. Seams should be staggered. The seam of the first gore should be on the side opposite to the seam of the second gore. This gives the elbow a

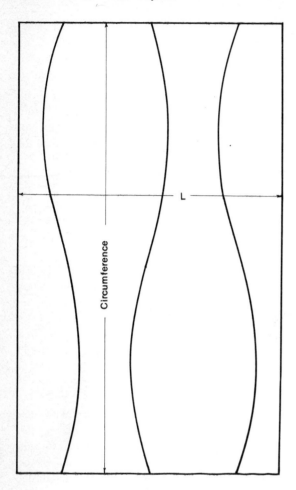

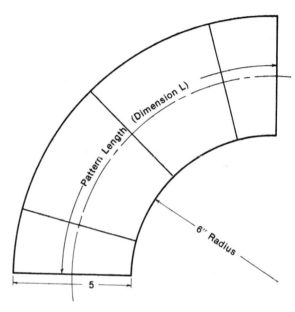

Fig. 11-7 Figuring the Size of Metal for the Total Pattern.

more balanced appearance and also avoids the annoyance of the seams catching in one another when the gores are twisted. The staggered seams are made both in rolling the gores and in running them through the elbow machine. The gores should be run through the rolls in the same position as they lie in the pattern in Fig. 11-8. When the edges are run through the elbow machine, they must be arranged so that the seams are properly staggered.

3. Only the first gore is laid out. The middle pattern is made by flipping the end gore pattern. In Fig. 11-8, dimension 2 on the second gore is always twice dimension 1 of the first gore pattern.

Note that dimension 1 is only the pattern length. Usually an inch or two is added to the end gores for ease in handling or to allow for lap joints. This addition is not counted in figuring dimension 2. If the elbow has to be extremely accurate, the seam allowance for an elbow-machine seam is $3/16$ in for each edge of each seam. This is figured as part of dimension 1 and is doubled along with dimension 1 when dimension 2 is figured.

4. In the pattern in Fig. 11-8, the cross marks along the center line indicate prick marks that should be on each piece. These marks should be at least ½ in from the edge of the pattern so that the elbow machine does not obliterate them. The

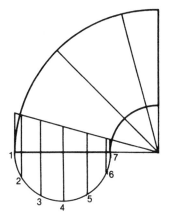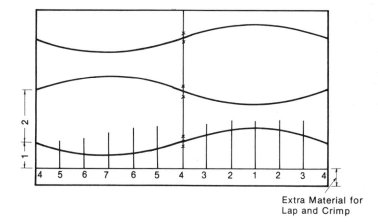

Extra Material for
Lap and Crimp

Fig. 11-8   Standard Layout for Round Elbow.

purpose of the prick marks is to help align the elbow when it is fabricated. Since the seams are staggered, these marks will be exactly even with the seams of the next gore. When the gores are assembled, the marks are kept in line with the seams of the previous gore, thus saving time in adjusting the elbow later.

5. The seams on the elbow can be either riveted, grooved, or spot welded. An elbow that has riveted longitudinal seams is easier to run in the elbow machine than a groove-seamed elbow. However, many mechanics prefer to use a groove seam because it is tighter and faster to make.

6. When the pattern is developed, the lines on the side view and on the pattern are numbered. This saves time by eliminating chances of error and having to recount lines.

Laying out by quarter points

A sheet metal worker's time is costly, and his or her value to the employer is judged by how well time is utilized. Therefore, it is important that common sense be used in choosing the method of laying out an object. If a hundred or so of the same object are to be made, the most accurate method of layout should be used for laying out the pattern. Time will be saved by making an exact pattern.

But if only one elbow is required and it is desirable to do it as quickly as possible, some sort of jump method should be used. A jump method of laying out by quarter points is shown in Fig. 11-9. The gore spacing is exactly the same; however, only the first miter line need be drawn. Also, only the

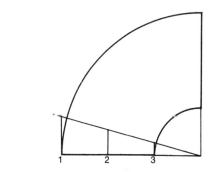

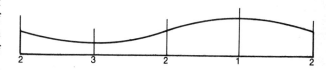

Fig. 11-9   Elbow Pattern by Quarter Points.

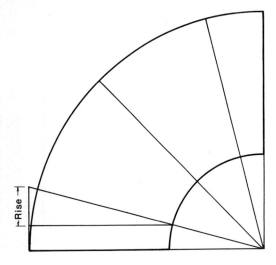

Fig. 11-10   Elbow Pattern by Rise.

Table 1. Constants for 90° Elbow

Pieces	90°
2	1.00
3	0.414
4	0.268
5	0.199
6	0.159
7	0.132
8	0.113
9	0.098
10	0.089
11	0.0787
12	0.0714

Table 2. Constants for Other than 90° Elbows

Pieces	60°	45°	30°
2	0.577	0.414	0.268
3	0.268	0.199	0.132
4	0.176	0.132	0.088
5	0.132	0.089	0.066
6	0.105	0.078	0.052
7	0.088	0.066	0.044
8	0.075	0.058	0.037

side lines and the center line are drawn in on this first gore. Since the center line is halfway between the side lines, no profile is needed. The pattern is divided into quarters as shown, and the lengths of the various lines are transferred from the side view to the pattern. By holding a flexible rule through the points and drawing around it, a fairly accurate pattern can be made. Remember that the miter line is an even, smooth curve; there are no sharp turns or abrupt changes of direction.

Elbow patterns by rise

Many metal workers prefer to lay out their elbows by the *rise* of the miter line. Figure 11-10 illustrates what is meant by the rise of the elbow. Figure 11-10 also shows the layout of the pattern by use of the rise. The diameter of the two half circles in the pattern is equal to the rise of the elbow. The important thing to remember in this layout is that the circle of the rise must be divided into six equal parts; therefore, the circumference of the pattern is divided into twelve spaces.

Layout by rise is used quite often in large fittings. An advantage is that the rise can be figured mathematically, without the use of a side view. This is done by multiplying the diameter of the elbow by a constant that is determined by the number of pieces in the elbow. Table 1 lists these constants. Table 2 gives the constants for elbows of commonly used angles other than 90°.

Tables 1 and 2 are used in the following way: To find the rise of a four-piece, 90° elbow of diameter 6 in, look at Table 1 for the constant for a four-piece, 90° elbow. This is found to be 0.268. Multiplying 0.268 by the diameter (6) gives 1.608 in ($0.268 \times 6 = 1.608$). This is the rise of the elbow, and the layout is done as described previously.

Elbow by quarter pattern

The advantages of the quarter pattern are that, for large elbows, the patterns are small and easy to

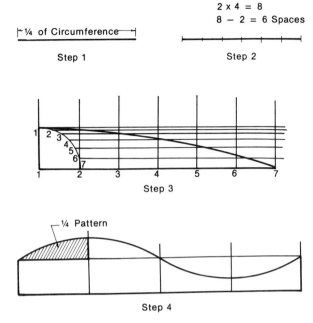

2 x 4 = 8
8 − 2 = 6 Spaces

⊢ ¼ of Circumference ⊣

Step 1

Step 2

Step 3

¼ Pattern

Step 4

Fig. 11-11 Elbow Pattern by Quarter Pattern.

store, and can be easily and quickly laid out. Figure 11-11 shows the use of this pattern. The quarter pattern is moved and marked four times in order to make a full pattern.

Figure 11-11 shows a short method for developing a quarter pattern, but any method of elbow layout can be used. A description of the steps shown in the figure follows:

Step 1. Draw a line equal to one-quarter of the circumference of the elbow diameter.

Step 2. Calculate 2 times the number of pieces in the elbow minus 2. Divide the line into this number of spaces. This is exactly the same as calculating the number of spaces in which to divide the throat of an elbow.

Step 3. On one end of the line, draw a quarter circle of radius equal to one of these spaces. Divide the quarter circle into the same number of spaces as are on the line. Project the spaces from the circle and from the line. Mark off the points of

intersection and draw a curve through them. This gives the finished quarter pattern.

PRACTICE PROBLEMS

Problem 11-1

Purpose. To learn some of the methods of laying out and fabricating round-pipe elbows.

Study. All of Chapter 11.

Assignment. Answer the following questions:

1. Do you think that a good layout worker should know more than one method of laying out the patterns for a round elbow? Give your reasons.

2. What are the sections of a round-pipe elbow called?

3. In laying out a four-piece, 90° elbow, into how many spaces should the throat or heel be divided?

4. How many spaces for a six-piece, 60° elbow?

5. In the layout for a five-piece, 90° elbow what should be the angle of the first gore?

6. What is the size of the piece of metal needed to lay out all the patterns for a four-piece, 5-in diameter elbow with a 6-in throat radius? Allow for a ¼-in groove seam, but do not allow for the elbow locks.

7. When an elbow has an odd number of gores, will the groove seams of the two end gores be on the same side or on opposite sides of the elbow?

Problem 11-2

Purpose. To learn how to lay out the pattern for a round elbow by the standard method.

Study. Introductory paragraphs of Chapter 11, *Allowance for growth, Standard layout of round elbows.*

Assignment.

1. Lay out the pattern for the first gore for the elbow shown in Fig. 11-12.

2. Make all the patterns and form up the elbow, using elbow locks to join the gores. You may add 1 in on the uncrimped end for ease in handling.

Problem 11-3

Purpose. To learn how to lay out an elbow pattern by quarter points and to practice estimating the amount of material needed for the pattern.

Study. Introductory paragraphs of Chapter 11; *How to figure the size of the pattern, Laying out by quarter points.*

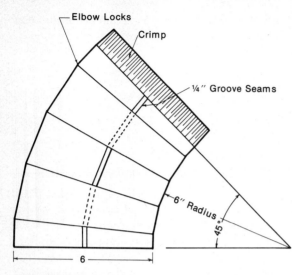

Make in 5 Pieces

Fig. 11-12 Problem 11-2, Laying Out a Round Elbow by the Standard Method.

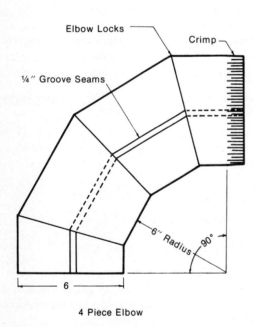

4 Piece Elbow

Fig. 11-13 Problems 11-3, 11-4, 11-5, and 11-6, Comparing Elbow Patterns Made by Different Short-cut Methods.

Assignment.

1. Estimate the size of the piece of metal that will be needed for the complete set of patterns for the elbow shown in Fig. 11-13. Allow material for the groove seam and crimp, and allow $3/16$ in for each edge of the elbow lock.

2. Lay out the pattern for the first gore by use of quarter points only.

3. Make up all the patterns for the elbow and fabricate it.

4. Save the pattern for comparison with those of other methods.

Problem 11-4

Study. *Elbow patterns by rise.*

Assignment.

1. Lay out the pattern for the first gore of the elbow shown in Fig. 11-13, using the rise method.

2. Make all the patterns and form up the elbow completely.

3. Compare this pattern with that from problem 11-3; this pattern is more accurate. Save the patterns from both problems for later use.

Problem 11-5

Study. *Elbow by quarter pattern.*

Assignment.

1. Lay out the quarter pattern for the first gore of the elbow shown in Fig. 11-13.

2. Form up the first gore and check the miter to see if it fits on a flat surface.

3. Compare this pattern with those of problems 11-3 and 11-4. If there is variation, the pattern from problem 11-4 is probably the most accurate, with the one from problem 11-5 next. Save the patterns from all three problems.

Problem 11-6

Purpose. To practice laying out elbow patterns by use of the radius method.

Study. *Elbow pattern by radii.*

Assignment.

1. Lay out the pattern for the first gore of the elbow shown in Fig. 11-13 by using the radius method.

2. Compare this pattern with the patterns of the elbow made in problems 11-3, 11-4, and 11-5.

Y branches are not made often now, but they are used frequently enough so that the efficient journeyman should know how to lay one out quickly and accurately. Since the proper method of laying out a Y is comparatively long, the mechanic must be familiar with shortcuts that can be used.

Sectors

Y branches primarily involve triangulation, and therefore present problems for the layout worker who is unfamiliar with triangulation principles. One problem may be lack of understanding of sectors. A sector is the same as the profile in other layout problems. It is the shape of the Y branch at the point where the two halves of the fitting join.

Figure 12-1 shows a Y branch, plus the side and plan view. In Fig. 12-1a, half the side view is shown as it is drawn to start the layout. The quarter circle attached to the line *AC* is a profile of the end of the fitting. The quarter ellipse attached to line *AB* is the sector. The purpose of the sector and the purpose of the profile are the same. They are divided into equal spaces in order to locate equal spaces on the pattern.

Sector by quarter circle

One method of developing the sector is by simply drawing in a quarter circle. This method is based upon the fact that the sector can be made in any shape desired as long as it is pleasing to the eye. Refer to Fig. 12-1a. The distances *AD* and *AE* represent the same distance—the distance that point *A* is out from the center of the fitting. On any

Y branch these two lines must always be the same length because they represent the same distance.

Since *AD* must be the same length as *AE,* if the sector is to be a quarter circle, line *AB* must also be the same length as *AD*. Therefore, in drawing the side view of the sector, the distance *AB* must be made the same length as *AC*. If this is done, both the sector and the profile can be quarter circles.

This method will result in an accurate sector and an exact pattern. The only disadvantage is that, when line *AB* is the same length as *AC,* the fitting is not as well proportioned as it should be; the result is a rather short, dumpy fitting. A better-looking fitting can be had when line *AB* is made longer than *AC,* but this cannot be done when a quarter circle is used for the sector.

Sector by development

In order to make line *AB* in Fig. 12-1 longer than line *AC,* it is necessary to develop the sector by another method, shown in Fig. 12-2.

To start the development of the sector, first draw the side view of half the Y branch, as outlined by points *ABDEC* in Fig. 12-2. The length of line *DE* is the diameter of the end of the Y branch, and line *AC* is equal to the *radius* of the large end of the Y branch. In order to make a proportionate fitting, line *AB* should be made about 1¼ times as large as *AC;* however, it can be drawn to any length desired.

After the side view is drawn, draw the profile of line *AC*. This profile will be a quarter circle, since

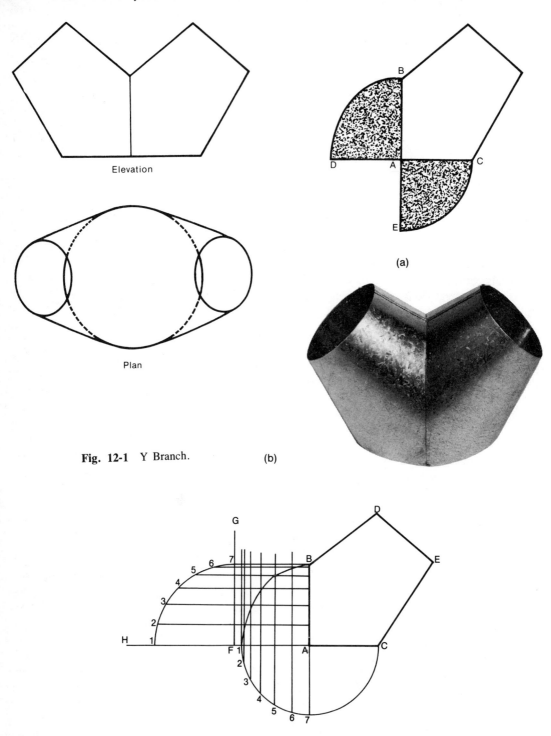

Elevation

Plan

B

D   A   C

E

(a)

(b)

Fig. 12-1 Y Branch.

G

D

6 7   B   E

5

4

3

2

H   1   F 1   A   C
             2
             3
             4
             5 6 7

Fig. 12-2 Layout of Y-branch Sector by Development.

the shape of the fitting at this point is a circle. Using point *A* as center, swing a quarter circle of radius equal to *AC*. Continue this circle to form a full half circle as shown.

Next extend line *AC* out to point *H,* as also shown in Fig. 12-2, and draw another quarter circle using *AB* as radius. The center point *F* of this circle can be located at any point as long as it is clear of the end of the profile half circle. After this quarter circle is drawn, divide it into equal spaces. Also divide the quarter circle of the profile into the same number of spaces. After both these quarter circles are divided, lines are projected up and across from these points as shown. The intersection of the corresponding lines gives the points through which the curve of the profile is drawn.

Sector by freehand drawing

The third method of developing the sector is by drawing it in freehand. Since the only requirement of a sector is that it provide a pleasing form for the fitting, it can readily be drawn freehand. The only point to remember is that the sector is going to determine the shape of the fitting at that point; therefore, it should be drawn in as a well-proportioned curve.

To sketch in the sector, first draw the side view as in the other methods. This is shown in Fig. 12-3*a*. Line *AB* may be drawn to any length that looks well proportioned. Point *D,* in Fig. 12-3*a,* is found by making *AD* equal to *AC*. This must be true in any Y branch.

After points *B* and *D* are located, draw in a smooth curve freehand between these two points. This curve should not be drawn to a point, as shown by the solid curve in Fig. 12-3*b*. Neither should it be drawn with a hump in it, as shown by the dotted curve in the same figure. Both these curves would produce a poorly shaped fitting. Instead, the sector should be shaped like the one in Fig. 12-3*c*. The portion of the curve indicated by arrow 1 should be drawn so it runs almost square to line *AB*. The portion of the curve that is indicated by arrow 2 should run almost square to line *AD*.

In actual practice, drawing in the curve freehand is usually the quickest and most satisfactory

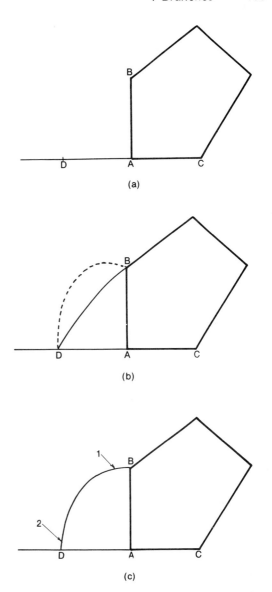

Fig. 12-3 Sector by Freehand Drawing.

method. Beginners tend to use one of the other methods because they require less judgment. However, the layout worker should study the sector curve and learn to draw it in freehand, since with very little practice this is as satisfactory as the other methods.

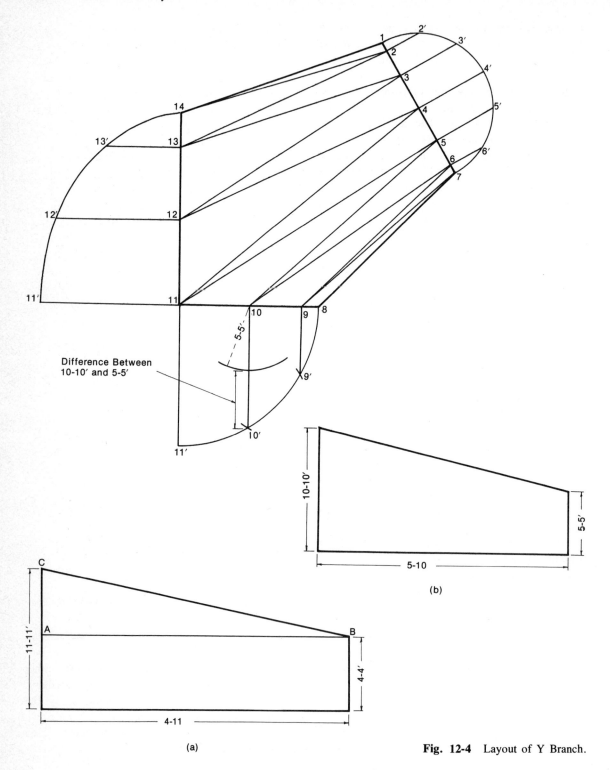

Fig. 12-4 Layout of Y Branch.

Pattern by triangulation

Since Y branches are not frequently made, shortcut methods are not common in the actual layout. It is usually triangulated out, following the methods used on any round taper. However, although the general methods of triangulating the pattern are the same, the method of determining the true length of the lines differs from the usual triangulation problem.

Before the true length of the layout lines can be found, the half side view must be drawn and the profiles drawn in and divided into equal spaces, usually three spaces to a quarter circle. The number of spaces may vary, however, according to the size of the fitting. In Fig. 12-4, note that the profile at line 1-7 is a half circle and that it is divided into six equal spaces. The profile at line

8-11 is a quarter circle, and consequently it is only divided into three equal spaces. The sector at line 11-14 is also divided into three equal spaces, since the number of spaces of the quarter circle and the sector must equal the number of spaces in the half circle of the other end. After the profiles and the sectors are divided up as described, the layout lines are drawn as shown.

To find the true lengths of the layout lines, it is necessary to determine how much each line slants out. In order to find the true length of line 4-11, for example, we must first determine how far points 4 and 11 are out from the center of the fitting. The distance that point 4 is out can be determined by measuring line 4-4' from the profile. Similarly, the distance 11-11' is the distance that point 11 is out from the center of the fitting. When these distances are known, the true length of the line 4-11 can be

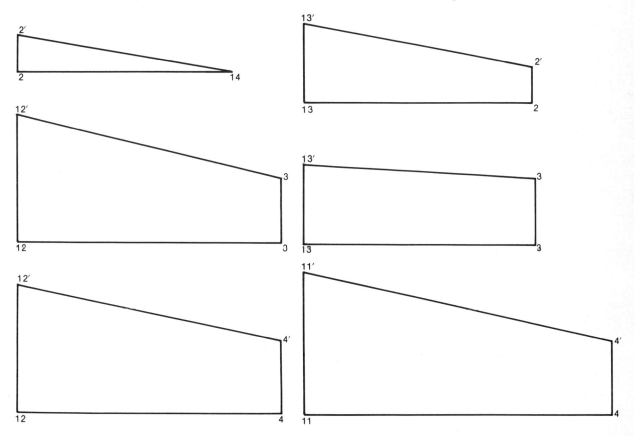

Fig. 12-5 True Lengths for Fig. 12-4.

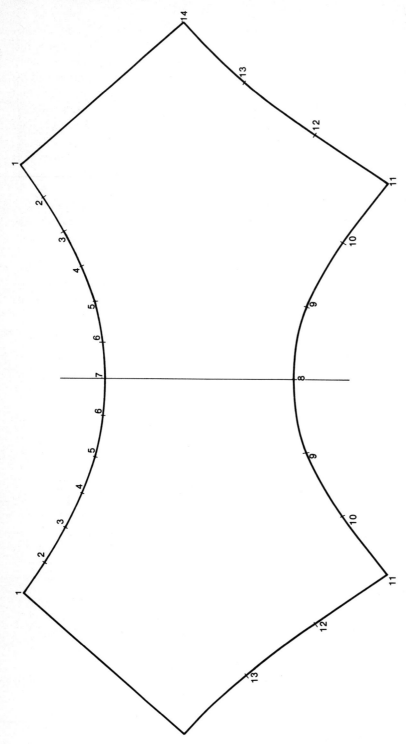

Fig. 12-6 Pattern for Fig. 12-4.

found as shown in Fig. 12-4*a*. The method used in obtaining the true length of line 5-10 is shown in Fig. 12-4*b*.

The true lengths for the remaining lines are found in the same manner. It should be noted that lines 1-14 and lines 7-8 in Fig. 12-4 differ slightly from the others because each represents a line running parallel to the center line of the fitting; as such, they are true lengths on the fitting. Figure 12-5 shows the true lengths for some of the other layout lines of the fitting.

After all the true lengths have been found, the pattern may be laid out as shown in Fig. 12-6. To start the pattern, first draw line 7-8 to the proper length. Then triangulate the other points just as for any round taper. Line 7-8 is the center line of the fitting, and the fitting is developed in both directions from this. Note that the distances between points around the sector are greater than the distances between points around the profiles, and the proper space between points must be used.

Shortcut in finding true lengths

Instead of finding the true lengths as previously described, a shorter method can be utilized to eliminate the need for squaring up two lines for every true length found.

Refer back to Fig. 12-4*a*. If line *AB* is drawn parallel to the base line 4-11 and with point *B* the distance of 4-4' above it, the portion of the development above *AB* is an ordinary true-length triangle. Line *AB* is the length of 4-11, and *AC* is actually the difference between lines 11-11' and 4-4'. Figure 12-7*a* shows the true length of line 10-5 found by this short method. To find the difference between the two heights, set the dividers at the length of the shorter one and deduct it from the longer. In Fig. 12-4, set the dividers to the length of 5-5', and mark this distance on line 10-10' by swinging it from point 10. The distance from this arc to point 10' is the difference between line 5-5' and 10-10' and is the height of the true-length triangle shown in Fig. 12-7*a*.

The true length of line 9-6 found by this same method is shown in Fig. 12-7*b*.

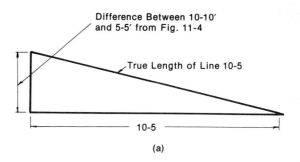

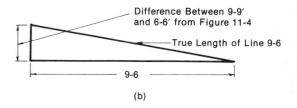

Fig. 12-7   Short Cut in Finding True Lengths.

PRACTICE PROBLEMS

Problem 12-1

Purpose. To practice developing sectors by the quarter-circle method and by laying out the pattern for a Y branch.

Study. *Sector by quarter circle, Pattern by triangulation, Shortcut in finding true lengths.*

Assignment.

1. Draw the half side view and develop the sector by the quarter-circle method for the fitting shown in Fig. 12-8. To use this method, change the height of the sector from the 5 in shown to 3½ in.

2. Lay out the full pattern for half the Y branch.

3. Form up the complete fitting from the pattern developed. Save the fitting for comparison with one to be made in problem 12-2.

Problem 12-2

Purpose. To practice developing the Y-branch sector by the development method and by laying out the pattern for a Y branch.

Study. *Sector by development, Pattern by triangulation, Shortcut in finding true lengths.*

Assignment.

1. Draw the half side view and develop the sector by the development method for the fitting shown in Fig. 12-8.

2. Lay out the full pattern for half the Y branch.

3. Form up the complete fitting from the pattern developed and compare it with the fitting made in problem 12-1. Note the difference in appearance that the change in height of the sector makes. Save both fittings for comparison with the one to be made in problem 12-3.

Problem 12-3

Purpose. To practice developing the Y-branch sector by freehand drawing and by laying out the pattern for a Y branch.

Study. *Sector by freehand drawing, Pattern by triangulation, Shortcut in finding true lengths.*

Assignment.

1. Draw the half side view and develop the sector by freehand drawing for the fitting shown in Fig. 12-8.

2. Lay out the full pattern for half the Y branch.

3. Form up the complete fitting from the pattern developed and compare it with the fittings from problems 12-1 and 12-2.

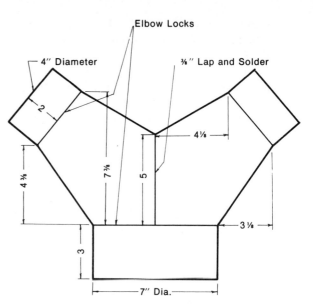

¼″ Groove Seams

Fig. 12-8 Problems 12-1, 12-2, and 12-3, Laying out Y Branches.

Today most roof jacks and caps are mass-produced, but the sheet metal worker is still called upon to make jacks and caps of special sizes and shapes or of special materials, such as copper.

Through the years certain designs for caps and jacks have proved practical in both fabrication and use. The competent layout worker must be familiar with these designs in order to apply them and vary them to fit the requirements of special jobs.

Roof pitch

Whenever sheet metal workers talk of roof jacks, the pitch of the roof is always mentioned. The pitch is the vertical measurement that a roof rises in 12 in horizontal measurement. Figure 13-1 illustrates this on a roof with a pitch of 4 inches in 12. A "4-in-12 pitch" means that the roof is rising 4 in for every 12 in of horizontal measurement. Notice in Fig. 13-1 that for the 12-in measurement

there is a corresponding vertical measurement of 4 in, and that for the 24-in measurement there is vertical measurement of 8 in on a 4-in-12 pitch roof. With a 4-in-12 pitch a 10-ft horizontal measurement will mean a rise of 40 in.

It is sometimes difficult to measure roof pitch exactly because of the unevenness of the roof. Remember that roof pitches are usually standard; an odd pitch is unusual. For instance, if a roof pitch is measured to be 5¼ in in 12, it is probably a 5-in-12 pitch roof and the ¼ in is due to extra-thick shingles or a high spot in the roofing paper. Normally roof pitches are in full inches, except that a 4½-in-12 pitch is common. When possible, it is best to measure on the underside of the roof rafters, either in the attic or under the eaves. This will give a more accurate measurement. Also, it is always best to make as long a measurement as is practical, since this will lessen the chance of inaccuracy due to a rough spot in the roof. Most levels are longer than 24 in, so a common method is to measure off 24 in from the end of the level and take the vertical measurement from that point. If a 24-in span on the level is used, the vertical measurement must be divided in half in order to obtain the pitch per foot. For instance, if the vertical measurement at 24 in is 10 in, the roof pitch is 5 in 12.

Figure 13-2 illustrates obtaining a roof pitch. A 24-in span is marked off on the level; then one end of the level is held against the roof, and the level is moved until the bubble shows a level position. The measurement is taken from the 24-in mark down

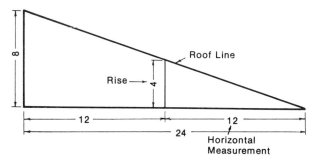

Fig. 13-1 Pitch of Roof.

Fig. 13-2   Obtaining a Roof Pitch.

vertically to the roof. If a 24-in span is used, half this amount is the pitch.

The simplest way to draw the roof pitch on a sheet of metal is to use the 2-ft framing square. The pitch can be obtained by laying the square so that the 24-in mark touches the bottom edge of the sheet and the proper measurement for the desired pitch is on the other blade and even with the bottom edge of the sheet. For a 4½-in-12 pitch, the square would be laid so that the 24-in mark of the blade is touching the bottom of the sheet and the 9-in mark of the tongue is touching the bottom edge of the sheet. Figure 13-3 illustrates this method.

Layout of round tapered jacks

Since a round roof jack is the same as a round taper on a pitch, the layout methods described in Chapter 9 are used to lay out the patterns. In Chapter 9, the sections on *Tapers on a pitch* and *Short method of radial lines* give the exact procedure for laying out the pattern for the round jack. In order for these methods to be used, the roof jack must be designed so that it is a regular cone tapering equally on all sides. The best method of accomplishing this is shown in Fig. 13-4. First draw the regular cone outlined by *ABCD,* with the top, *DC,* to the diameter desired. Normally the bottom of a jack does not have to be any particular diameter, and line *AB* can be made to any diameter that produces a taper of pleasing proportions. After the taper is drawn, draw the pitch line from point *A* and lay the jack out like any round taper.

Trimming a jack

Often, especially when only one jack is needed, a round taper is swept out, and, after it is formed, the pitch is trimmed on the bottom. By setting the taper on a bench, as shown in Fig. 13-5, and measuring up the correct distance on the back and

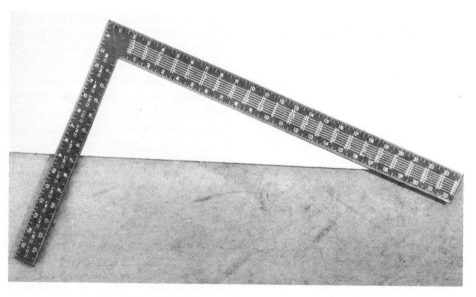

Fig. 13-3   Drawing a Roof Pitch on a Sheet of Metal.

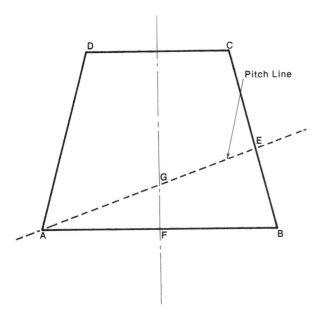

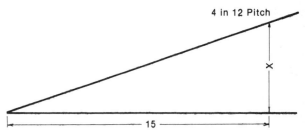

Fig. 13-6 Determining the Amount to Trim a Taper.

Fig. 13-4 Starting the Layout for a Tapered Roof Jack on a Pitch.

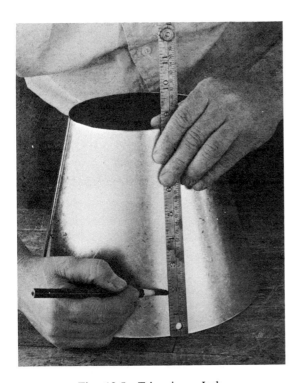

Fig. 13-5 Trimming a Jack.

center, a sufficiently accurate pitch line can be drawn in. If the line must be exact, the fitting can first be trimmed to this pitch line and then another line scribed in the manner described in Chapter 16 in the section called *Marking miters.*

The amount that the taper must be trimmed can be determined as illustrated in Fig. 13-6. If line *AB* in Fig. 13-4 is 15 in long and the roof pitch is 4 in 12, first draw a 4-in-12 pitch line. By measuring over 15 in, as shown in Fig. 13-6, the vertical measurement indicated by *X* is found to be 5 in. This is the distance measured up on the back of the roof jack. Half this distance, or 2½ in, would be measured up at the center of the fitting in order to give an extra point to which to draw the curve. In Fig. 13-4, the 5 in would be line *BE*, and the 2½-in measurement would be line *FG*.

T-top cap

A cap that is commonly made by the sheet metal worker is the T-top cap. It is used more often than other types of caps because the patterns are usually handy in the shop and it can be made from one piece of metal with no waste. Figure 13-7 shows T-top caps.

The pattern for the T top is shown in Fig. 13-8. Line *CE* is made equal to the circumference of the pipe desired. Line *AB* is drawn parallel to *CE* and any distance up from it. This distance is determined by the length of pipe desired on the cap. Next, line *AB* is stepped off into six equal spaces. The dividers are set to one of these spaces, and arcs are swung from points *A*, *D*, and *B*, as shown

Fig. 13-7 T-top Cap.

in Fig. 13-8. After these arcs are swung, line *FG* is drawn parallel to *AB* and at a distance from line *AB* equal to half the length of *AB*. On any size T top this distance is always half the circumference.

After line *FG* is drawn, edges are added as shown for the ¼-in groove seam. The outside of the pattern is trimmed and notched as shown, and cuts are made on the lines and arcs indicated by heavy lines in the figure. However, no metal is removed by these cuts.

To form the T top, the edges for the groove seam of the pipe are turned; the ¼-in edges for the top groove seam are not turned at this time. The pipe is then rolled and the groove seam finished.

The next step in forming the T top is to straighten out the portion that forms the cap. The edges are bent for the top groove seam and the top is rolled. These two edges are then hooked together and grooved. This forms the finished T top shown in Fig. 13-7.

China cap

A round, cone-shaped cap, called a *China cap,* or *coolie cap,* is used on large-diameter roof jacks. The actual method of laying out the pattern for the cap is simply that of sweeping a taper, described in Chapter 9, but the layout worker must be familiar with the common design features of the caps.

The design of China caps will vary slightly from shop to shop, but the essential features are basically the same. Figure 13-9 illustrates a common design of a China cap. The slant of the cap can be any measurement that makes for a well-proportioned cap; usually this is about a 4½-in-12 pitch. The brackets that hold the cap to the pipe are called *stays*. These are usually made out of 1-by-⅛-in band iron, but on smaller caps they are made of 16-gauge strips. On small caps, three stays are used; the larger sizes require four or more. On the cap itself, it is good practice to crimp

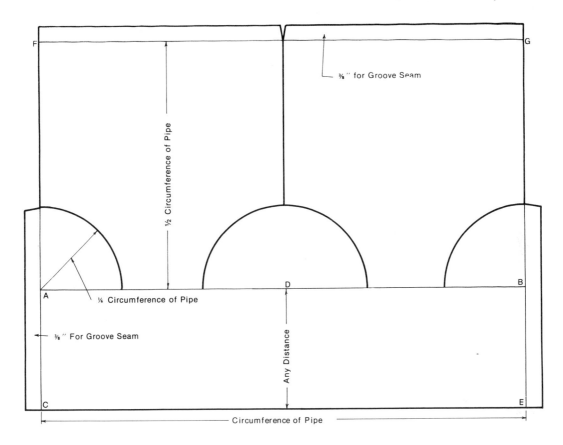

F

G

⅜" for Groove Seam

½ Circumference of Pipe

A

¼ Circumference of Pipe

⅜" For Groove Seam

D

B

Any Distance

C

E

Circumference of Pipe

Fig. 13-8 Pattern for T Top.

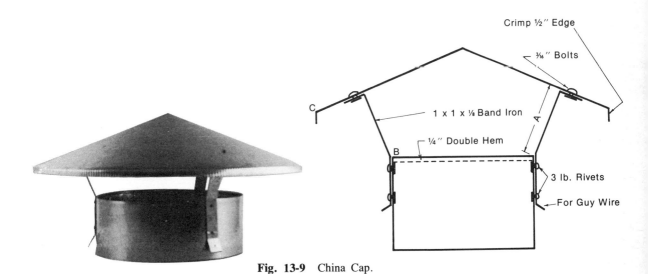

Crimp ½" Edge

³⁄₁₆" Bolts

C

1 x 1 x ⅛ Band Iron

A

¼" Double Hem

B

3 lb. Rivets

For Guy Wire

Fig. 13-9 China Cap.

about ½ in of the edge so that it bends down straight. This not only stiffens the outside edge but also gives the cap a more finished appearance.

The sectional view in Fig. 13-9 shows a typical arrangement of the stays. Two rivets are necessary to hold them to the pipe, and one rivet or a $^3/_{16}$-in stove bolt in each stay holds the cap on. It is easier to fasten the cap to the stays if the stays are bent at a 90° angle with the cap. The stays may be riveted on either the outside or the inside of the pipe. Often they are placed on the outside so that the bottom of each stay can be punched and bent out for a tie for a guy wire. The length of the stay is determined by the distance *A* in Fig. 13-9. This distance is actually the free area through which all the air from the pipe must flow, and it should be made so that the area at this point (figuring all around the pipe) is equal to at least 1½ times the area of the pipe.

Usually, if *A* is made 3½ in long, it is long enough for a well-proportioned cap and also gives plenty of free area. If there is a doubt whether there is enough free area, multiply the distance *A* by the circumference of the pipe. This gives a rough approximation of the free area, and it can be checked to see whether it is about 1½ times the area of the pipe.

For instance, if the pipe has a 10-in diameter, its area is approximately 75 sq in. One and one-half times that figure is 112 sq in, the amount of free area needed at *A*. The circumference of a 10-in diameter is approximately 32 in. Multiplying 32 × 3½, the length of *A*, gives 112 sq in, the free area needed.

As can be seen by the above, it is only necessary to make a rough approximation of the free areas to see that they are close to the proper proportions. In general, anything under 10 in in diameter will be in good proportion and have plenty of free area if the stays are made 3½ in long. In larger caps, over 10 in in diameter, the stays will have to be increased in length to maintain the proper amount of free area.

Although there are rules for determining the diameter of the cap for a particular pipe size, the best and easiest rule to remember is that the cap should be large enough and run down low enough so that an ordinary rain cannot blow into the cap. In other words, in Fig. 13-10, angle *a* should be less than a 45° angle, preferably about 30°.

Layout of China cap

To start the layout of a China cap, it is first necessary to draw half the side view, as shown in Fig. 13-10. The first step is to draw the center line *AB* and square the base line *CD* to it. Both these lines are of indeterminate length and position. Next, draw line *CJ*, which represents the pitch of the cap. Normally it is drawn to a 4½-in-12 pitch. Line *EF* represents the side of the pipe and is drawn parallel to the center line *AB* and out from it a distance equal to the radius of the pipe. After *EF* is drawn, hold a square on line *CJ* and slide along the line until the 3½-in mark of the blade hits line *EF*. This is shown by line *GH* on the drawing. Line *GH* is the line of the stays. Point *H* is the top of the pipe opening. Point *K* is marked ½ in below point *G* and represents the rivet hole for the stays; point *I* is the end of the cap and is determined by the angle it forms with point *H*. The angle indicated by *a* is small enough so that no rain can blow under the cap and into the pipe. An angle between 45° and 30° is usually desirable. After these points have been found, the pattern can be laid out.

To start the pattern, first sweep out the cone by setting the dividers at *JI* from the side view and swinging the arc at the most economical point on the sheet. The true radius of the finished cone is shown by *IS* in the side view, and from the length of *IS*, the circumference of the bottom of the cone can be calculated. This circumference can be measured around the arc with a steel rule as in sweeping out any taper, or it can be determined by setting the dividers at the distance of *IS* and stepping this distance around the arc six times. Stepping the distance around the arc is not quite as accurate as measuring, but for a China cap it produces satisfactory results. Another method of determining the stretchout of the arc, also based upon six times the radius, is to take the difference

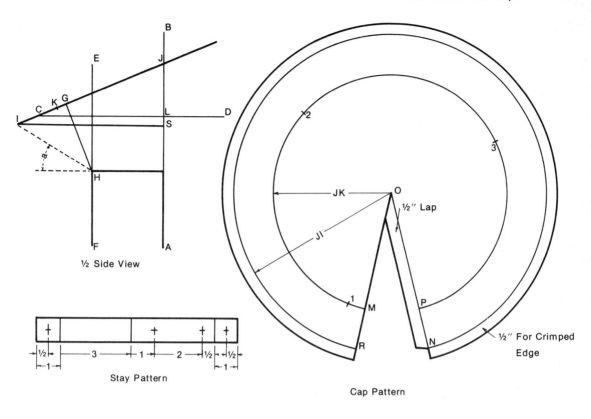

½ Side View

Stay Pattern

Cap Pattern

JK

½" Lap

½" For Crimped Edge

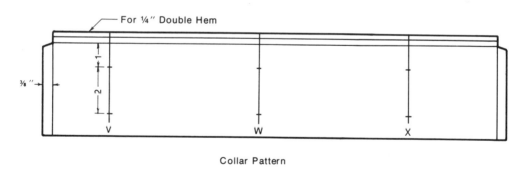

For ¼" Double Hem

Collar Pattern

Fig. 13-10 Patterns for China Cap in Fig. 13-9.

between lines *JI* and *IS* and step this amount around the arc six times. Rather than giving the stretchout of the arc, this method gives the amount of cutout from the circle. The short distance from *N* to *R* in Fig. 13-10 is the amount of cutout for this pattern.

After the basic pattern is found, the dividers are set at the distance *JK* in the side view and this arc is also swung on the pattern, using the same center as before. This circle gives the line for the rivet holes for the stays. To locate the rivet holes, adjust the dividers so that the large arc from *P* to *M* is

Fig. 13-11   Marking the Stays a Cap.

stepped off into three equal spaces. (If four stays are being used, the arc should be divided into four spaces.) After the dividers are set at the proper spacing, locate the first rivet hole (shown by point 1) about an inch away from the seam and step the spacing around to locate rivet holes 1, 2, and 3. Add the laps and allowances as indicated, and the pattern for the cap is completed.

The pattern for the pipe collar is also shown in Fig. 13-10. This is just a simple round-pipe pattern, usually with a double hem allowed on the top for stiffening. If the stays are to be riveted on, the rivet holes should be laid out, since laying out and prepunching the rivet holes results in a faster

Fig. 13-12   Square Caps.

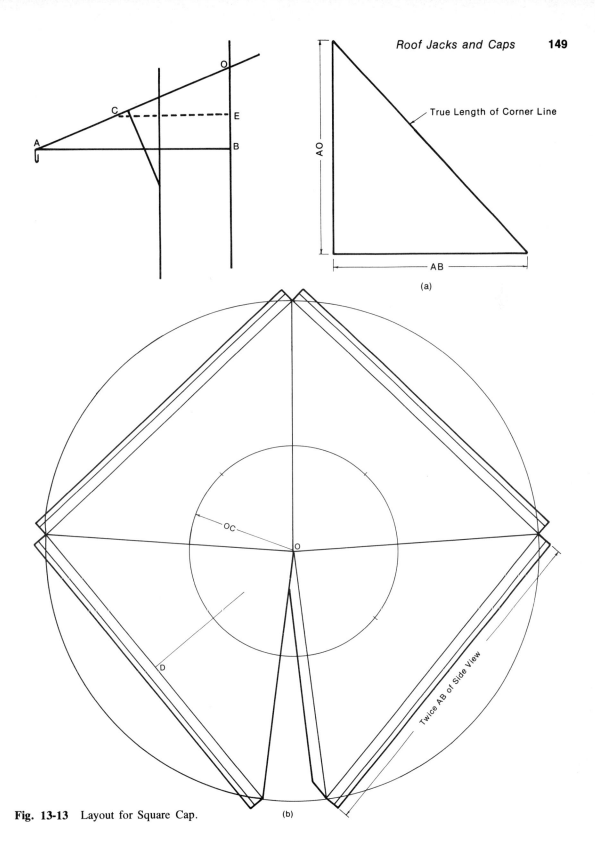

(a)

(b)

Fig. 13-13 Layout for Square Cap.

assembly job and allows less chance of getting the cap on crooked. The distance between *V* and *W*, and between *W* and *X,* is one-third of the circumference of the pipe, since this cap will have three stays.

The stays are normally made out of 1-by-⅛-in band iron. The pattern for one of the stays is also shown in Fig. 13-10. If only three stays are needed, they are usually marked separately. However, if a number of stays are needed, two stays are marked out, and the remaining stays are set between them inside a square, as shown in Fig. 13-11. Then, with the two marked stays on each end, lines are drawn across all of them. After the stays are marked and punched, they are bent to fit the cap. In the side view of Fig. 13-10, the angle *GHF* is the angle at which the stay must be bent.

Square caps

Many vents in commercial buildings must be made square, such as the one shown in Fig. 13-12. In laying out the patterns for the roof jack, few problems are encountered. However, the design of the cap involves a few new problems. Although small caps are made in one piece, the larger ones are made in four pieces with standing seams on the corners.

In pitch, size, and free area, the design of a square cap is exactly like that of the round China cap. The layout is basically the same.

Figure 13-13 shows the layout for a one-piece square cap. This is started just as with a China cap, by drawing half a side view.

To draw the pattern, set the dividers at the true length of line *OA* of the side view. This true length is found, as shown in Fig. 13-13*a,* by taking *AB* from the side view as the base of the triangle and *AO* as the height. The true length of *OA* must be found because the side view shows the length of the cap at the center line, and the pattern requires the true length of the corner line. With this true length, swing a circle for the start of the pattern. Then hold a rule so that chords, equal to twice *AB,* are formed in this circle. Lines from the ends of these lines up to the center point form the

basic pattern for the cap, as shown in Fig. 13-13. Next, swing *OC* (taken directly from the side view), on the pattern to locate the rivet holes for the stays. On a square cap the stays are usually located in the center of each side. Square up a line from the center of each side, as shown at *D* in the pattern, to locate the point on the arc where the rivet hole will be.

Some shops prefer the stays on the corners. If the stays are to be located on the corners, the intersection of the corner lines and an arc of radius equal to the true length of *OC* locates the points where the rivet holes should be. This length of *OC* is found by a true-length triangle of base *CE* and height *OC*.

The edge of a square cap is usually bent down vertically about ½ in, with a ¼-in hem. This is added as shown in Fig. 13-13. A lap for spot welding is added to complete the pattern.

PRACTICE PROBLEMS

Problem 13-1

Purpose. To study the design principles of roof jacks and caps.

Study. All of Chapter 13.

Assignment. Answer all the following questions:

1. If the pitch of a roof is 6 in 12, what is the amount it rises in 8 ft?

2. If the pitch of a roof is 4 in 12, what is the amount of rise in 17 in? (Figure this by drawing a side view of the roof.)

3. When measuring the pitch of a roof, why is it better to measure over as long a span as is practical to use?

4. Make a freehand sketch of how to lay a square on a sheet of metal in order to mark out a 7-in-12 pitch.

5. What job conditions would make it advisable to trim out a round tapering roof jack rather than to lay it out?

6. In trimming a round tapering roof jack with a bottom diameter of 14 in, what would be the measurement up on the back and what would be the measurement at the center in order to obtain a 6-in-12 pitch line? (Figure this by a drawing.)

7. In the pattern for the T-top cap shown in Fig. 13-8, the distance from *A* to *F* is made half the circumference in order to provide enough free area. Can you suggest how the dimension of half the circumference was arrived at?

8. In laying out a China cap for an 18-in-diameter pipe, approximately how much space would the stays have to provide in order to maintain a free area 1½ times the area of the pipe?

9. In Fig. 13-10, why does six times the distance *IS* give the stretchout of the pattern?

10. What basic method of layout is used in laying out the pattern for both the China cap and the square cap?

Problem 13-2

Purpose. To learn how to lay out a T-top cap.

Study. *Roof pitch, T-top cap.*

Assignment.

1. Lay out the pattern for a T-top cap and jack *to fit over* a 5-in-diameter, uncrimped pipe on a 5-in-12 pitch roof. Make the collar part of the cap 4 in long. Use ¼-in groove seams. Lay out the pattern so that the groove seam of the pipe is on the side of the jack and not on the back or front. This makes the T-top seam line run parallel to the ridge of the roof.

2. Make up the complete cap and jack.

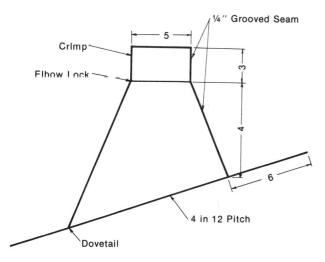

Fig. 13-14 Problem 13-3, Laying Out a Roof Jack.

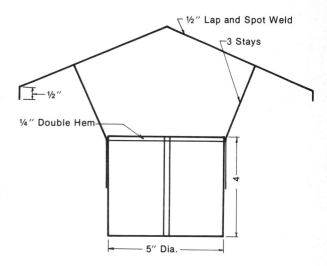

Fig. 13-15 Problem 13-4, Laying Out a China Cap.

Problem 13-3

Purpose. To practice laying out the pattern for a round tapered roof jack.

Study. *Roof pitch, Layout of round tapered jacks.*

Assignment.

1. Lay out the patterns for the roof jack shown in Fig. 13-14 by radial lines.

2. Lay out the pattern for the roof jack by the short method of radial lines and compare it with the first pattern.

3. Make up the complete roof jack from the pattern developed in 1.

Problem 13-4

Purpose. To learn how to lay out all the patterns for a China cap.

Study. *China cap, Layout of China cap.*

Assignment.

1. Lay out all the patterns for the China cap shown in Fig. 13-15. Lay out all rivet holes in the cap, stays, and collar. Use your own judgment for the length of the stays and the diameter of the cap.

2. Make the complete cap and connect it to the roof jack made in problem 13-3.

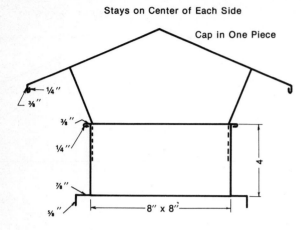

Stays on Center of Each Side

Cap in One Piece

¼″

⅜″

⅜″

¼″

⅜″

⅜″

4

8″ x 8″

Fig. 13-16   Problem 13-5, Laying Out the Patterns for a Square Cap.

Problem 13-5

Purpose. To learn how to lay out the patterns for a square cap.

Study. *Square caps.*

Assignment.

1. Lay out all the patterns for the square cap shown in Fig. 13-16. Lay out all rivet holes.

2. Make the complete cap.

Like roof jacks, most louvers are mass-produced and sold much more cheaply than the custom sheet metal job shop can possibly make them. However, many large and specially shaped louvers still have to be made to order. In addition, the sheet metal worker may make louvers out of special materials such as copper, brass, or stainless steel.

Design of louvers

The layout of louvers is simple parallel-line layout. If the sheet metal worker understands certain basic design principles, the actual layout of the patterns is simple. Figure 14-1 shows a typical louver.

Figure 14-2 shows a sectional view of two louver blades. These illustrate two basic principles of louver design. First, all louver blades should be lapped. The blades should be arranged so that the points D and C in Fig. 14-2a are even with one another. Lapping keeps rain out and prevents seeing through the blades. The second important design feature is that the angle of the louver blades should be about 45°. This angle may be flattened to suit certain job conditions, as will be explained later, but it should never be flattened to less than a 30° angle.

Figure 14-2 also illustrates the basic shape of the louver blade. The distance from A to B varies from ¼ to ½ in, depending on the size of the louver. The distance from B to C varies from ⅜ to ¾ in, also depending on the size of the louver. Figures 14-2b and 14-2c show variations in the shape of the louver blade.

The frame for the louver blades will vary with the requirements of the job. Figure 14-3 shows the construction of a typical louver frame. It also shows a sectional view of the same frame. This type of frame is used in new construction, since the ¾-in dimension is a plaster stop, which provides a stiff, straight surface for the plasterer to work up to.

In order to fasten the louver to the frame, a ¾-in lap is turned up on the end of each louver blade for spot welds or rivets. This is shown in Fig. 14-4.

All louver blades are spot welded or riveted to the louver frame, but the bottom blade is also soldered so that any water that runs down the side of the frame will be caught and will run out on the bottom blade. In addition to being soldered, the bottom blade is also bent in a different manner than the other blades, so that the blade and the bottom frame are combined in such a way that the water

Fig. 14-1 Typical Louver Installed in the Job.

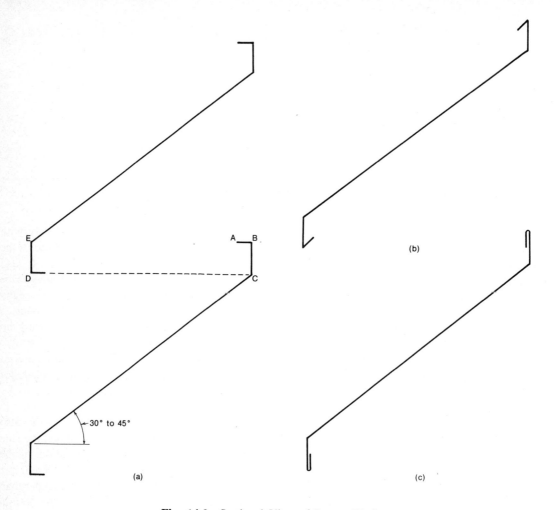

E

A   B

D   C

←30° to 45°

(a)

(b)

(c)

Fig. 14-2 Sectional View of Louver Blades.

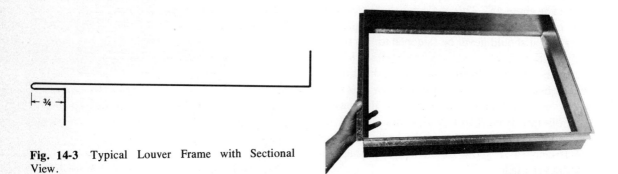

←— ¾ —→

Fig. 14-3 Typical Louver Frame with Sectional View.

³/₄" Turned up for riveting or spotwelding

Top Frame

Fig. 14-4 Formed Louver Blade and Turn-up on Each End for Spot Welding or Riveting.

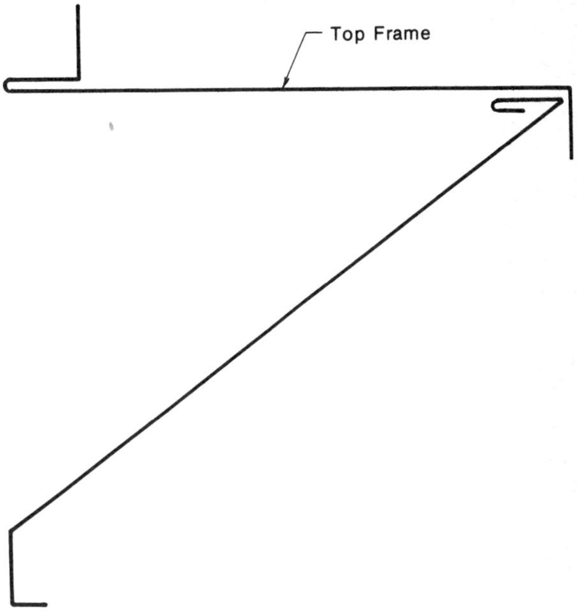

Fig. 14-5 Sectional View of Top Frame of Louver.

will drip free of the louver frame. The side view in Fig. 14-6a shows one way in which the bottom blade is bent. Instead of the face of the blade being bent down in the conventional manner, it is continued out straight. It sticks out past the other blades and also past the front of the frame to provide a drip for the louver. Since this drip sticks out past the surface of the wall, it lets all the water running off the louver drip free instead of running down the wall and streaking it.

The top blade of the louver is also bent in a slightly different manner. The top edge of this blade is bent as shown in Fig. 14-5 so that it can fit up into the corner of the top frame.

Layout of louver

Figure 14-6a gives the details for a louver that will serve here to explain the principles of laying out louver patterns.

The first step is to lay out the pattern for the side frame as shown in Fig. 14-6b. After this pattern is laid out, the louver lines are located on it. To do this, first set the dividers at the width of the frame, which is the distance AB, and step this off on line AC. This spacing probably will not come out evenly, so adjust the dividers and step it off again until the spacing is even between A and C. Always try to close the dividers rather than opening them so that the finished spaces will be slightly smaller than the length of AB. With the same spacing on the dividers, step off line BD also. By using the same spacing on both lines, points F and E (and all other corresponding points) are even with each other. Draw the slanted lines as shown in Fig. 14-6b to indicate the line of the louver blades. A prick mark on the end of each of these lines, as shown on line AE, will provide marks so that the louver blades can be spot welded in rapidly and still be straight.

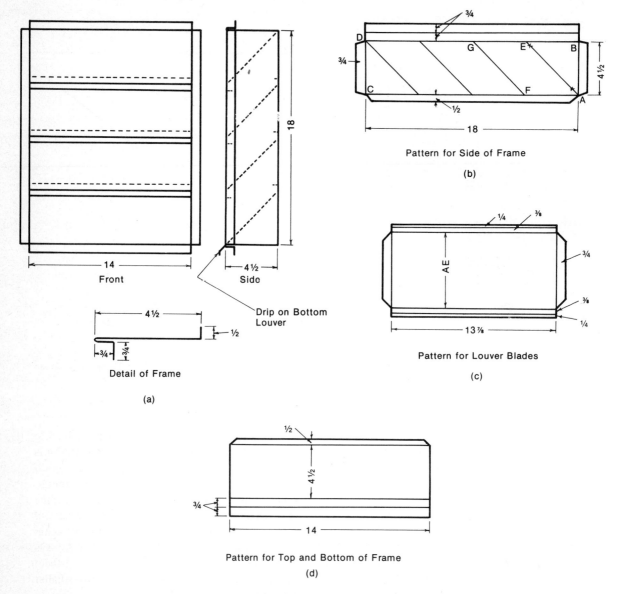

Front

14

Side

4 1/2

18

Detail of Frame

4 1/2

1/2

3/4

3/4

(a)

Drip on Bottom Louver

Pattern for Side of Frame

(b)

3/4

3/4

1/2

18

4 1/2

D

C

G

E

F

B

A

Pattern for Louver Blades

(c)

1/4

3/8

3/4

3/8

1/4

AE

13 7/8

Pattern for Top and Bottom of Frame

(d)

1/2

4 1/2

3/4

14

Fig. 14-6 Rectangular Louver and Layout of the Patterns.

After the louver lines are drawn on the side frame, the louver blade can be laid out. The pattern for the louver blade is shown in Fig. 14-6c. The distance *AE* is taken from the side-frame pattern. The distance is actually made $^1/_{16}$ in shorter than *AE* so that the blade will fit easily into the frame.

Allowances are added to the blade for edges and laps. All the blade patterns are exactly the same on a square or rectangular louver. The top and bottom blades are bent differently, as we have seen. The layout for the top and bottom frames is shown in Fig. 14-6d.

Forming the louver

To assemble the louver, first form up all the blades and frames. The angle to which the blades must be bent can be taken from the side-frame pattern. This is angle *GEA* in Fig. 14-6*b*.

After all the pieces are formed, fasten the two side frames to the bottom frame. The top frame should not be fastened at this time. The next piece to assemble is the bottom blade. The bottom blade is either spot welded or riveted in. If it is to be riveted, the rivet holes should have been punched before the patterns were formed to assure exact alignment of the blade. If it is to be spot welded (as the majority of louvers are) the blade should be carefully lined up with the prick marks on the side frame. The bottom blade must be soldered completely. On small louvers, this bottom blade should be soldered before the other blades are set in place. On larger louvers the bottom blade can be soldered after all the blades are in place.

Working up from the bottom, fasten all blades in place. After the top blade is set, fasten the top frame into place to finish the louver. If the guide marks have been pricked on the side frame and if the blades have been carefully set to these marks, the louver blades will all be straight and parallel.

Layout of a triangular louver

Though the layout of a triangular louver is not a common job, it will serve here to illustrate the principle involved in the construction of any irregular-shaped louver. Louvers made in a sheet metal shop are often of irregular shape and cannot be bought ready-made. Therefore, it is important that the sheet metal worker know how to approach such a problem.

The first step in laying out a triangular louver is to draw the outline of the front view, as shown in Fig. 14-7*a*. If the louver is symmetrical, as this one is, only half the front view need be drawn, since the other half will be exactly the same. The dotted lines in the front view indicate the part of the fitting that need not be drawn.

After the outline of the front view is drawn, draw the side view to establish the lines of the blades on the front view. This is done in exactly the same manner as for a rectangular louver.

When the blade lines are established on the side view, project lines over to the front view to locate the blade lines on it. Line *MH* on the front view, for example, shows a blade line. After this is done, the layout of the blade patterns may be made.

To lay out the blade pattern, take the stretchout of the blade from the side view and the length of the blade from the front view. The layout for the bottom blade is shown in Fig. 14-7*b*. All blade patterns will be the same width, which is the distance *BF* from the side view. Draw a center line for the blade, and mark the distance *KB* from the front view on each side of center to obtain the length of the bottom line of the pattern. Mark off the distance *JF* from the front view on each side of the center line of the pattern to obtain the length of the top line of the pattern. Draw lines as shown to close off the ends, and the basic pattern for the bottom blade is complete. Laps and edges must be added to the pattern in order to complete it. These will be the same as those shown on the blade pattern in Fig. 14-6*c*.

Since this is a triangular louver, the side has the same slant all the way up, and all the blade patterns will be the same except that the length of each one will be different. If the louver were round in shape, the curve of the circle would be different at every point and each blade would have to be laid out separately.

The bottom line of the second blade of this louver will be twice the length of line *JF* of the front view. To start the pattern, draw a line to this length, as shown in Fig. 14-7*d*. Then set the pattern of the bottom blade, already laid out, so that its bottom line is directly over line *F'F* and its corner is directly on point *F*. When the bottom-blade pattern is in this position, mark the right-hand half of the pattern to form the end for the second blade. This same process is repeated. Set the bottom-blade pattern over point *F'* and mark the left-hand half of the pattern. This makes the pattern the proper length without having to repeat the layout process. Note that this can only be done if the angle of the side frame remains the same all

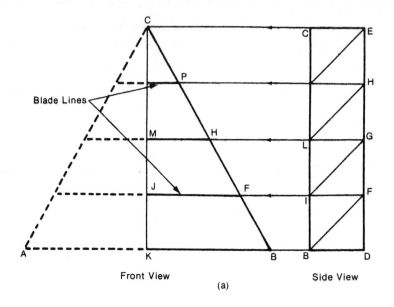

Front View

Side View

(a)

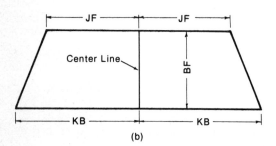

(b)

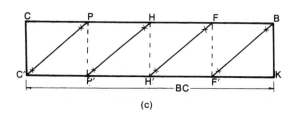

(c)

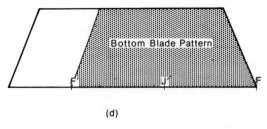

(d)

Marking the Second
Blade Pattern

Fig. 14-7 Layout of Patterns for Triangular Louver.

the way up. If the allowances for laps and edges have already been added to the bottom-blade pattern, they will automatically be added to the second-blade pattern when the bottom pattern is used to mark the ends.

Mark all other blades by the same process; the length of the bottom line for the third louver will be twice the length of *MH* in the front view.

In laying out the patterns for the side frames, all the lengths are taken from the front view because the side view does not show the true length of the pattern. Figure 14-7*c* shows the basic pattern for the side without any allowances for laps and edges. The length *BC* of the pattern is taken from the front view. The distances *BF*, *FH*, and *HP* are also taken from the front view and transferred to the pattern as shown. After these points have been located, lines are squared from them across to line *KC'* to establish the other point of the blade line. The line drawn from *B* to *F'*, and other similar lines, are the blade lines, and they should be prick marked at each end to provide a guide for spot welding the blades into place.

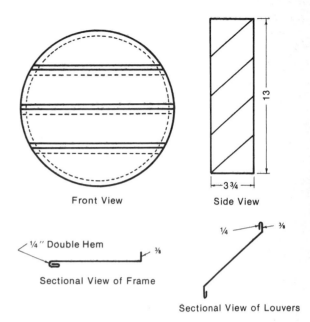

Front View   Side View

Sectional View of Frame

Sectional View of Louvers

Fig. 14-8   Problem 14-3, Laying Out a Round Louver.

PRACTICE PROBLEMS

Problem 14-1

Purpose. To practice designing and laying out the patterns for a rectangular louver.

Study. *Design of louvers, Layout of louvers, Forming the louver.*

Assignment.

1. Design and lay out all the patterns for a rectangular louver 14 in wide and 12 in high. Make it deep enough to extend through a 2-by-4-in stud wall that is to be plastered on one side. Build the frame with a plaster stop. Spot weld construction.

2. Make up the complete louver.

Problem 14-2

Purpose. To learn how to lay out the patterns for a triangular louver.

Study. All of Chapter 14, with emphasis on *Layout of triangular louvers.*

Assignment.

1. Design and lay out a triangular louver to fit a 2-by-4-in stud wall that is plastered on one side. Make a plaster stop on the frame. The louver will be an equilateral triangle with sides 14 in long.

2. Make up the complete louver.

Problem 14-3

Purpose. To learn how to lay out a round louver.

Study. All of Chapter 14, with special emphasis on *Layout of triangular louvers.*

Assignment.

1. Lay out all the patterns for the round louver shown in Fig. 14-8. No specific instruction has been given on this particular type. However, it is almost the same as the layout of the triangular louver and, therefore, a good test of the student's ability to adapt his or her knowledge to varied jobs.

2. Make up the complete louver. At points where the curve of the circle is extreme, no end lap is allowed on the blades, and they are only butted and soldered.

A short method of developing a complicated pattern is to roll it out. This procedure is usually referred to by sheet metal workers in a half-joking manner as *rollation*.

The theory behind rollation is that the surface of any fitting can be generated by rolling it over a flat surface and marking the edges as it is rolled. Fig. 15-1 shows the curve generated by rolling and marking the edges of a round cone as it turns one revolution. Since the sheet metal worker cannot have the finished fitting to roll, a template is used that produces the same results.

To make a template for rolling out a fitting, draw a side view of the fitting and attach a profile at each end of it. Bend up the profiles square to the side view, and this template can be used for rolling and marking the fitting on metal or paper.

Fig. 15-2a shows the side view of a simple cone to be rolled out. The first step is to draw an exact side view of the fitting and attach a profile to each end, as shown in Fig. 15-2b. Cut out this template and make square bends on lines *AB* and *CD*. It is important that these bends be exactly square, since any variation in the angle will result in inaccuracy in the pattern. After the template is cut and bent, as shown in Fig. 15-3a, place it on the sheet, as shown in Fig. 15-3b, and slowly roll it, marking points along the edge as it is turned. When the

Fig. 15-1 Taper Pattern Being Generated by Rolling and Marking the Edges of a Taper.

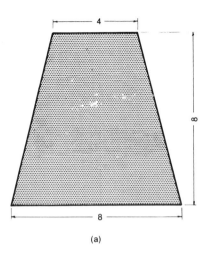

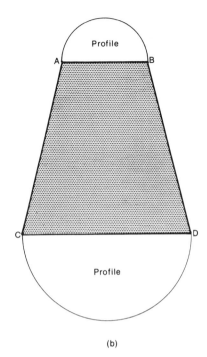

Fig. 15-2 Side View of Round Taper and "Rolla-tion" Template for Rolling the Pattern.

template has been rolled to the other edge of the side view, it has developed a half pattern of the fitting (Figure 15-3c).

Limitations of rollation

One of the greatest faults of rollation is that too often the beginning sheet metal worker, seeing it for the first time, is led by its apparent simplicity to adopt it as a universal layout method. Like any other shortcut method, rollation has its limitations, and the sheet metal worker should learn to use it only where it offers a definite advantage. Some employers feel so strongly about it that they will not hire a sheet metal worker who depends principally on rollation. In fact, some employers will fire any worker they observe using rollation, on the assumption that anyone who uses it does not know the proper layout method.

Another disadvantage of rollation is that it is an approximate method. No matter how carefully the template is made and used, human error leads to enough inaccuracy that the finished pattern usually has to be trimmed to fit.

Though rollation can be used to lay out a great number of fittings, it is limited to wrap-around fittings such as square to rounds, Y branches, and round-pipe fittings. Duct fittings, louvers, and hoods cannot be developed by rollation.

Rollation also involves some waste of metal because the template is of no use after the fitting has been made. On a small fitting, such as the one illustrated in Fig. 15-3, the amount of metal used is negligible. However, with a fitting 24 inches in diameter and 36 in long, the amount of metal used on the template would be considerable.

It is also difficult to keep the template profiles of large fittings at an exact 90° angle, and usually much time is wasted constructing braces and spot welding them into position in order to hold the profiles square.

Another limitation of rollation is that it is difficult to lay out a fitting that is offset in both directions. The square to round shown in Fig. 8-18,

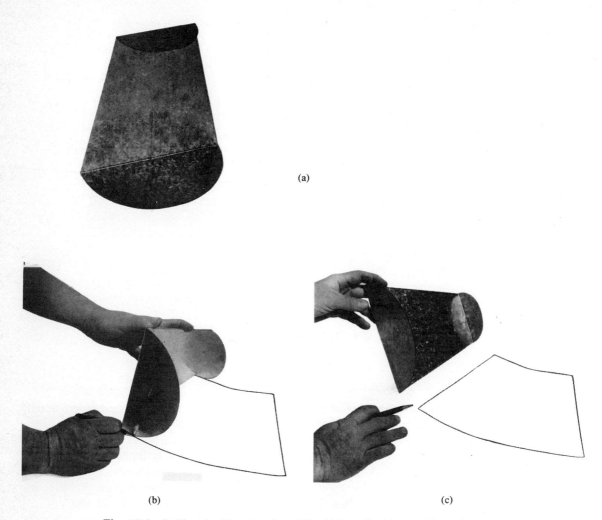

(a)

(b)   (c)

Fig. 15-3   Rolling the Template from Fig. 15-2 to Develop the Taper Pattern.

for instance, can theoretically be laid out by rollation, but it would not be practical for shop purposes because rollation would take more time than laying it out in a more conventional manner.

In spite of its many limitations, the sheet metal worker should have a good working knowledge of rollation technique. Problems frequently arise in the shop that can be solved most efficiently by this method. If only one size of a certain Y branch is needed, for instance, and if it is not extremely large, rollation will probably be faster than conven-

tional layout. The same would be true of one four-piece square-to-round elbow. When used with moderation and good judgment, rollation is a valuable asset to the sheet metal worker.

Using rollation

Sheet metal patterns are seldom laid out on paper in the ordinary shop, but it is much faster to develop rollation patterns on paper if any is available. The reason is that it eliminates the need for marking the edges of the template with a pencil

Fig. 15-4   Using Oil on the Edge of Template Pattern.

as the template is rolled around. A small amount of oil can be applied to the edges of the profile, and then, when the template is rolled over the paper, a smooth, even mark is left on the paper by the oil, as shown in Fig. 15-4. This outlines the pattern without any need for marking with a pencil. After the pattern is developed on paper, the paper is laid over the metal and the pattern prick marked through onto the metal.

Templates for rollation

The success of rollation depends upon the correct layout of the template. The templates of some typical problems follow.

Figure 15-5 shows the template for a square to round that is offset in one direction. This template is for the square to round shown in Fig. 8-1. Note that it is simply a side view with the profiles attached. The distance *AC* is half the square end of the fittings. Square bends would be made on lines *AB* and 1-7 in order to finish the template.

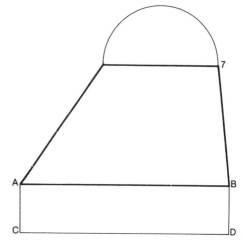

Fig. 15-5   ''Rollation'' Template for Off-center Square to Round from Fig. 8-1.

Figure 15-6 shows the template for a square to round on a pitch. This template is for the square to round shown in Fig. 8-16.

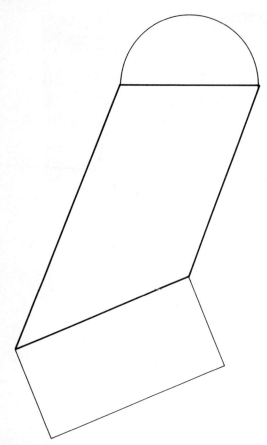

Fig. 15-6   Template for Square to Round on a Pitch Shown in Fig. 8-16.

Fig. 15-7   Template for Round Taper from Fig. 9-5.

Figure 15-7 shows the template for another class of fitting commonly laid out by rollation. In this case, the round taper is centered and is for the fitting in Fig. 9-5.

Figure 15-8 illustrates the template for a round taper on a pitch. This template is for the fitting shown in Fig. 9-16.

Although such things as a round-elbow gore are usually not rolled out, Fig. 15-9 shows the template for the first gore of the elbow shown in Fig. 11-13.

Note that in this fitting (Fig. 11-13) the profile at the miter line is not a circle but an ellipse. Whenever a round pipe is cut on a miter, the profile at that point must be elliptical.

To develop the ellipse for the miter line, draw the profile *AB* in Fig. 15-9 the same as the profile on the bottom of the pipe. Divide the bottom profile into six equal spaces, square them up to the miter line, and then square them from the miter line. The profile at *AB* is divided into three equal spaces and these lines are projected over parallel to *AB*. The intersection of these corresponding lines gives the points of ellipse.

Figure 15-10 illustrates another form of template. This one is for the Y branch in Fig. 12-1. In this case, there are three profiles because there are three open, curved surfaces. The development

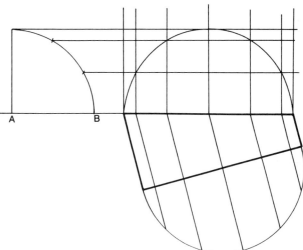

Fig. 15-9 Template for First Gore of the Round Elbow from Fig. 11-15.

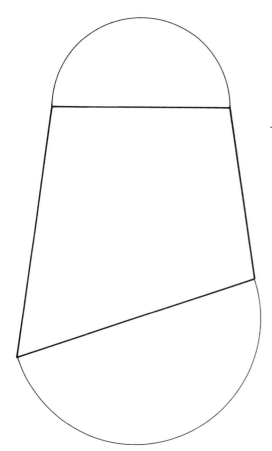

Fig. 15-8 Template for Round Taper on a Pitch from Fig. 9-16.

of the profiles and sector is done in the manner described in Chapter 12. After the template is cut out, all three profiles are bent at right angles.

PRACTICE PROBLEMS

Problem 15-1

Purpose. To learn how to roll out the pattern for a square to round.

Study. All of Chapter 15, with emphasis on Fig. 15-5.

Assignment.

1. Lay out the template for rolling out the square to round shown in Fig. 8-14.

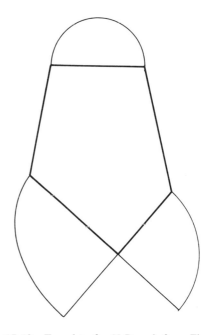

Fig. 15-10 Template for Y Branch from Fig. 12-1.

2. Form up the template and roll out the half pattern for the fitting.

3. Make up the complete fitting.

Problem 15-2

Purpose. To learn how to lay out the patterns for a square to round on a pitch.

Study. All of Chapter 15, with emphasis on Fig. 15-6.

Assignment.

1. Lay out the template for rolling out the square to round shown in Fig. 8-17.

2. Form up the template and roll out the half pattern on paper. Compare the pattern with the one made previously for the same fitting.

3. Make up the complete fitting.

Problem 15-3

Purpose. To learn how to roll out the pattern for a round taper on a pitch.

Study. All of Chapter 15, with emphasis on Fig. 15-8.

Assignment.

1. Lay out the template for rolling out the fitting in Fig. 9-16.

2. Form up the template and roll out the half pattern on paper. Compare it with the pattern made previously for the same fitting.

3. Make up the complete fitting.

Problem 15-4

Purpose. To learn how to roll out the fitting for a Y branch.

Study. All of Chapter 15, with emphasis on Fig. 15-10.

Assignment.

1. Lay out the template for rolling out the fitting in Fig. 12-8.

2. Form up the template and roll out the half pattern. Then reverse the bends on the template and roll out the other half pattern in order to make a full pattern. Compare this pattern with the one made previously for the same fitting.

3. Make up the complete fitting.

16
Trimulation and Trimming

The two terms sound similar, and they do stand for almost the same operation, but there is considerable difference between *trimulation* and *trimming*. Both terms refer to a method of avoiding a long layout for a pattern, and both terms refer to forming an approximate shape of sheet metal and then trimming it down to the proper size. The great difference between the two is that trimulation is usually a term of derision. When a mechanic reports using trimulation to lay out the pattern, it is meant jokingly that he or she did not know how to lay out the pattern and, therefore, formed up a shape as close as possible and trimmed it down by guesswork. Trimming, on the other hand, is a legitimate procedure for the skillful sheet metal worker. When a sheet metal worker says the pattern was *trimmed out,* it means that trimming was chosen as the most practical means of making that particular fitting.

Just as with rollation, trimming must be used with judgment and only at the proper times. It is not a cure-all for avoiding proper layout methods. Often it is used in the shop in conjunction with rollation when the proper layout method would take too much time to be practical. Trimming is also used frequently on the job. On gutter jobs, for instance, the sheet metal worker often takes only straight lengths of downspout and gutter to the job, with the intention of trimming all the miters at the job site. This simplifies transporting the material to the job and is usually faster than trying to lay out all the miters in the shop. Trimming is also used on

emergency fittings that must be made on the site. Often a fitting is needed on the job, and a trip back to the shop would be too time-consuming, so the fitting is trimmed out of the duct or pipe available on the job.

To sum up, trimulation is poor practice: the term implies that the worker does not know any other way to make the fitting. On the other hand, trimming is a legitimate method of layout which must be used with judgment.

Trimming is based upon certain principles; this section covers the basic principles of trimming, with the aim of providing students a basis for developing their own personal trimming techniques.

45° miters

The miter is the joint where two pieces join to form an angle. When two pieces of gutter, downspout, or anything else join to form a 90° angle, the miter

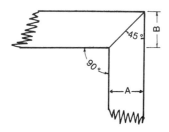

Fig. 16-1 Miter Line for 90° Angle.

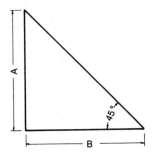

Fig. 16-2 45° Triangle.

line is always a 45° angle, as shown in Fig. 16-1. Since a 90° joint is the most common one in sheet metal work, the sheet metal worker should know how to make a 45° angle easily. The method used to draw a 45° angle is based on the fact that in a 45° triangle both legs are the same length. Therefore, in Fig. 16-2 sides *A* and *B* are equal. This means that in Fig. 16-1, whatever the width of the metal, (dimension *A*), the distance up from a squared-off line (dimension *B*) is just the same. In other words, if *A* is 6 inches wide, *B* must be measured up 6 in from a squared-off line to form the 45° angle.

Laying out other miters

In cases where the miter is not for a 90° angle, the sheet metal worker must determine the cut of the angle by other means. The usual way is to draw out the angle either full size or to scale and then measure the cut.

In Fig. 16-3, if the angle formed by *ABC* is the desired angle, the first step is to draw *DE* parallel to *AB* with the distance *W* equal to the width of the pipe that is to be mitered. Line *EF* is drawn parallel to *BC* and the same distance away. After these lines are drawn, the miter line may be drawn from *B* to *E,* completing the side view of the pipe. To determine the cut for the miter, line *EG* is drawn square to *EF* to intersect *BC*. The distance *BG* is the amount that the miter is cut off a square line, as shown in Fig. 16-4. Figure 16-4 is a side view of the pipe that is to be mitered to the angle shown in Fig. 16-3. Line *EG* is squared up at any point where the miter is desired, and the distance of the cut is then taken from Fig. 16-3 and measured off on the pipe. This is shown as distance *BG*. After the distance of the cut is measured off, lines are drawn from *E* to make the cut. The shaded portion of Fig. 16-4 is the material to be cut out. No lap is allowed for on this illustration, but ordinarily it would be allowed for on the actual job.

This method of determining the cut for a miter is used on downspout, conductor pipe, gutter, duct work, flashing, and any other material that must be mitered. Each job involves slightly different methods of cutting and allowing for laps, but the basic method of determining the amount to cut out is always the same.

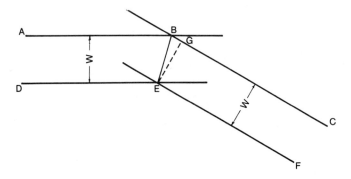

Fig. 16-3 Finding the Cut for a Miter.

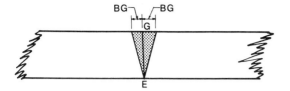

Fig. 16-4 Marking the Cut for a Miter.

Length of offset

When cutting miters on the job, it is difficult to determine how long the offset part of the pipe must be in order to make the pipe come out to the correct length and amount of offset. An offset measured on the job is usually determined by dimensions rather than by the amount of the angle. The fitting shown in Fig. 16-5 is designated as offsetting 6 in 12 in.

The usual method of determining this offset is by drawing it out on the floor or sidewalk to full scale, if this is feasible, or otherwise to half or quarter scale. After the offset is drawn to scale, the cut of the miter and the length of the offset can be determined.

Assuming that Fig. 16-5 shows the side of a rectangular pipe, the cut for the miter can be determined by squaring up line *BC* and getting distance *CA*. This will be the cut for both the angles, since the miter at *AB* and *A'B'* will be the same angle on any offset.

The length of the offset is the distance *AB'* (*A'B* is the same distance). Care must be taken to mark this distance on the right spot on the pipe, since it

is easy to mismeasure this length. In Fig. 16-5 the points *A* and *A'* represent the point of bend of the pipe, and points *B* and *B'* represent the sides of the cut. Figure 16-6 shows how this length would be measured on the side of the pipe. Notice that *A* is the point where the pipe will bend and *B'* is to the side of the cut. This is an important item to remember when cutting miters: always check to see where the measurement should be taken from.

Laps on miters

Whenever a pipe, gutter, or other object is mitered, the usual method of joining the two pieces is by lap and solder, occasionally with metal screws or rivets for strength. Therefore, an important consideration in cutting miters is an allowance for laps. Three types of laps are shown in Fig. 16-7. Laps are generally made from ¼ to ⅜ in wide, depending on the job. They are usually not made much larger than this unless there is a definite need for it, because a larger lap will not bend and lay up against the metal as neatly as a smaller lap. The corners of any lap are always notched as shown in Fig. 16-7; at any place where the lap is on a curved surface, the lap is notched to allow the metal to shrink or stretch when it is bent. If the lap is on a curve, requiring the metal to stretch, only a straight cut is made at intervals in the lap; if the lap is where the metal must shrink in bending, small wedges are cut from the lap. When notching a lap, it is good practice to avoid cutting exactly up to the line. Instead, cut to within about $1/16$ in so that the actual bend line will not show the notches and will appear from the outside to be a solid bend.

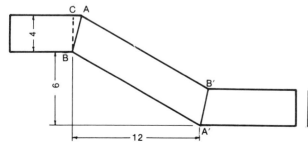

Fig. 16-5 Offset in Rectangular Pipe.

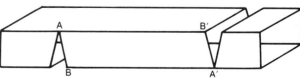

Fig. 16-6 Measuring Length of Offset.

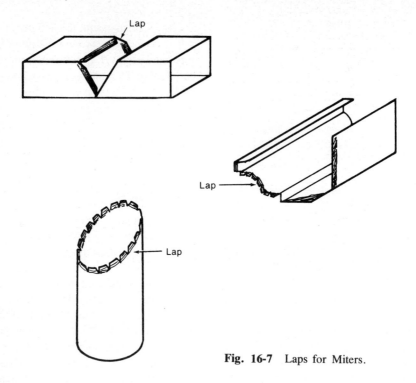

Fig. 16-7   Laps for Miters.

Stops on laps

When connecting two pieces of metal by lapping, it is often difficult to hold the metal in position, especially if the pieces consist of curved surfaces. In connecting two pieces of round pipe, for instance, it is difficult to hold the metal in the proper position while tacking. It is helpful to bend three or four of the tabs from the lap out square for the other piece of pipe to rest against while it is soldered in place. Figure 16-8 illustrates this method. The lap on the piece of pipe is notched and bent in the usual manner. However, four of the tabs are bent out to a 90° angle, as shown in Fig. 16-8, the top photograph. After this, the second piece of pipe is connected to the first piece, with the lap fitting inside. The four tabs act as *stops* for the second pipe to fit against, thus holding it in the proper position and angle while the joint is tacked in place. After the joint is tacked in place and before it is soldered, the four tabs are cut off as close to the pipe as possible and the remaining portion is tapped down against the pipe. If these tabs are cut off closely, they will not be apparent from the outside of the pipe and the miter will still present a neat appearance after it is completely soldered as shown in Fig. 16-8, the bottom photograph. Using stop tabs on round pipe and such miters as gutter greatly speeds up making the lap and also ensures a more accurate joint.

Marking miters

On a curved surface such as a round pipe, the beginner has difficulty marking the line for the miter, since it is hard to follow the curved surface and still retain a line that follows a straight plane. Figure 16-9 illustrates how the line for the miter should run. When looking at the side of the pipe and trying to mark the miter line, try to visualize the flat surface that is drawn in the photograph. The pencil line should be the same as the line where this flat surface and the pipe intersect.

Visualizing this flat piece of metal intersecting the curve at the miter angle applies not only to round pipe but to any curved surface. Any miter on

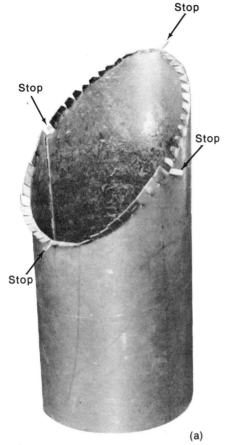

Fig. 16-9 A Miter Must Fit Against a Flat Plane.

Fig. 16-8 "Stops" on a Lap.

a curved surface should fit against a flat plane after it is cut. This applies to the curve on ogee gutter, half-round gutter, downspout, stovepipe, or any other miter that is curved or partially curved.

Another illustration of how the miter must fit a flat plane is seen in the old-time method of cutting miters. Back in the days when sheet metal workers seldom knew pattern drafting, every worker was, of necessity, a trimming expert. One trick for marking miters on stovepipe, and even for marking gores for round elbows, was to throw some coal dust or lampblack in a bucket of water and then dip the pipe into the water at the proper angle. The

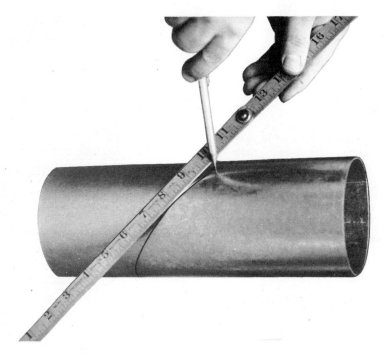

Fig. 16-10   Using a Rule as a Guide to Marking a Miter.

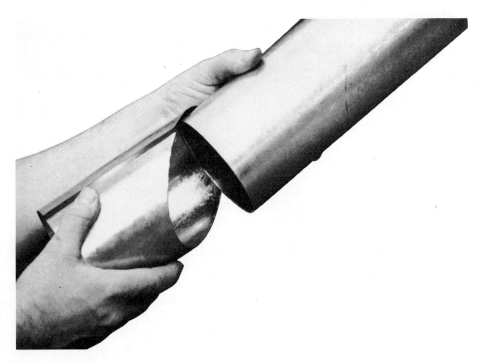

Fig. 16-11   Using a Template to Mark a Miter.

Fig. 16-12 Trimming a Miter to a Flat Surface.

lampblack on the surface of the water would stick to the pipe, leaving a black line where the pipe intersected the water; the line of the miter. This further illustrates the concept of a flat surface cutting across the pipe to get the line of the miter.

One aid to marking the miter is to hold a rule or a straight strip of metal against the pipe, as shown in Fig. 16-10. Note that the rule is not wrapped around the pipe, as this would give a spiral cut instead of the desired straight cut. The rule is held in a straight line and against the pipe at the angle of the miter; the pencil is held at right angles to the rule and slid along it to mark the pipe. It is important that the pencil be at right angles to the rule, for otherwise the miter will not fit a straight plane after it is cut.

Another method of marking a miter is shown in Fig. 16-11. This method consists of having a template cut to the proper angle and formed to fit over the pipe or other object. The miter is marked by slipping the jacket template over the pipe and drawing around it. This method is practical only when a large number of the same miter have to be

cut or when the same type of miter is cut on various jobs, such as standard offsets for downspout or miters for gutter.

Scribing a miter

After a miter is cut to the marked miter line, if the job calls for speed rather than neatness, the miter can often be used after the first trimming cut. However, in most cases, and especially where a miter must fit accurately, the miter must be scribed to closer accuracy. The following method of scribing the miter to exactness uses the concept that the miter of any object must fit against a flat surface. After the miter is trimmed to the initial miter line and checked to see whether its angle is correct, it is then set on a relatively flat surface such as a bench top, as shown in Fig. 16-12. The fitting is held firmly so that it cannot rock on any high spots, and a pencil is laid flat on the bench, as shown in Fig. 16-12, and moved around the pipe, marking a line. By this means, a line parallel to the flat surface of the bench top is marked around the pipe. The fitting is trimmed to this line to obtain an accurate miter free of high or low spots. A pencil is generally used because it marks a line about $3/16$ in above the bench top, which is usually enough to take care of most imperfections. If the waves in the miter are too large to mark out with a pencil, a second marking is necessary or else dividers may be used in place of a pencil. If dividers are used, they are opened wide enough to reach the highest spot of the miter. Care must be taken that the divider legs are held square to the bench top and not allowed to tip forward or backward, because this will cause inaccurate marking.

Scribing is often used when a piece of metal is to be trimmed to fit against an irregular curve. The metal is cut roughly to the shape by guess, and then held in the position it is to fit while the curve is scribed in with dividers, as shown in Fig. 16-13. Usually several scribe marks and several trimmings must be made before an exact cut is achieved, because it is almost impossible to hold the dividers at right angles to the curve when there is a large gap to span. Many mechanics use a

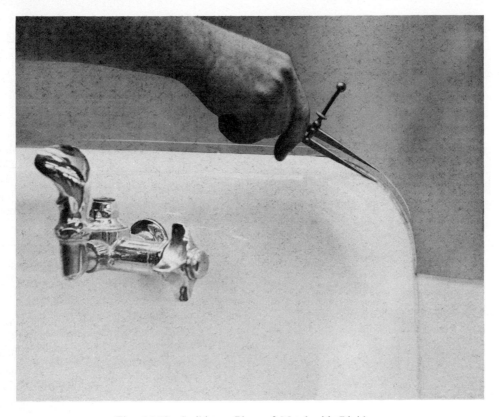

Fig. 16-13 Scribing a Piece of Metal with Dividers.

pencil in the manner described above after the line has been scribed down close enough with dividers.

PRACTICE PROBLEMS

Problem 16-1

Purpose. To test your knowledge of trimming.

Study. All of Chapter 16.

Assignment. Answer the following items:

1. Explain the difference between trimulation and trimming.

2. What is the advantage of trimming out a fitting when you know how to lay out the pattern?

3. Give three specific examples of jobs that would be trimmed rather than laid out.

4. If a downspout offsets at an angle of 150°, what is the angle of the miter?

5. On a rectangular pipe, an angle of 90° must be made. The width of the side of the pipe on which the miter is cut is 4 in.
   a. What is the angle of the miter?
   b. What is the cut for the miter?

6. Find the cut for a 75° miter (the pipe forms a 150° angle) by the trigonometric method. The pipe is 5 in wide.

7. Find the cut for 6 by construction and compare it with the results of 6.

8. What is the purpose of stops on laps?

Problem 16-2

Purpose. To practice trimming a rectangular pipe.

Study. *Laying out other miters, Length of offset, Laps on miters.*

Assignment. Do one of the following:

1. Make a section of rectangular pipe 4-by-3-in and 24 in long, using a double seam on one of the 4-in sides.

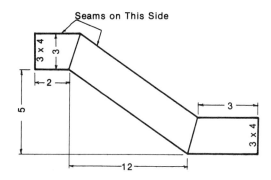

Fig. 16-14 Problem 16-2. Offset Rectangular Pipe.

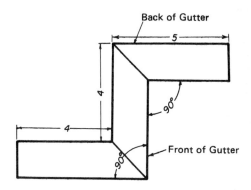

Fig. 16-16 Problem 16-4, Miters in Ogee Gutter.

After the pipe is made, trim the miters, allow for laps, and solder together to make the offset shown in Fig. 16-14.

2. Instead of making the pipe, draw a full-sized side view of the straight pipe and mark the cuts and laps, indicating all dimensions.

Problem 16-3

Purpose. To practice cutting miters on round pipe.

Study. *Laying out other miters, Length of offset, Laps on miters, Stops on laps, Marking miters.*

Assignment. Make a length of 3-in-diameter pipe long enough to trim out the offset shown in Fig. 16-15. Use a groove seam to join it. After the pipe is formed, trim it, allowing for laps, notch the laps, and use four stops to help connect the miter.

Problem 16-4

Purpose. To practice trimming ogee gutter.

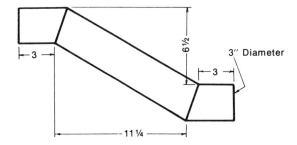

Fig. 16-15 Problem 16-3, Offset Round Pipe.

Study. *Laps on miters, Stops on laps, Marking miters, Scribing a miter.*

Assignment.

1. Either make or obtain a length of preformed ogee gutter about 24 in long.

2. Trim the miters to form the shape shown in Fig. 16-16. Lap and solder the joint.

Problem 16-5

Purpose. To practice scribing a miter to an exact fit.

Study. *Laps on miters, Stops on laps, Marking miters, Scribing a miter.*

Assignment.

1. Make two pieces of 4-in-diameter pipe, 12 in long.

2. Mark and trim one end of each piece to a 45° angle.

3. Scribe the trimmed miters with a pencil until they fit against a flat surface perfectly.

4. Hold the two miters together to check fit and whether they form a 90° angle.

5. Make a notched lap on one piece; turn out four stops; solder and finish lap.

6. Save the fitting for problem 16-6.

Problem 16-6

Purpose. To practice scribing a pipe to an irregular surface.

Study. *Scribing a miter.*

Assignment. Using one of the uncut ends of the pipe used in problem 16-5, scribe and trim it to fit exactly an irregular surface or corner that your instructor selects.

17
Sheet Metal and Sheet Metal Gauges

Sheet metal layout requires knowledge other than pattern drafting. The drafter must know the common types of sheet metal available and the gauges for each type. On large jobs the type of sheet metal and the gauges are specified, and the layout worker must follow specifications closely. On small jobs, the worker must recommend the type and gauge of metal that should be used. To do this, the properties of each type of sheet metal and the advantages and disadvantages of each under different conditions must be understood.

Terms

To understand the properties of different types of sheet metal, you must first understand some of the common terms used to describe metals. Study the following terms until you are able to define each of them in your own words.

Iron. Strictly speaking, *iron* means the pure element of iron. However, pure iron is rarely seen since it is too soft for commercial use and rusts very easily, so the term iron is used to mean *steel*. For example, *galvanized iron* is a term commonly used to mean galvanized sheet steel.

Alloys. An alloy is a mixture of two or more different metals. The greatest part of an alloy is a parent metal (such as iron) to which is added small amounts of other metals. Stainless steel, for example, is an iron alloy to which nickel and chromium have been added in small percentages. In addition, there may be even smaller amounts of many other

different metals present, depending upon the type of stainless steel.

Steel. Steel is an iron-based alloy that contains varying amounts of carbon. When only carbon is added the steel is called *carbon steel*. Tool steels and other special steels contain small percentages of many other metals such as tungsten, molybdenum, chromium, and vanadium, in addition to carbon.

Carbon steels. Carbon steel is different from tool steel and other alloy steels in that only carbon has been added to the iron. In carbon steels the carbon content does not exceed 2 percent.

Mild steel. *Mild steel* is another name for *low carbon steel*. It is the steel used for the sheet metal, bars, and angles normally found in the sheet metal shop. It is a plain carbon steel (no alloys other than carbon). The amount of carbon it contains is small—up to $3/10$ of 1 percent carbon. This content is often stated as ".3 percent" or as "3 points".

Cold-rolled and hot-rolled steel. Mild steel may be obtained in either *cold-rolled* or *hot-rolled form*. It is hot rolled if, when the steel ingot comes out of the furnace, it is run through a series of rollers while it is still hot in order to shape it into an usable form such as an angle, a flat bar, or sheet metal. However, most of the products in the sheet metal shop are cold-rolled steel. Cold-rolled steel is formed hot-rolled steel that has been run through finishing rolls after it has cooled. It therefore has the same composition as hot-rolled steel, but has a closer grain, a better finish and more clearly defined edges.

Ferrous. Ferrous means *containing iron*. A ferrous metal therefore is one containing iron. A nonferrous metal is one that does not contain iron (such as copper, brass, or lead).

Oxides. An oxide is a chemical that results from combining a metal and oxygen. Since a large percentage of the atmosphere is oxygen, any metal that is exposed to air will form an oxide (moisture speeds up the oxidizing process). One of the most common examples of oxide is rust, which is iron oxide.

Types of sheet metal

Coated and solid sheets. All sheets used in the sheet metal shop can be classed into the two general categories of *solid sheets* and *coated sheets*. Solid sheets are made of the same metal throughout. Examples are stainless steel, copper, and black iron sheets. Coated sheets are those in which the parent metal is covered with a thin coating of another metal, either to improve its appearance or to improve its corrosion resistance properties. The most common example of a coated sheet is galvanized iron, which is an iron sheet coated with zinc.

Whether the metal is coated or uncoated sometimes determines the fabrication processes for an object. The durability and appearance of a coated sheet is effective only as long as the coating is not destroyed. For example, if a galvanized iron sheet is welded, the zinc coating is burned off and the sheet metal in the area of the weld is no more rust resistant than black iron. Solid sheets, on the other hand, can be welded and ground with no effect upon their performance because they are of the same composition throughout. Stainless steel is a solid sheet that can be welded and ground without changing its performance characteristics. Coated sheets have the advantage of lower cost, and for many applications will perform as well as more costly solid sheets. For example, galvanized iron

sheets used for ductwork in a building will generally last as long as the building is in existence.

Effect of oxides. Before examining specific types of metal, the effect of oxide on the characteristics of a metal should be understood. Remember that an oxide is a chemical that results from the metal combining with oxygen in the air. All metals form surface oxide. This means that the characteristics of the oxide form what we generally think of as the characteristics of the metal.

For example, rust (iron oxide) forms relatively quickly on iron sheets. Iron oxide is porous and forms in flakes. The result is that an iron sheet forms a rust coating quickly and, since this oxide is porous, it does not protect the iron from the oxygen in the air. Oxide continues to form on the surface of the metal. As the oxide builds up, it flakes off, exposing the iron to even more air and continuing the oxidation process. In this way, iron rusts through completely in a relatively short time.

On the other hand, the oxide of stainless steel is transparent, tough, impervious to most chemicals, and forms quickly. This means that the actual stainless steel is seldom exposed to the atmosphere because the oxide reforms quickly whenever the oxide surface is scratched. Oxide is a key to the beauty of stainless steel; its transparency preserves the luster of the metal, and its imperviousness to most chemicals protects the stainless steel metal itself. The stainless steel is really never in contact with the chemicals—only the oxide is.

Copper has a long life because copper oxide, once it is formed, is tough and does not react to oxygen. Copper oxide is not as transparent as stainless steel oxide and this explains why copper that has been exposed to air for a period of time is duller (and often has a green color) than a newly polished piece of copper.

Aluminum oxide makes aluminum impractical to solder. This oxide forms almost immediately and is a tough, insoluble chemical. It can be quickly dissolved by some chemicals but only at specific temperatures. Since solder must penetrate the pores of the metal in order to stick, the oxides from the surface of the metal must be removed.

Unless the oxides are removed, the solder lays only on the oxides and does not penetrate the metal. This is why aluminum can be soldered only with special fluxes and only when one has developed the skill to recognize the proper temperature at which to apply the flux.

Iron-based sheets. Iron is still the cheapest and most plentiful of all metals and therefore is the most common type of sheet metal used in sheet metal shops. *Iron* is the common term used in the shop for mild steel sheets. Mild steel sheets are available either as solid or coated sheets.

Solid mild steel sheets are commonly known as *black iron*. They are available as either hot-rolled or cold-rolled sheets. Because cold-rolled sheets have a better finish, flatter surface, and straighter edges, they are the most commonly used in the sheet metal shop. Since black iron is a solid sheet, it performs the same as iron. It will rust comparatively quickly, especially when exposed to moisture, and will eventually rust completely through.

The most common of the coated iron sheets are those coated with zinc or with lead. Zinc sheets can be coated by dipping them into melted zinc or by applying the zinc by an electrolytic process similar to electroplating. If the black-iron sheets are dipped into melted zinc, the result is *galvanized iron*. Galvanized iron is recognizable by the typical spangled appearance of the zinc. Iron sheets on which the zinc has been deposited electrically do not have the typical spangles of galvanized iron, but instead are a uniform, grey color. Most of the characteristics of either type of zinc coating are the same, except that the electrically deposited zinc provides a much better surface for paint without any extra processing. Hot-dipped galvanized iron requires washing with acid before paint will stick to it satisfactorily.

Terne plate is iron sheets coated with lead. As long as the lead coating of terne plate is not damaged, the iron sheet is protected from exposure to air and therefore cannot rust. Terne plate provides the rigidity of iron sheets plus the durability of lead. The most common use of terne plate in the sheet metal trade is for roofing.

Iron alloys. The most common iron-alloy sheet used in the sheet metal shop is stainless steel. This is an alloy of steel, chromium, nickel, and other metals, depending upon the type of alloy. The advantages of stainless steel are its long life and its ability to retain its luster even after long use. Stainless steel is a solid sheet and is never coated because coating could not improve its appearance or long life.

It is important to realize that *stainless steel* is a general name and that there are many different types of stainless steel. When a job calls for stainless steel, the sheet metal worker consults a catalog from the supplier to determine the type of stainless steel which is best for the particular job conditions.

Copper. Copper is usually used as a solid sheet in the sheet metal shop. It has a warm appearance and long life. Like stainless steel, it is much more expensive than iron sheets. Although copper lasts almost indefinitely when exposed to the atmosphere, it is not as impervious to attack by some extremely corrosive chemicals as is stainless steel.

Copper can be obtained as either cold-rolled or hot-rolled sheets. Hot-rolled copper sheets are extremely soft (almost as soft as lead). They are generally used when the metal must be stretched or formed in a die.

Most copper sheets used in the sheet metal shop are cold-rolled sheets because the cold-rolling process gives the sheets the necessary stiffness for most sheet metal jobs. Copper and lead are not gauged by thickness, but by their weight per square foot. The copper gauge is given in ounces per square foot. Thus, *16-oz copper* means copper sheet of such thickness that 1 sq ft of it weighs 16 oz.

Copper is most commonly used for architectural applications in the sheet metal trade, such as copper roofs, canopies, and inside and outside hoods.

Lead. Lead sheet has limited use in the sheet metal shop because of its softness, weight, and high cost. Because it is soft, lead is delivered in wide rolls rather than in sheet form. It is always used as a solid sheet, because lead is not changed by the atmosphere and is impervious to almost any chemical. This resistance to attack is the greatest advantage of lead. That is why it is often used to line tanks that hold acids and other highly corrosive chemicals. The limitations of lead are that it is too soft to maintain its shape without other support and that its weight makes an extremely heavy installation. Lead is gauged by pounds per sq ft. A *3 lb lead*·is lead of such a thickness that 1 sq ft weights 3 lb.

Gauges

The ferrous sheets used in the sheet metal shop (black iron, galvanized iron, terne plate, stainless steel, etc.) are gauged by the U.S. Manufacturer's Standard Gauge (Table 17-1). In the shop, the sheets are stored in racks or stacks with the gauge clearly marked so that they can be quickly selected. Also, sheet metal workers are able to determine the gauge of a metal by bending the corner and judging the metal's resistance to bending. Because there is only a very slight difference in thickness from one gauge to another, sheet metal shops only stock the even-numbered gauges, such as 10, 12, 14, and so on.

Except in precision work (which is a specialized area of the sheet metal industry) sheet metal work is seldom figured to more precise tolerances than $^1/_{16}$ in (0.0625). Therefore, gauge tables are normally only used to determine the pounds per square foot of a particular gauge to estimate weight and cost of a job. These tables are seldom used to determine the thickness because metal thickness need not be this precise. As a general rule of thumb, the sheet metal worker figures that 10 gauge is approximately ⅛ in thick and every six gauges reduces this thickness by 50 percent.

10-gauge——⅛ in

16-gauge——$^1/_{16}$ in

22-gauge——$^1/_{32}$ in

28-gauge——$^1/_{64}$ in

Table 17-1. U.S. manufacturers' standard gauge for uncoated sheet and stainless steel

Standard Gauge Number	Pounds per Square Foot	Thickness in Inches
10	5.6250	0.1345
11	5.0000	0.1196
12	4.3750	0.1046
13	3.7500	0.0897
14	3.1250	0.0747
15	2.8125	0.0673
16	2.5000	0.0598
17	2.2500	0.0538
18	2.0000	0.0478
19	1.7500	0.0418
20	1.5000	0.0359
21	1.3750	0.0329
22	1.2500	0.0299
23	1.1250	0.0269
24	1.0000	0.0239
25	0.87500	0.0209
26	0.75000	0.0179
27	0.68750	0.0164
28	0.62500	0.0149
29	0.56250	0.0135
30	0.50000	0.0120
31	0.43750	0.0105
32	0.40625	0.0097
33	0.37500	0.0090
34	0.34375	0.0082
35	0.31250	0.0075
36	0.28125	0.0067
37	0.26562	0.0064
38	0.25000	0.0060

Table 1 gives the thicknesses of gauges for *uncoated* sheets and stainless steel. Coated sheets such as galvanized iron and terne plate, are sheets whose thickness is that of the uncoated sheets shown in Table 1. The coating on galvanized sheets and terne plate increases the thickness and the weight per square foot, making them slightly heavier and thicker than uncoated sheets. The actual thickness of galvanized sheets is shown in Table 17-2. As a rule of thumb, sheet metal workers estimate that a galvanized sheet is two gauges thicker and heavier than an uncoated sheet.

Table 17-2. Galvanized sheet gauges

Gauge Number	Pounds per Square Foot	Thickness in Inches
10	5.7813	0.1382
11	5.1563	0.1233
12	4.5313	0.1084
13	3.9063	0.0934
14	3.2813	0.0785
15	2.9688	0.0710
16	2.6563	0.0635
17	2.4063	0.0575
18	2.1563	0.0516
19	1.9063	0.0456
20	1.6563	0.0396
21	1.5313	0.0366
22	1.4063	0.0336
23	1.2813	0.0306
24	1.1563	0.0276
25	1.0313	0.0247
26	0.9063	0.0217
27	0.8438	0.0202
28	0.7813	0.0187
29	0.7188	0.0172
30	0.6563	0.0157
31	0.5938	0.0142
32	0.5625	0.0134

For example, an 18-gauge galvanized sheet is approximately the weight and thickness of a 16-gauge uncoated sheet.

PRACTICE PROBLEMS

Problem 17-1

In the blank space next to the number, write the letter that indicates the term in the right hand column that best matches the statement. Some terms may be used more than once.

_____ 1. The basic alloy of steel
_____ 2. Forms steel when added to iron
_____ 3. In the trade it is used as an interchangeable term with *steel*
_____ 4. A mixture of two different metals
_____ 5. An iron alloy of nickel and chromium
_____ 6. Contains iron and carbon
_____ 7. Mild steel
_____ 8. Same composition as hot-rolled steel
_____ 9. Means *containing iron*
_____10. A chemical that results from oxygen and metal combining

A. Steel
B. Iron
C. Oxides
D. Alloys
E. Cold-rolled steel
F. Stainless steel
G. Ferrous
H. Carbon

Problem 17-2

In the blank to the left of each term write "coated" or "uncoated" to indicate whether the sheet names is a coated or uncoated sheet.

_____ Stainless steel
_____ Galvanized iron
_____ Terne plate
_____ Lead
_____ Copper

Problem 17-3

Give the thickness in inches and weight per square foot of the following gauges of uncoated steel sheets

Gauge	Weight	Thickness
16	_____	_____
22	_____	_____
28	_____	_____

Even though a pattern has been developed accurately, the finished product can be inaccurate, poor in appearance, or difficult to install if the pattern has not been notched properly. The layout worker is expected to be able to notch the pattern correctly. Although notching ability must be gained by experience, there are standard notches for certain types of seams and edges that every sheet metal worker must know.

Most notches are dictated by common sense. Visualizing the final shape of the metal will usually make clear what is needed. On unusual items that are difficult to visualize, mark a piece of paper from the pattern and fold it into the finished form. This will usually make clear how the pattern should be notched.

Reasons for notching

The two basic reasons for notching are to speed the fabrication of the object and to improve its appearance. The specific reasons for notching are twofold.

1. To remove those areas of metal that interfere with bending. Removal of areas of metal that interfere with bending is shown in Fig. 18-1. The corner where two 90° bends meet must be notched out or the metal will wrinkle.

2. To remove areas where there are multiple thicknesses of metal that will interfere with later fabrication. Seams such as Pittsburgh seams have three or four thicknesses of metal. Therefore,

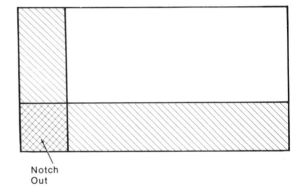

Notch
Out

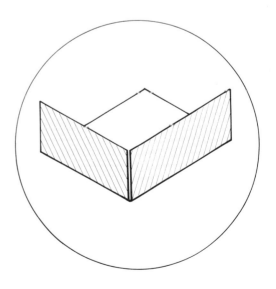

Fig. 18-1 Corner where two 90° bends meet.

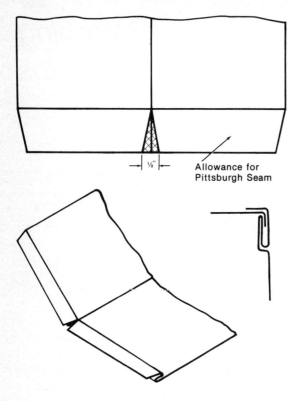

Fig. 18-2   Notch for bend in Pittsburgh Seam.

when a bend is to be made across a Pittsburgh seam, a notch is usually needed. (See Fig. 18-2.)

Examples of notching

Figures 18-3 through 18-11 show typical examples of notching. Dimensions are given only to give an approximate idea of the notch. In actual practice, notches are seldom measured but are estimated as they are cut with the snips. The exception to this is notches that are measured for exposed miters that must fit precisely; for very precise work, where uniform appearance is important; and on high-cost metals such as stainless steel and copper where appearance of the finished job is extremely important.

Pittsburgh seam and government lock

Figure 18-3 shows the notch for a Pittsburgh seam, along with the notches for a government lock on a piece of duct. Note that the Pittsburgh seam allowance is notched about ¼ in back from a 90° notch. This is so that the multiple thickness is back far enough so that it will not interfere with a bend or with any clip that is fastened to the duct. Remember that the ¼-in measurement is approximate. It should not be less than ¼ in, but may be as much as ⅜ in. The square notch on the left-hand side of this pattern is typical for a 90° flange. On the right side of the pattern, the cut at approxi-

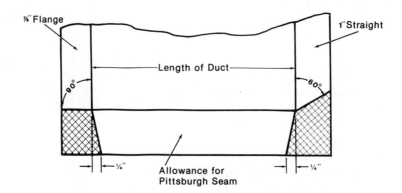

Fig. 18-3   Notch for Pittsburgh Seam and Government Lock.

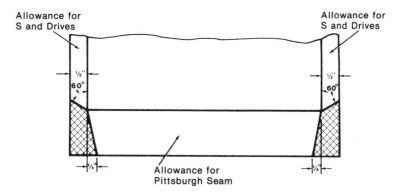

Fig. 18-4 Notch for Pittsburgh Seam and S and Drive Clips.

mately 60° is typical for a government clip. This is to assure that the corners do not touch one another and to make it easier to slip on the government clip.

Pittsburgh seam and s-and-drive clips

The notching for a Pittsburgh seam on a piece of duct on which allowance has been made for S-and-drive clips is shown in Fig. 18-4. Note that the notching for the Pittsburgh seam is exactly the same as in Fig. 18-1. The notch for the S-and-drive clip is at approximately 60°. This is to make it easier to start the S-and-drive clips.

Groove seam and dovetail

Figure 18-5 shows a typical notch for a groove seam. Note that the allowance for the groove seam

is notched slightly less than 90° (approximately 75°). This is to ensure that the end of the groove seam does not interfere with the bottom edge of the pipe—as it is likely to do if the notch is made at 90°.

This figure also shows the typical notches for a dovetail seam. These are straight cuts at 90° to the pattern line—no metal is removed. The width between cuts on a dovetail seam will vary with the width of the allowance for the dovetail and with the diameter of the pipe. In general, the distance between cuts on a dovetail seam is approximately equal to the width of the dovetail seam allowance. For example, if the allowance for the dovetail is ⅜ in, then the distance between cuts should be approximately ⅜ in. Note that the distance between cuts is seldom measured (except on an extremely precise job). Also, no marks are made for these cuts; they are snipped holding the snips

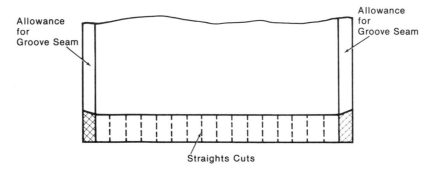

Fig. 18-5 Notch for Groove Seam and Dovetail Seam.

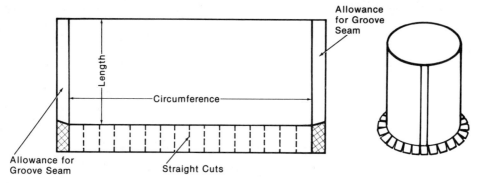

Fig. 18-6 Notching for a large flange to the outside of a round pipe.

approximately square to the line and judging the spacing by eye.

Notched flange to the outside

Sometimes a round pipe must have a large flange that is too wide to be turned on a bench machine.

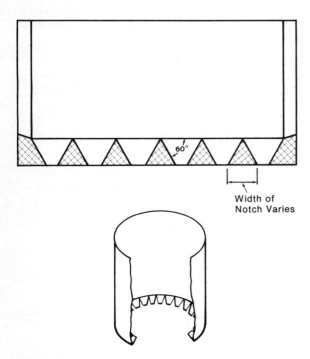

Fig. 18-7 Notching for a large flange to the inside of a round pipe.

In such cases, straight cuts are made (Fig. 18-6) to allow a series of single tabs to be bent out to form a notched flange. In the case of a flange turned to the outside of a round pipe, the outside edge of a formed flange has a greater circumference than the bend line. Therefore, only straight cuts need to be made on the pattern, and no metal need be removed. When the flange is formed, the distance between cuts is approximated and not marked. The distance between cuts is generally equal to the width of the flange. Note that the groove seam on the ends of this pattern is notched at a slight angle from 90°. This is the typical notch for a groove seam. No angle is cut at the top of the groove seam allowance because this is a raw edge on this particular pattern and there is no need to cut back the groove seam allowance to avoid interference with a bend or another seam.

Flange to inside of a pipe

When a large flange must be bent to the inside of a curve (Fig. 18-7), a V notch is removed from the flange because an inside flange must shrink. This is different from an outside flange which must stretch and so has only a straight cut (Fig. 18-6). The amount of notch that is taken from an inside flange will vary according to the width of the flange and the diameter of the curve. In general, the notch is at approximately a 60° angle.

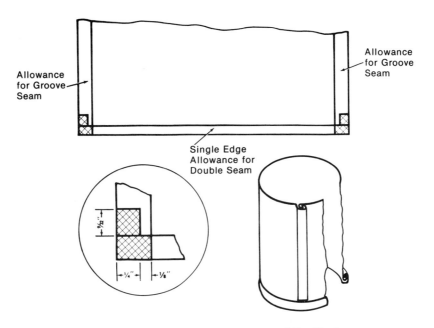

Fig. 18-8 Notching for Groove Seam and Double Seam.

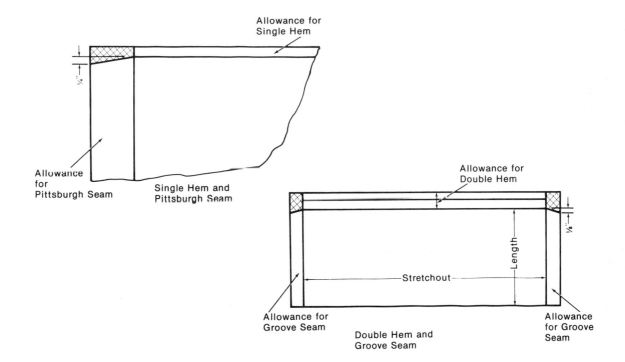

Fig. 18-9 Notching for hems.

Groove seam and double seam

The groove seam and the double seam are both four thicknesses of metal. Therefore, if they are not notched there will be an unsightly bump where the 4 thicknesses of the two seams cross. For a neat job, the groove seam is notched as shown by the inset in Fig. 18-8. This results in only a single thickness of metal along the groove seam. The double seam can then be formed over a single thickness, as shown in the pictorial view. For this particular notch, the widths of the notches are measured instead of estimated so that a neat finished job is possible.

Notching for hems

The notch for a hem is 90° to the hemline (Fig. 18-9). Since the allowance for a hem is usually around the top of an object such as a pipe, the notch is combined with the standard notch for the type of vertical seam on the object. For example, Fig. 18-9 shows the notch for a hem combined with that of a groove seam and with that of a Pittsburgh seam.

Tap-in lock

Figure 18-10 shows a typical notch for a tap-in lock. Note that the two inside allowances are cut square so that they form 90° flanges when they are formed, as shown in the pictorial view. The outside edge is notched at approximately 60° so that it can easily be inserted in the hole that is cut in the duct. The outside edge allowance is usually cut in straight, as shown by the grey lines. This makes it easier to bend the flange inside of the duct when it is installed.

Note the rest of the notching in Fig. 18-10. This is typical notching for S and drives and Pittsburgh seams, and illustrates how the many different types of notches are combined as needed.

Flange on a square to round

The notching for a 90° flange on a square to round (Fig. 18-11) is typical of a 90° flange on most fittings. Note that the notch is made so that it is 90° to the pattern line so that when the flange is formed, its ends form a 90° to the pattern line.

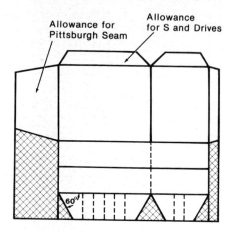

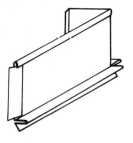

Fig. 18-10   Notching for a Tap-in Lock.

PRACTICE PROBLEMS

Problem 18-1

Purpose. To learn the notching for a Pittsburgh seam and government lock.

Study. *Pittsburgh seam and Government lock.*

Assignment.

1. Lay out on paper two sides (in one piece) of a duct 4-by-2 in and 3½ in long, with allowances for a Pittsburgh seam and government lock.

2. Mark, and shade with a colored pencil, the areas of the pattern that should be notched out.

3. Mark the pattern on metal, and form it up.

Problem 18-2

Purpose. To learn the notching for a Pittsburgh seam and S-and-drive clips.

Study. *Pittsburgh seam and S-and-drive clips.*

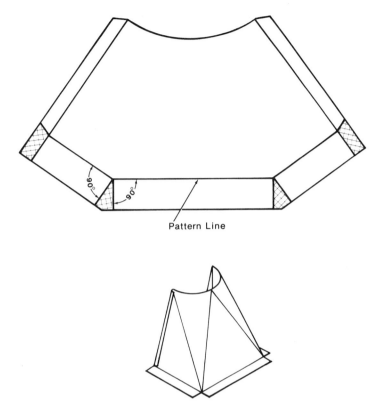

Pattern Line

Fig. 18-11 Notching for a 90° Flange.

Assignment.

1. Lay out on paper two sides (in one piece) of a duct 3½ in-by-2 in and 4 in long with allowances for a Pittsburgh seam and S-and-drive clips.

2. Mark, and shade with a colored pencil, the areas of the pattern that should be notched out.

3. Mark the pattern on metal, and form it up.

Problem 18-3

Purpose. To learn the notching for a groove seam, dovetail, and hem.

Study. *Groove seam and Dovetail, Notching for hems.*

Assignment.

1. Lay out on paper the pattern for a 3-in-diameter pipe, 3 in long, with a ⅜ in dovetail on one end and a ¼ in single hem on the other.

2. Work, and shade with a colored pencil, the areas to be notched. If there are straight cuts (no metal removed) mark an arrowhead at the end of each cut line.

3. Mark the pattern on metal, and form it up.

Problem 18-4

Purpose. To learn the notching for a groove seam and double seam.

Study. *Groove seam and double seam.*

Assignment.

1. Lay out on paper the pattern for a 3-in-diameter pan, 3 in high, with the bottom fastened with a ¼ in double seam. The vertical seam will be a ¼-in groove seam.

2. Mark, and shade with a colored pencil, the areas of the pattern that should be notched out.

19

Cutting Patterns

After a pattern is developed on metal, it must be cut out and properly notched. Often the pattern will be used as a master to mark several more pieces from, and this means that it must be especially accurate. The straight lines of a pattern are often cut on a squaring shear, and the curved lines and the notches are done by hand snips. Knowing how to use squaring shears and snips properly ensures that an accurate pattern will be cut out with little lost time.

Squaring shears

The foot-powered squaring shears (Fig. 19-1) should be used for quick blanking of material for patterns. For single cuts, the marked line is aligned by sight with the bottom blade of the shear. For a large number of cuts of the same width, either the back gauge (Fig. 19-2) or the front gauge (Fig. 19-3) is used. These are set by measuring from the bottom blade of the shear. The back gauge is used when narrow pieces of metal are to be cut. With narrow pieces, the metal is shoved in from the front of the shear until it hits the back gauge. For wide pieces of metal, the back gauge is more awkward to use because the metal will sag, so the front gauge should be used.

Squaring bars (Fig. 19-1) are on the right-hand and left-hand side of the shear. These bars are square to the blade so that any piece of metal held tight against either of the bars will be cut 90° to the side of the sheet. Some mechanics prefer to use the right-hand bar because the position for holding the

metal seems more comfortable. Other mechanics prefer to use the left-hand bar because the cutting action of the shear blade pushes the metal tight against the squaring bar so that there is no danger of the metal slipping and cutting out of square.

Safety. The foot-powered squaring shear is a very dangerous piece of equipment. It is extremely easy to cut the tip of one's finger off. Both federal and state safety regulations require that a safety guard (Fig. 19-4) always be in place on the squaring shear. This guard prevents fingers from being placed in danger under the blade. *Never use a shear that does not have this safety guard.*

The safety guard on the front of the shear (Fig. 19-5) does not prevent a person from reaching behind the shear and getting a finger in the blade. To prevent this, *never* try to hold a small piece of metal at the back of the shear. A good rule is that if the edge of the sheet metal is not clearly visible, do not try to hold it. Let it fall to the floor and pick it up.

Another danger with the foot-powered squaring shear is that of smashing one's toe underneath the foot treadle. It *is* possible to smash one's own toe (or that of someone else standing on the other side of the shear). Always keep feet clear of the treadle. Most shears are equipped with a stop underneath the foot treadle that prevents the treadle from going down completely to the floor. This does not mean that someone's foot cannot be smashed under the treadle. The only safe practice is to keep feet clear of the treadle.

Fig. 19-1 A foot powered squaring shear.

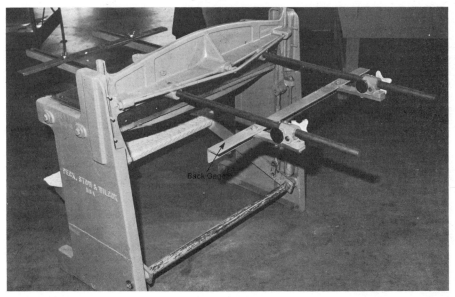

Fig. 19-2 The back gauge.

Fig. 19-3 The front gauge.

Fig. 19-4 Safety guard on squaring shear.

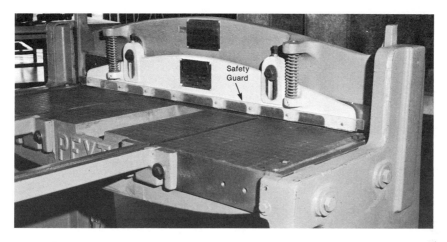

Fig. 19-5   Required safety guard.

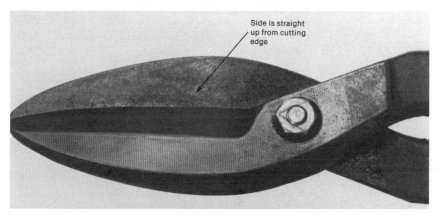

Fig. 19-6   Straight blade.

An important safety rule for squaring shears—or any sheet metal machinery—is; when working in pairs, each person must always be aware of the other's movements and location. It is everyone's responsibility to watch out for fellow workers.

Hand snips

There are many different types of snips. They vary in size, type of leverage, and length of cut. However, all snips use one of two basic types of blades; the *combination blade* and the *straight blade*.

A sectional view of the straight blade is shown in Fig. 19-6. Notice that the sides of the blades run straight up from the cutting edge. This type of blade is the easiest type to use when cutting straight lines. It is difficult to use when cutting curves, because the cut metal strikes the upper part of the blade and this makes it difficult to turn the metal or the snips to follow the curve.

The combination blade (Fig. 19-7), has sides that are curved away from the cutting edge. This blade can be used for cutting straight lines and curves, since the cut metal will roll over the top of the blade (Fig. 19-8), allowing the snips to be turned to follow the curve.

Types of snips

To cut patterns, sheet metal workers generally use three types of snips; *bulldog snips, general-purpose snips,* and *aviation snips.*

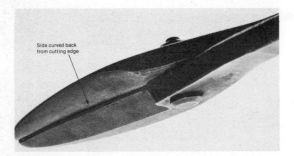

Fig. **19-7** Combination blade.

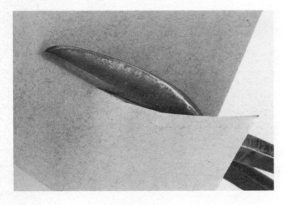

Fig. **19-8** Cut metal will roll over the curve of the combination blade.

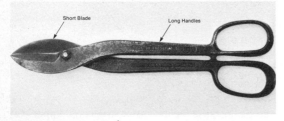

Fig. **19-9** Bulldog snips (combination blade).

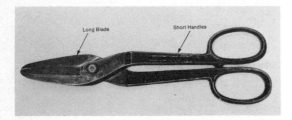

Fig. **19-10** General purpose snips (combination blade).

Fig. **19-11** Aviation snips.

Bulldog snips (Fig. 19-9) are designed for cutting heavy gauges. They have a short cutting blade, and long handles to provide sufficient leverage. In general, bulldog snips are used for cutting metal from 22 gauge up to a thickness of 16 gauge. Bulldog snips may be of either the straight blade or combination blade type.

General-purpose snips (Fig. 19-10) are used for general cutting of 26 gauge or lighter. Since they are designed for cutting lighter metal than the bulldog snips, the snip length is longer and the blades are shorter. General-purpose snips may also be either the combination blade or straight blade type.

Aviation snips (Fig. 19-11) are also called airplane snips. These snips are shorter than the general-purpose snips. They are capable of cutting even thicker metal than the bulldog snips because of their short blade and because of the compound leverage designed into their handle.

The blade design of aviation snips is similar to that of the combination blade, but their special

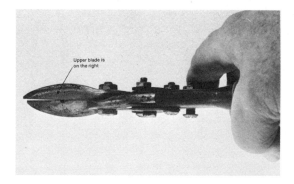

Fig. 19-12 Right-hand airplane snips.

Fig. 19-13 Left-hand airplane snips.

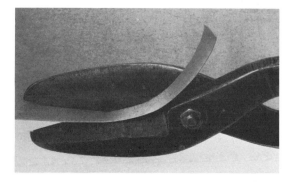

Fig. 19-14 Metal curling over bottom blade of snips.

Fig. 19-15 A cut from this direction is difficult with right-hand snips.

Fig. 19-16 A cut from this direction can be done easily with left-hand snips.

design permits cutting very small-radius curves and circles because of the short blade. Aviation snips are available in right-hand, left-hand, and straight design. Sheet metal workers generally carry both the right-hand and left-hand snip in order to cut in either direction easily. Most snips are right-hand snips. When right-hand snips are held for cutting, the top blade is on the user's right (Fig. 19-12). When left-hand snips are held for cutting (Fig. 19-13), the top blade is on the user's left.

Left-hand snips are important because the greatest problem in cutting metal with snips is not the actual cutting, but getting the metal to slide out

Fig. 19-17 Notching.

Fig. 19-18 Starting cut for cutting out a hole.

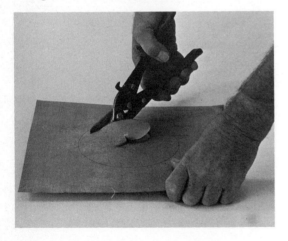

Fig. 19-19 Rough cut for hole.

of the way over the snip blades. Cutting is easier if the smaller piece of scrap is over the bottom blade of the snips so that it curls out of the way and allows the snips to be reinserted for a new cut (Fig. 19-14). Right-hand snips would be difficult to use for the cut shown in Fig. 19-15, because the large piece of metal is over the bottom blade of the

snips. The cut is made easily with left-hand snips (Fig. 19-16), because the small piece of metal curls over the bottom blade of the snip and is out of the way.

Using snips

We have seen that the small scrap of metal should be kept over the bottom blade of the snips. For right-hand snips (the most commonly used) the smallest piece of metal is kept to the left-hand side. If both pieces of cut metal are large, the usual practice is to cut out the pattern about ¼ in to ½ in away from the cut line. This removes the excess metal which will otherwise make it difficult to cut to the line. After the pattern is roughed out, it is cut on the line. The narrow allowance strip will curl out of the way, making a neater cutting job possible.

When using snips other than the aviation snips, always rest the snips on the bench, allowing the strength of the upper arm and shoulder to aid in cutting. If the snips are unsupported, the hand muscles do most of the work, and will quickly tire.

When notching, the end of the snip blade should be at the end of the notch (Fig. 19-17). This is a fast and sure way to notch because the cut can be made with one quick movement and will not go beyond the end of the notch. If the blades are placed past the notch, then the cut must be made slowly and carefully to avoid cutting too far.

When cutting holes, first a hole or slit is made in. the center of the circle (Fig. 19-18). Then right-hand airplane snips are used to make a spiralling cut until the excess metal is trimmed out to within about ¼ in from the cut line (Fig. 19-19). After this is done, the circle can be trimmed neatly to the cut line.

When cutting a square hole, both right-hand and left-hand airplane snips are used. First a starting hole is made near the center, then the excess metal is trimmed in the same way as for a round hole. The right-hand snips are used to cut the line to one corner (Fig. 19-20), and the left-hand snips are used to cut to the corner from the other direction (Fig. 19-21). The remaining corner cuts are made

Fig. 19-20 Cut to corner with right-hand aviation snips.

Fig. 19-22 Making a 90° cut with right-hand aviation snips.

Fig. 19-21 Cut to corner with left-hand snips.

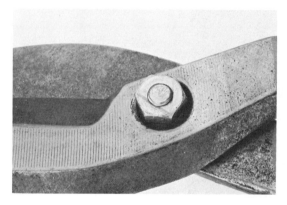

Fig. 19-23 Swivel bolt.

in the same way. On light metal, the use of left-hand snips can be avoided by holding the right-hand snips into the corner and rotating them 90° (Fig. 19-22). This usually results in slightly marring and distorting the corner, but for most work this is unimportant.

Care of snips

The most important rule for using snips is to use them only for what they are designed to do. Cut only what can be comfortably cut without resorting to the use of levers or pounding on the handles. This will surely *spring* the blades. Springing

means that the middle of each blade is slightly deformed so that the clearance between the two blades is too much. Snips with sprung blades will either leave a burr or simply bend the metal without cutting it, and have to be discarded.

Use snips to cut sheet metal only. If they are used to cut wire (even soft wire) the blades will be nicked. This is because the angle of the cutting blades and the clearance between the blades is designed for cutting sheet metal, not wire or nails.

The swivel bolt (Fig. 19-23) must have the proper tension. If it is too loose, there will be too much clearance between the blades, and the snips will seem to be sprung. If the bolt is too tight, the snips will be tiring to use.

Fig. 19-24 Center punch on swivel bolt nut

A general procedure for testing the tension of the swivel bolt is to set the snips on the bench and let the upper handle fall of its own weight. If the swivel bolt is at the proper tension, the handle will fall freely to within about ¼ in of the bottom handle. Sometimes snips that seem to be too tight need a little oil at the pivot. When oiling snips, be careful to place the oil only at the swivel bolt. Oil on the snip blades will cause them to slip and make cutting more difficult.

Good-quality snips have a swivel bolt and a self-locking nut designed to remain at the same tension even though the blades are always pivoting on the bolt. If the nut on the swivel bolt does work itself loose, a remedy is to adjust the snip to the proper tension and then put a centerpunch mark at the juncture between the bolt and the nut (Fig. 19-24). This jams the bolt and nut so that they will not move unless turned with a wrench.

Sharpening must be done by those who have had special training in sharpening scissors and snips. The cutting angle at the edge of each blade must be a precise angle. If this angle is changed in sharpening, the snips will be ineffective or useless until they are resharpened by an expert who can reestablish the proper angle. Sharpening is always done on the top cutting edge and never on the side of the blade because this ruins the clearance between the blades.

PRACTICE PROBLEMS

Problem 19-1

Identify the snips in these figures as *straight blade* or *combination blade*.

1.

Fig. 19-25

2.

Fig. 19-26

Problem 19-2

Identify the snips in the following figures as *right-hand* or *left-hand*.

1.

Fig. 19-27

2.

Fig. 19-28

3.

Fig. 19-29

2.

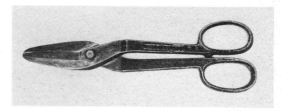

Fig. 19-31

Problem 19-3

Identify the snips shown in the figures as *bulldog* or *general purpose*.

1.

Fig. 19-30

Index